AS IF IT WERE

Robert K. Beecham poses in his officer's uniform as a captain in the Twenty-third United States Colored Troops.

AS IF IT WERE
Glory

ROBERT BEECHAM'S CIVIL WAR
FROM THE IRON BRIGADE
TO THE BLACK REGIMENTS

Edited with an introduction by
Michael E. Stevens

MADISON HOUSE
Madison, Wisconsin · 1998

Michael E. Stevens, ed.
As If It Were Glory: Robert Beecham's Civil War
From the Iron Brigade to the Black Regiments

Library of Congress Cataloging-in-Publication Data

Beecham, R. K. (Robert K.), b. 1838.
As if it were glory : Robert Beecham's Civil War from the Iron Brigade to the
Black regiments / ed with an introduction by Michael E. Stevens. — 1st ed.
      p.   cm. Includes index. ISBN 0-945612-55-9 (acid-free paper)
1. Beecham, R. K. (Robert K.), b. 1838. 2. United States. Army. Iron Brigade
(1861–1865) 3. United States. Army. Colored Infantry Regiment, 23rd (1863–
1865) 4. United States—History—Civil War, 1861–1865—Participation, Afro-
American. 5. United States—History—Civil War, 1861–1865—Personal
narratives. 6. Soldiers—United States—Biography.
7. Afro-American soldiers—Biography.
I. Stevens, Michael E.
E493.5.I72B43   1997
973.7'415—dc21   97-26826
CIP

Printed in the United States of America on acid-free recycled paper.

Designed by Gregory M. Britton.

Madison House Publishers, Inc.
P.O. Box 3100 · Madison, Wisconsin 53703

FIRST EDITION

Illustration credits: Frontispiece, Marc J. Storch Collection, U.S. Army Military History Institute (hereafter USAMHI); pg. 2, WHi(X32)17350, State Historical Society of Wisconsin (hereafter SHSW); pg. 20, Mass. Commandery Military Order of the Loyal Legion, USAMHI; pg. 36, WHi(X3) 11029, SHSW; pg. 58, WHi(X3)11291, SHSW; pg. 84, Mass. Commandery Military Order of the Loyal Legion, USAMHI; pg. 100, WHi(X3)43442, SHSW; pg. 120, Wisconsin Mss. 121S, SHSW; pg. 142, Mass. Commandery Military Order of the Loyal Legion, USAMHI; pg. 160, Henry Kurtz Collection, USAMHI; pg. 176, Mass. Commandery Military Order of the Loyal Legion, USAMHI; pg. 190, WHi(X3)12870, SHSW; pg. 218, R. K. Beecham, *The Fields of Gettysburg With Other Poems and Stories* (Everett, Washington, 1905?).

For Elisabeth, Martha, and Emily

CONTENTS

INTRODUCTION

Although four decades had passed since he had first put on his country's uniform, Robert K. Beecham still vividly recalled the trip that began his four-year stint in the Union army. The men and women who cheered the trainloads of midwestern soldiers as they headed east in June 1861 "seemed to wave us on, as if it were glory and not years of bitter war that awaited us." The Civil War was a defining moment for a generation of men who served in the Union and Confederate armies. Disabled veterans had daily reminders of the cost of the war, but even those veterans who escaped serious injury remembered the war as a great national drama of almost religious importance that transcended their own lives. In the half century after the war, many veterans, both Northern and Southern, wrote their recollections either to make a few dollars to supplement their pensions or to impress on succeeding generations the importance of their sacrifices or, perhaps, as a catharsis to resolve in their own minds the conflict between the glorification of battle and their recollections of the "years of bitter war."

Robert K. Beecham, the author of this memoir, served in the Union army for four years—from May 1861 through May 1865. A private in the famed Iron Brigade and later one of the white officers in the newly formed units of African-American recruits, Beecham remained an unreconstructed Union man throughout his long life. Writing more than forty years after his enlistment, Beecham took special delight in attacking the conventions of his time and used his memoir to counter the misrepresentations he saw at the dawn of the new century. He satirized the altered recollections of fellow veterans that stressed triumphs and downplayed defeats. He bitterly censured those who would whitewash the South's wartime motives in the name of national reconciliation, and he rejected the growing mythology developing around Robert E. Lee. Not confining his criticism to the Southern cause, Beecham also maintained a healthy disrespect for those aspects of the Union war effort that favored privilege at the expense of the common soldier, and in his narrative he always championed enlisted men over officers. Perhaps most striking in that era, he insisted that the black troops under his command equaled or even surpassed the all-white "Iron Brigade" with whom he served at Gettysburg.

The son of an Irish-born Protestant farmer, Robert Beecham was born in the Canadian province of New Brunswick on March 25, 1838.[1] Beecham's parents moved the family in 1843 to Sun Prairie, Wisconsin Territory, a small farming community about ten miles northeast of the recently established capital of Madison. Young Robert seemed to have been endowed with a temperamental fire that flared up against oppression or misuse of authority. He also showed a strong dislike of the institution of slavery. In July 1856, at the age of eighteen, Beecham joined two hundred other midwesterners in Colonel Jim Lane's "army" in Kansas to counter Southern efforts to add another slave state to the Union.[2]

Returning to Wisconsin, Beecham worked as a farmer until the outbreak of the war. He enlisted in the Union army on May 10, 1861 and was formally mustered into service on June 11, 1861 in the Second Wisconsin Infantry, Company H. Two of Robert's brothers followed him into the Union forces. Henry enlisted in the fall of 1861 and survived the war after being wounded; Charles Beecham joined the army in spring 1862 and died of pneumonia in July 1864.

Beecham and over a thousand other young men of the 2nd Wisconsin left for the east on June 20, 1861, and were cheered at the various train stations along the way. They arrived in Washington, D.C., on June 25, the first regiment of three-year volunteers to reinforce the beleaguered capital, whose residents feared an imminent Confederate attack. Along with three New York regiments, Wisconsin recruits were placed under the command of Colonel William Tecumseh Sherman. On July 21, 1861, Sherman's newly formed brigade took part in the Union disaster at the first battle of Bull Run, leaving Beecham disillusioned with the future war hero. Following this battle, Beecham's 2nd Wisconsin was transferred to the command of General Rufus King, joining the 19th Indiana and the 5th and 6th Wisconsin in an all-western brigade. The unit that later became known as the Iron Brigade took its final shape with the replacement of the 5th Wisconsin by the 7th Wisconsin in October 1861 and the addition of the 24th Michigan a year later.[3] The winter of 1861–62 was spent parading and drilling at Fort Tillinghast, near Arlington, with one brief operation in March 1862 in Centreville.

The 2nd Wisconsin would see plenty of action in 1862, but Beecham missed most of it because of illness. Having come down with a fever, he spent three weeks in April 1862 at the Prince Street Hospital in Alexandria, an experience that confirmed his views of the mismanagement of the army hospital system. Beecham rejoined his unit, then at Fredericksburg, but soon a relapse forced him in and out of military hospitals and convalescent camps for the remainder of the year. He returned to his regiment in winter quarters outside Belle Plain Landing, Virginia, in December 1862 in time for General Burnside's infamous "Mud March" in January 1863.

Beecham saw action in the Chancellorsville campaign and took part in the fierce fighting on the first day of the battle of Gettysburg. The 2nd Wisconsin lost nearly 40 percent of its men in the morning's fighting and 77 percent by the end of the day. Beecham was taken prisoner of war on the evening of the first, and by the fourth he and nearly three thousand other prisoners were marched south, ending up at Belle Isle, a Confederate prison camp on an island in the James River. By early August Beecham was released in the final general exchange before the agreement between the North and South broke down.

Even before Gettysburg, Beecham had hopes of becoming an officer, and opportunity presented itself when President Lincoln authorized the creation of the United States Colored Troops (USCT). Eventually more than 186,000 black enlisted men and a largely all-white cadre of officers served in the USCT. In December 1863, after appearing before an army examining board, Beecham received a first lieutenant's commission and was assigned to the 23rd USCT. Beecham and other white officers who commanded black troops not only encountered prejudice from their fellow Union officers, but faced the explicit threat of execution if captured by the Confederacy. Only the threat of Union retaliation on Confederate prisoners saved captured officers of the USCT.[4]

Beecham spent the winter of 1863–64 drilling recruits, mostly from Baltimore and Washington, D.C. Receiving a leave of absence in March 1864, Beecham went home to Sun Prairie where he married the English-born Emma Watkinson, who had been awaiting his return since his enlistment. The couple returned to camp, and Emma, despite some initial trepidations, helped open a school for the men of the 23rd USCT. For several weeks, she spent her evenings teaching them to read and write before returning to Sun Prairie.

Beecham and the 23rd USCT spent the spring and early summer of 1864 guarding supply lines. He saw action during the bloody battle of the Crater in July 1864, where he was wounded and again taken prisoner by the Confederates. Beecham was held in Columbia, South Carolina, until February 1865, and escaped while being evacuated as General Sherman approached the city. After living by his wits for about a week, Beecham learned that an exchange of prisoners was scheduled to be made at Wilmington, North Carolina, and he returned and surrendered at Charlotte on February 21, 1865. A week later he was exchanged and headed home for Wisconsin on a leave of absence. He returned to his regiment, then near Petersburg, after Lee's surrender and was promoted to captain in May; but, with the war now over, Beecham resigned, settled his accounts, and began the trip home. At 8:00 p.m., on June 7, 1865, Beecham arrived in Sun Prairie, where, as he put it, "My days of war were over; before me were the paths and the vocations of peace."

* * *

Civil War veterans who recorded their memoirs met a popular need for tales of valor, glory, and gore. By the opening of the twentieth century, the desire for national reconciliation between North and South led many to stress the valor of both sides and to downplay the causes and youthful enthusiasm that propelled many volunteers into battle. In addition, growing racism led many to minimize slavery's role in causing the war. Even some of the most idealistic veterans—the white officers who commanded the all-black units—fell under the sway of the respectable racism of the late nineteenth century.

Beecham resisted these trends in his memoir. Rather than filling his account with stories of combat, he focused on the social history of the war. His memoir contains accounts of camp life, conditions in army hospitals, and other everyday elements of life in the Union army, stories that usually celebrated the ingenuity of the enlisted man at the expense of officers who were portrayed as arrogant and sometimes incompetent. He used humor to make his points and even poked fun at himself, noting on one occasion that "it seemed easier to retreat than to advance—it generally does on a battlefield."

Looking back on the war, Beecham worried that stories shaped by the needs of a new age were beginning to replace authentic memories of the war. On visiting Gettysburg in 1900, he complained that he could not find a single veteran guiding tourists because those "who visit the field have no use for one, but prefer to be guided and instructed by some pink-and-white kid." The youthful guides assumed "fine and pompous airs" as they explained "the intricacies of some military position or maneuver." Yet while insisting on the preeminence of veterans' accounts of the war, he also discounted the distorted, exaggerated tales of some of his colleagues. He satirized fellow warriors who recalled only glory. A survivor of the first battle of Bull Run, Beecham claimed that he never met a Union man at veterans' reunions who admitted serving in that disaster. At the same time, he poked fun at the selective memories of Confederate veterans. Beecham claimed to "have met thousands of ex-Confederates who were survivors of the First Bull Run, and could tell me more of its glories than I dreamed it possessed," adding, "No wonder we were beaten. The Confederates were all there."

While a veteran's overstated war claims could be forgiven, Beecham had little tolerance for advocates of the Lost Cause. Popular magazines that published accounts of the sufferings of former Confederates while ignoring the plight of the victims of the Confederacy angered him. After all, they "might lose a Southern subscriber, you know." Nor could Beecham forgive the Confederates for their detestable policy towards Union prisoners. Twice held prisoner, Beecham charged the Confederates with a deliberate policy of neglect that caused the death of thousands prisoners. "Death" Beecham remembered "was among us, gathering in his victims from day to day." Postwar claims that the Confederates had not intentionally starved their prisoners outraged him. Beecham charged that the Confederate treatment of Union prisoners "was a savage, inhuman and cowardly policy, inaugurated by a set of men better qualified by nature, and by their education, to become henchmen of the prince of darkness than the rulers of a nation which they sought to establish."

While the treatment of white Union prisoners was bad, Beecham stressed that black prisoners in the South suffered even more. Southerners justified this inhumanity because "they were only 'niggahs'." Race and slavery remained at the center of his explanation of the war, and he explicitly argued that it "grew directly out of the question of slavery." He reminded his readers that "this boasted 'land of the free and home of the brave' had been in fact a land of oppression for a whole race of people." He blamed "the high mightiness of the proud and haughty Southerner of those days" and he had only contempt for "the cause for which Davis planned, Lee fought and Jackson prayed."

Beecham ridiculed the myth of the happy slave, recalling that "liberty-loving masters . . . had gone forth to war for the right to keep them [slaves] and their children in everlasting servitude." While foraging for supplies in Westmoreland County, Virginia, he "saw many a highbred Virginia lady in sorrow and in tears entreat her Dinah in vain to return to the old homestead and take care of her kind and helpless mistress in the hour of her need." Southerners maintained that blacks who fled for freedom "were foolish, of course. People always are who want a greater degree of liberty than they are enjoying, in the eyes of those who deny them such rights, and the man or woman who has once tasted liberty is never wise enough to go back to slavery voluntarily."

Not only did Beecham refuse to downplay the sectional differences that led to war, he declined to participate in the glorification of Confederate military prowess and the canonization of Robert E. Lee. While conceding Lee's genius, he asserted that the Confederate leader blundered at Gettysburg. Beecham argued that subsequent generations should not "glorify the military genius of a man who deserted the nation that educated him in the art wherein he was gifted, and turned the strength of his genius against the sword of God and the might of his truth." To Beecham, Lee was a great yet tragic man, for he suffered from a fatal flaw. Lee deserted "a nation dedicated to liberty" in order "to swear allegiance to decrepit old Virginia, the mother of the abomination of the age and the breeding ground of human chattels for the marts and shambles of the cotton states, in her mad effort to become the cornerstone in an edifice of state to be erected on the foundation of slavery and oppression. . . . Such a man can never take his place in the pages of history as one free from guile and perfect in thought and in deed."

While critical of those who mythologized Lee, Beecham also reproached Union leaders when he felt they deserved it. He gently chided General Sherman for his leadership at the first battle of Bull Run, criticized General Halleck for his policy on captured prisoners, and maintained that General McClellan "delighted in reviews more than in battles." As a survivor of the "Mud March," he rejoiced that the weather prevented General Burnside from his "last effort to hurl his defeated and demoralized army into the jaws of destruction." Beecham saved his strongest barbs for General Meade for his "gross injustice and inhumanity" in refusing to allow Union soldiers captured on the first day of the battle of Gettysburg to accept a Confederate parole and avoid Confederate prison camps.

Beecham's problems with the Union army went beyond the competence of its generals. Having spent much of 1862 in military hospitals, Beecham feared that the practice of medicine in army hospitals was nearly as great a threat to Union soldiers as the Confederate army. He claimed that convalescents were poorly fed and that surgeons and officers actually siphoned off donations of food meant for recovering soldiers.

Imbued with "the feelings of a freeborn American citizen who had grown to manhood in the glorious West," Beecham had little use for the arrogance and elitism of the officer corps. As a young private, Beecham assumed that the army would place little premium on rank. He quickly learned that rank brought privileges. Shortly after signing his enlistment papers, Beecham visited Lieutenant Colonel Henry W. Peck. Imagining that "no soldier of the republic was a menial," Beecham neglected to remove his hat. Peck's withering response, "Take off your hat, sir, when you come into the presence of your superiors," still rankled Beecham four decades later, and he resolved that if he should ever become an officer, he would "treat a private soldier as a gentleman and as an American citizen."

Beecham eventually rose to the rank of captain in the USCT and enjoyed the perquisites of officers. In seeking his commission, he encountered army red tape, but used his ingenuity to work around it. When ill, he enjoyed the superior meals served to officers at military hospitals and advised "all soldiers in the American or any other army, who are so unfortunate as to be sent to the hospital, to get into an officers' hospital, if possible." Despite his rank, Beecham never claimed superior moral status and refused to join veterans organizations that limited membership to officers.

Writing in an era of resurgent racism, Beecham saved some of his strongest prose to remind Americans of the contributions of blacks in the Civil War. Using the Bible and the Declaration of Independence to support his claims, he insisted on the "universal brotherhood of the human race." Because of the oppression suffered by blacks, Beecham felt that "the most remarkable fact connected with that great war" was "that the Afro-American came forward cheerfully and volunteered his strength, his brawn, his heart's blood to save the honor of the flag that to him and his race had been the symbol of every dishonor."

Beecham used his memoir "to disprove some of the theories or ideas that are held by white people generally, and are frequently advanced, relative to the Afro-American race." He explicitly countered racial slurs and maintained that the men of the USCT were cleaner, had greater respect for women, and were less likely to abuse alcohol than the white troops with whom he served. Indeed, he declared, "I would prefer to command a company or regiment of black, rather than white soldiers."

Beecham defended the valor of the black soldiers. He recalled with pride that "a soldier feels safe when he is with reliable men who possess the courage and the ability to meet any danger on the shortest possible notice and stand together like soldiers till the last man falls, if necessary. When in the field with the old Iron Brigade I never felt one whit safer than I did with the regiments of the Black Division."

Beecham took special aim at critics who blamed the USCT for events at the disastrous battle of the Crater. Union troops had built a five hundred foot tunnel near the besieged city of Petersburg, Virginia, and Beecham and his men did guard duty and built trenches. On the morning of July 30, 1864 Union forces set off nearly four tons of gunpowder and the ensuing explosion created a crater, 170 feet long and 30 feet deep. The white troops who led the assault after the explosion mistakenly went into the crater and then stopped rather than going around it. The black troops who had followed the lead troops were blocked by the men who had gone before them. In the ensuing confusion, the disorganized Union troops became easy targets for the Confederates, and the entire disastrous operation cost 4,000 Union casualties. General Burnside originally planned to have the USCT lead the assault, but Generals Meade and Grant overruled him. Grant feared that "if we put the colored troops in front . . . and it should prove a failure, it would then be said, and very properly, that we were shoving those people ahead to get killed because we did not care anything about them."[5]

Twenty years after the war, Colonel Henry Thomas, one of Beecham's superior officers, recalled that the black troops had been specifically drilled for the operation, and modern historians followed Thomas's lead.[6] Yet Beecham argued that his men received only three or four hours of training during the immediate weeks prior to the assault. General Burnside testified to a court of inquiry that he had ordered General Edward Ferrero, who commanded the all-black 4th Division, to drill his men and that Ferrero had reported that he had done so. Ferrero, on the other hand, seemed to corroborate Beecham's claim when he testified before the same court that the men of his division had not had as much as two weeks of total training from the day of their enlistment to the day of the battle.[7]

The USCT took heavy losses at the Crater, including 74 men killed, 115 wounded, and 121 taken prisoner or missing in the 23rd alone.[8] Some Confederates killed the black troops rather than take them prisoner. Beecham confirmed these killings and charged that Southerners "deny the truth of the cold-blooded and inhuman murders committed by their soldiers that day" against the black soldiers. Beecham himself was among the 1,600 Union soldiers (1,100 white and 500 black) who were captured and marched through Petersburg after the battle. While officers of the 4th Division were accustomed to marching with black troops, officers of all-white units found the parade humiliating and called the white officers of the USCT "nigger officers." Beecham praised the valor of the black troops at the battle of the Crater, calling them "the bravest and best soldiers that ever lived." He stressed that more blacks died that day than the U.S. army lost during the entire Spanish-American War and that military service had earned black Americans "the right to life, liberty and the pursuit of happiness, with each and every other right that belongs to any American citizen."

*   *   *

After the war, Robert and Emma Beecham left Wisconsin for Meeker County, Minnesota, where the couple started a family. The Beechams and their three children moved to Neligh, Nebraska, in 1880, returned to Sun Prairie, Wisconsin, in 1886, and finally settled in Everett, Washington, around 1894. Robert Beecham supported his family by working as a lawyer and insurance agent, and in 1904 he became jury bailiff for the superior court in Everett, where he was widely known as a civic activist.

Beecham had written some poems during the Civil War, including one about a snowball fight among Union soldiers while stationed at Alexandria, Virginia. After moving to Washington, he resumed his interest in poetry and between 1898 and 1913 published five slim volumes of poetry, focusing largely on historical themes, such as the Civil War, the Spanish-American War, and western history.[9] He also began writing prose works around the turn of the century, including the memoir that appears in this edition. The Washington, D.C., *National Tribune,* a weekly paper aimed at veterans and the predecessor of *Stars and Stripes,* first serialized the memoir between August 14 and December 18, 1902, under the title "Adventures of an Iron Brigade Man."

The serialization of his memoir whetted Beecham's appetite for further publication. One Civil War veteran from Cleveland, Ohio, wrote to the paper that he thought that Beecham's account of Gettysburg was "the most readable and easiest understood of any account of that greatest of battles I ever read."[10] Beecham soon began working on a manuscript, which was published in 1911 as *Gettysburg: The Pivotal Battle of the Civil War.*[11] Unlike his memoir, the Gettysburg book includes almost no first-person accounts of Beecham's own experiences, with the exception of his return to the battlefield in 1900. It incorporates some of the language found in chapters 4 through 6 here, but deletes Beecham's descriptions of his own wartime efforts. One contemporary reviewer, a former Confederate officer, found the book to be largely an "excellent account," although criticized Beecham for his prejudice against Lee.[12]

Beecham died at the age of eighty-two on September 12, 1920. His wife, Emma, survived him for another seven years and died in December 1927. Robert Beecham's obituary appeared on the front page of the *Everett Daily Herald.*[13] It praised his civic activism, lauded his poetry, and recalled his service in the Iron Brigade. The article politely noted that Beecham had "consistently and insistently" presented his ideas about public affairs, implying that he continued to express his opinions as strongly during his final decades as he had during his youth. Ironically, the obituary made no mention of his service with the United States Colored Troops, an omission that likely would have provoked a pointed barb from the old man.

* * *

Beecham's original manuscript memoir no longer exists, and this edition is taken from the version that appeared in the *National Tribune.* While available to scholars who have been willing to use crumbling, yellowed copies of the *Tribune* or to view it on microfilm, the memoir has largely been inaccessible for the past century. The *Tribune* serialized the memoir over four months and divided the untitled segments based on the amount of space available in each issue rather than at logical breaks in the narrative. It seems likely that the title, "Adventures of an Iron Brigade Man," was supplied by the editor rather than Beecham. This new edition divides the narrative into chapters, with titles supplied by the editor, using quotations from Beecham's prose. It also silently corrects spelling and typographical errors, standardizes capitalization and block quotations, and omits the headings inserted by the compositor, which typographically broke up the newspaper version.

*   *   *

Many individuals helped make this book possible. Lance Herdegen first called my attention to the Beecham memoir and its importance. John Kaminski at the University of Wisconsin and Greg Britton of Madison House encouraged me to prepare this edition and offered useful advice along the way. Joe Glatthaar, Alan Nolan, and Leslie Rowland generously shared their expertise on the Civil War with me, and Marge Bodre of the Everett, Washington, Public Library provided information on Beecham's later years. The U.S. Army Military History Institute and the State Historical Society of Wisconsin supplied the photographs that appear in this edition. Marc J. Storch graciously gave permission to use the photograph of Beecham in uniform that appears as the frontispiece. (Full illustration credits appear on the copyright page.) Charmaine Harbort efficiently and accurately typed the original manuscript. My wife, Therese, helped in innumerable ways, not only by assisting with this book but even more by being there day in and day out.

NOTES

1. Beecham's statements about his Civil War career have been confirmed using a variety of public records. The most useful include his pension file in the National Archives; Regimental Muster and Descriptive Rolls (Blue Books), Series 1142, Vol. 8 and (Red Books), Series 1144, Vol. 8, State Historical Society of Wisconsin; Adjutant General's Office, *Official Army Register of the Volunteer Force of the United States Army for the Years 1861, '62, '63, '64, '65,* Part 8 (Washington, D.C., 1867), p. 194. Additional details about his life have been pieced together from federal census records

as well as R. K. Beecham, *The Fields of Gettysburg: With Other Poems and Stories* (Everett, Washington: Ray, The Printer, 1905?); *Everett Daily Herald*, September 13, 1920; Everett City Directory, 1894-95, p. 74; 1900, pp. 30, 193; 1901, pp. 81, 180; 1904, p. 61; 1907, p. 59; and *History of Dane County, Wisconsin* (Chicago: Western Historical Company, 1880), 2 vols., p. 1106. The State Historical Society of Wisconsin also holds three letters from Beecham dated July 27, 1862, August 5, 1863, and June 8, 1864, Wisconsin Mss. 121S.

2. Beecham, *The Fields of Gettysburg*, p. [17].

3. The best source on the 2nd Wisconsin is Alan T. Nolan, *The Iron Brigade: A Military History* (Madison: The State Historical Society of Wisconsin, 1975).

4. For the relationship between the officers and the enlisted men of the USCT, see Joseph T. Glatthaar, *Forged in Battle: The Civil War Alliance of Black Soldiers and White Officers* (New York: The Free Press, 1990).

5. Ira Berlin, Joseph P. Reidy, and Leslie S. Rowland, eds., *Freedom: A Documentary History of Emancipation,* Series II, *The Black Military Experience* (Cambridge: Cambridge University Press, 1982), p. 522n. Grant added that he believed that the assault would have been a success had the USCT led the attack.

6. Henry Goddard Thomas, "The Colored Troops at Petersburg, *The Century Illustrated Monthly Magazine* 34 (May–October 1887), 777–82. For modern accounts that follow Thomas, see Dudley Taylor Cornish, *The Sable Arm: Negro Troops in the Union Army, 1861–1865* (New York: Longmans, Green and Co., 1956), p. 274; Hondon B. Hargrove, *Black Union Soldiers in the Civil War* (Jefferson, N.C.: McFarland & Company, 1988), p. 184; Michael A. Cavanaugh and William Marvel, *The Petersburg Campaign: The Battle of the Crater, "The Horrid Pit" June 25–August 6, 1864* (Lynchburg, Va.: H.E. Howard, Inc., 1989), p. 18; Ervin L. Jordan, Jr., *Black Confederates and Afro-Yankees in Civil War Virginia* (Charlottesville: University Press of Virginia, 1995), pp. 276–77.

7. *The War of the Rebellion: A Compilation of the Official Records of the Union and Confederate Armies*, Series I, Vol. 40, Part 1, pp. 58, 93, 524.

8. Ibid., p. 248.

9. *The Battle of Gettysburg, a poem. . . .* (Everett, Washington: Office of the Independent, 1898); *The Latest Battles of the Great Race War Or Lifting the America's Cup. A Poem in Four Can't Os!* ([Everett, Washington]: Ray the Printer, 1903); *Sacajawea and Other Poems* (Everett, Washington: Ray the Printer, 1905); *The Fields of Gettysburg: With Other Poems and Stories* (Everett, Washington: Ray, the Printer, 1905?); *Old Glory at Gettysburg, 1863–1913: Souvenir Poem of the Fiftieth Anniversary of the Great Battle* (Everett, Washington: Puget Press, 1913?).

10. *National Tribune*, October 23, 1902.

11. (Chicago: A.C. McClurg and Co., 1911).

12. James M. Garnett, "Lee and Longstreet at Gettysburg," *The Dial,* September 1, 1911, pp. 126–28.

13. September 13, 1920.

AS IF IT WERE

The First Battle of Bull Run gave Beecham and members of the Second Wisconsin their first taste of combat.

ONE

"As if it were glory and not years of bitter war"

Bull Run and a Winter of Idleness
May 1861–April 1862

I enlisted May 10, 1861, in Co. H, 2d Wis. The 2d Wis. was a three-year regiment, and one of the first mustered into the service of the United States in the war of the rebellion.

From the date of my enlistment until some time in June we put in the time learning the art of war, hoping all the time that we would not be called upon to practice the art to any great extent. On June 11, 1861, we were mustered into the United States service, and, nine days later, started for Washington, D.C. In that ride we enjoyed, to some extent, the pomp of war.

The country through which we passed was full of enthusiasm and the people seemed to wave us on, as if it were glory and not years of bitter war that awaited us. We stopped one day at Harrisburg, Pa., where we received our arms—old Harper's Ferry smoothbore muskets—which we loaded afterward in the day of battle, with one ball and three buck-shot to each piece, with powder sufficient behind ball and buckshot to drive them out of the gun barrel and at the same time nearly knock the life out of the man who stood behind the gun.

When we marched through Baltimore, we loaded our pieces and fixed bayonets, as a precautionary measure. In those days Baltimore was a hotbed of treason, and on that march through the city the people delighted our ears with cheers for Jeff Davis; but they carefully refrained from the use of brickbats and stones, so we had no occasion to use our muskets; but the demonstration did not augur an early peace, by any means.

We arrived at Washington all safe and sound, in the latter part of June, and encamped for several days in the outskirts of the national capital, which, at that time, was nothing more or less than a great, over-grown village.

On July 2 our regiment crossed the Potomac River by the way of Long Bridge, into the state of Virginia. We were there brigaded with the 69th, 79th and, if my memory serves me, the 13th N.Y. The 69th was a famous Irish regiment, commanded by Col. (afterward General) Corcoran, and carried the green flag of the Emerald Isle beside the Stars and Stripes. The 79th was Cameron's Scotch regiment, and displayed the thistle of Scotia with the American flag, the same being borne aloft by two brawny, barelegged Scotchmen. The other regiment, which was only a common, everyday Yankee regiment like my own—only mine was from the West—had nothing peculiar about it to fix it in my memory, so I am not certain as to its number, but do remember that it was a New York regiment.

Gen. William Tecumseh Sherman was honored with the command of this brigade of four regiments of volunteers, and as it was Sherman's first important command, he was just as proud of his four superb regiments as an old hen could possibly be with four broods of chickens.

Sherman's Brigade was assigned to Gen. Tyler's Division, and further than that we knew but little about the organization of the army. Of course, we knew that Gen. Scott was the general-in-chief, or in supreme command, with headquarters in Washington, while Gen. McDowell commanded the army in the field; that Sherman's Brigade was a part of Tyler's Division, and that there were other divisions in McDowell's army; but we had very little knowledge of the situation, and I presume no army ever went into the field and into battle more completely unqualified to perform intelligently the duties of soldiers and officers. There was but little if any time to drill or study the art of war, for the Confederacy had taken the initiative and confronted us with an army better prepared for a campaign than we were, and that army actually threatened the capital; so we were obliged to put in our time building fortifications and preparing defenses. All that portion of Virginia opposite Washington seemed covered with woods, and the labor required in felling the thousands of acres of trees, that might be used in sheltering an advancing army of the enemy, was great. We participated in one or two brigade drills, or, more properly speaking, brigade parades, during the early days of July, while we occupied this position, but the bulk of our time was taken up with hard work in making the position of Washington more secure, until the advance of McDowell's army began.

About the middle of July the Bull Run campaign opened. The 2d Wis. and two or three others were three-year regiments; there were also a few two-year troops but the bulk of the army was composed of three-months men, whose terms of enlistment would expire within the next 30 days, or by the middle of August. Therefore, if McDowell's army was to capture Richmond and end the rebellion, it was necessary for it to make a forward movement without further delay, while we had soldiers to do the fighting, if fighting should become necessary. So the military authorities seemed to reason, and the army moved out on its first great campaign.

Sherman's Brigade was encamped along the Warrenton Pike—the main thoroughfare leading to Centreville and Manassas—about a mile west of Fort Corcoran. We were supplied with good, comfortable wall tents, but when we started on that campaign we left our encampment in charge of a lieutenant and, probably, a hundred sick and convalescent soldiers. As we had no such thing as shelter tents in those days, each soldier rolled a woolen inside of a rubber blanket, which served for both bed and shelter, except, on rare occasions, when we took shelter beneath a bush or slept under a rail.

The Confederate army, under the command of Beauregard, did not seem to dispute our advance at first, and abandoned the defenses at Centreville, retiring behind Bull Run.

On the afternoon of July 18 Tyler's Division encountered the enemy at Blackburn's Ford, where we had our first skirmish, in which the 2d Wis. lost one man. Tyler's Division did not gain a lodgment on the west bank of the Run, and withdrew from the contest at that place. For the next two days McDowell's army lay along the eastern bank of Bull Run, while he perfected his plans and prepared for a general battle. Beauregard stood on the defensive, and the sluggish waters of Bull Run wound their course between the opposing armies.

On Sunday, July 21, the first great battle of the Civil War, known in history as "The First Bull Run," was fought, lasting about six or seven hours. Sherman's Brigade had it very comfortable at first, and many of us thought our general was a born strategist. From our camp, near the Warrenton Pike, between Centreville and Cub Run, Sherman marched us down the pike, crossing Cub Run, and arriving near the Stone Bridge, which crosses Bull Run, where he led us to the right into a grand old forest which, with its friendly foliage, sheltered us from the scorching rays of the July sun until about 11 o'clock a.m. We held that position in fine shape (we could have held it longer) until Hunter's Division had made a wide detour to the right, crossing Bull Run at Sudley's Ford, far up the creek, thus striking Beauregard on the flank and opening the battle with apparent advantage to McDowell.

During the hours we held our position in the woods in the vicinity of Stone Bridge we were amused and encouraged by an occasional shot fired by a large 32-pounder smoothbore gun—the only big gun in McDowell's army. This was planted in a commanding position near Stone Bridge, and for several hours Sherman's Brigade had nothing to do but watch the effect of the bursting shells thrown by it from time to time within the lines of the enemy.

After Hunter struck Beauregard's left and the battle had waxed hot in that direction for an hour or two, some military genius discovered that Sherman's Brigade might be used to better advantage than supporting a one-gun battery on the safe side of Bull Run, and forthwith we received orders to advance. Then Sherman moved his brigade at a double-quick along the eastern shore of Bull Run for a mile or two. Once he halted us, not to rest, but to put us in light-marching order, and to that end he ordered us to pile up our blankets and haversacks in a convenient place by the wayside, where we might return and camp for the night when the battle was over—then we knew of a certainty that he was a born strategist, or, if not at that moment, we knew it a few hours later when night closed in upon us and the whole brigade could not muster a single hardtack, to say nothing about blankets.

After getting rid of our cumbersome blankets and useless provisions, we increased our speed, and shortly after arrived at Poplar Ford, pretty well fagged out, for the day was hot. At Poplar Ford we waded the Run, about waist-deep in water, which was exceedingly refreshing. Once across the Run, we moved over the fields in the direction of the Warrenton Pike, which we reached at a point in the valley where Spring Creek crosses the pike where stood a stone house that was used for a hospital.

From this point we moved up the hill eastward toward the Stone Bridge, and went into battle.

Our brigade line extended across the turnpike and nearly at right angles with it, while the enemy seemed to be posted between our position and Bull Run. For a time the battle seemed to progress favorably. The enemy was supposed to be in our front, but in the confusion it was not an easy matter to locate his position. When our line ceased to advance there was no well-defined battle line of the enemy opposing us, that I could discover, but we halted all the same, and continued to blaze away with our old smoothbore muskets.

About this time the smoke of battle became thick and the confusion great, and I lost all trace of Gen. Sherman, not seeing him again until after we had returned to the defenses of Washington. I also lost track of our lieutenant colonel commanding the 2d Wis. Our colonel, S. Park Coon, was on Gen. Tyler's staff, and Lieut.-Col. Peck commanded our regiment in his stead.

Col. Peck was calculated by nature for a great military leader. He knew the duties of enlisted soldiers, and was aware of the fact that officers were created out of superior clay, and, therefore, always insisted that soldiers should not forget to doff their hats when they came into the presence of their superiors. It was said that Col. Peck displayed superior leadership shortly after we went into battle, by leading straight out but to rearward. Whether or not that report was true, I cannot say; but I know that I never saw our gallant lieutenant colonel again. He was not killed that day, neither was he wounded nor a prisoner of war, and he arrived safely in Washington at an early hour the next morning, but when we returned to our old camp, later in the day, our lieutenant colonel commanding was not there to welcome us, and we took our hats off in his magnificent presence no more forever.

This battle, called "The First Bull Run," to distinguish it from another fought on the same ground a little more than a year later, was never considered a very glorious affair, so far as it applied to the Union army. The strategy was deficient in some important particulars, but neither Gen. Sherman nor his brigade were the only parties at fault.

Our battle losses, as compared with the wholesale slaughter of modern battles, prove that it was a small affair—a mere skirmish, and but little fighting was done on either side. My regiment lost about 150 men and Sherman's Brigade sustained nearly one-fourth of the entire loss in

McDowell's army, which was 401 killed and 1,071 wounded. The Confederates lost 387 killed and 1,582 wounded.

The retreat began some time during the afternoon, probably about 4:30 o'clock. I never learned just why we retreated, and am not sure that any one knew. It began in this way: After blazing away with our kicking muskets until the exercise became monotonous, we ceased firing and fell back down the hill to the creek that ran through the valley, to get a drink. While there we leisurely filled our canteens. Then, as it was getting toward night, it occurred to some of the boys that our blankets and haversacks were not safe where we had stored them, or would not be after dark—besides, we would need our haversacks about supper time, and our blankets before retiring for the night, and they concluded that it would be the proper thing to do to go back and get them, and back they started. Some historians say we ran, but that's false. There was no enemy in sight—nothing to run from, and nothing to run after, except our supper and beds, and it is not likely that we ran for fun, but it seemed easier to retreat than to advance—it generally does on a battlefield.

In retiring from the field we recrossed Bull Run above the ford where we crossed it in the morning, but struck the Warrenton Pike again between Stone Bridge and Cub Run. When I reached the bridge over the latter stream, lo and behold! there was that big 32-pounder that Sherman's Brigade had supported so gloriously all the forenoon, broken down and abandoned in the center of the highway, blocking the crossing of the bridge. Behind this gun along the turnpike stood a whole battery, guns, caissons and all, in complete order, but no horses and no artillerymen. I learned, later, that the artillerymen had taken their horses down to the Run to water them and soon after returned for their battery, which they secured all right, in fact, never intended to leave it there; but the old 32-pounder was not removed from the position where I last saw it as I crossed the bridge over Cub Run, until it was removed by Beauregard's men a day or two later. This was the source of great rejoicing on the part of the Southern Confederacy for months after. In capturing that old gun, which was of less actual value on the field than one musket well handled, Beauregard thought he had won the independence of the Confederacy.

I reached our old campground, west of Centreville, a little before sunset, but the ground was all that remained to us; for on our return trip from the battlefield we missed the locality where we had so carefully stored our blankets and haversacks at the request of Gen. Sherman, and we were truly orphans in a strange land.

While we were preparing our campground for a night's rest, who should dash along the pike headed toward Washington but a whole brigade or division of congressmen and newspaper correspondents, who had gone out with the army in carriages to see the fun, and, having seen enough to satisfy them, were going home. Most of them had lost their carriages and were mounted on horseback, having left the harness on just as they unhitched, in order that they might have something to cling to, and they were clinging fast enough. There was one newspaper man in the division by the name of Carleton, who wrote a great deal about the battle and the retreat afterward, having viewed the battle from afar, as he "stood on the roof of a house near Stone Bridge." I believe he lived in New York, for some of the 69th boys seemed to recognize him, and as the cavalcade dashed down the pike, one of them remarked to a comrade, as he pointed out a gallant horseman with a huge roll of manuscript in his pocket and a bunch of quills over his ear, while his soft felt hat served for a saddle: "Do yez moind that foin-looking lad in lade of the whole gang there, Barney? Well, that's Carleton; he wroits for the papers and is one of the raciest correspondents in the army." To which his comrade made reply: "Begorrah, Pat, and I belave yez roight; he's the raciest of that gang, at all events." I'm not so sure that Carleton's soft felt felt soft, but it must have been some improvement on the bareback of a harnessed steed. We cheered and laughed till the tears ran down our cheeks as long as the cavalcade was in sight, and to the day of my death I shall never be able to recall the vision without laughing.

This cavalcade reached Washington early the next morning, safe and sound, but a little sore. From them it leaked out and gradually worked into the papers that "McDowell's army was panic-stricken!"

We had settled for the night in our improvised camp when we were roused by the bugle call which sounded "Fall in." It seems that a council of war had been called by Gen. McDowell, which, by common consent, had resolved itself into a council of retreat, where it was soon decided to begin the retreat to the defenses of Washington that night; in fact, there was nothing for McDowell to do but retreat, as the terms of enlistment of half his army would expire within a week. There was no time to issue rations, and Gen. Sherman obtained leave to put his brigade in the advance, i.e., next to the congressional and journalistic cavalry, as his men were minus blankets and provisions, and, some of them being three-year troops, their lives were worth saving. We learned, also, in that mysterious way through which knowledge is often gained in camp, that Gen. Sherman had this very retreat in contemplation when he instructed us to pile our blankets and haversacks on the bank of Bull Run, so that we might be light of foot and fleet as the wind for the home stretch.

Sherman's Brigade took its place in the advance of the infantry, and during that memorable night-march we would have kept in sight of the flying cavalry, but for the thick darkness that concealed them from view. Soon it began to rain—a gentle mist at first, then a drizzle, and by daylight it was coming down in fine shape. On our homeward march we did not sing as much as we did on the advance, but we made better time. In fact, it was the old camp before breakfast, after which we might sing again.

We reached camp in sections, from 9 to 11 o'clock the forenoon of July 22, and I had the honor of being among the first. Our comrades who remained behind in charge of the camp, had caught a glimpse of the congressional cavalry an hour or two earlier in the day, and heard the voice of Carleton as he shouted in passing: "The whole army is panic-stricken." Then they put on the camp kettles and prepared coffee and hardtack and such other articles of food as they could obtain, for our refreshment. Immediately after breaking our 24-hour fast we seemed to hear a voice of command saying: "To your tents, O 2d Wis.," and we got there.

When we retired to our tents, we hoped to enjoy a season of sleep and repose, after our long and weary march; but about noon we were aroused from our slumbers, not to partake of a nicely prepared dinner—no, and really I never learned exactly for what purpose we were aroused. I intended to ask Gen. Sherman why it was, but the general left us and went west before I found the opportunity. However, we received orders to gather up everything we possessed, and, forming in line, we abandoned our camp and were marched to Fort Corcoran, where we stood around in the rain and mud all the afternoon, while our unoccupied tents, only a mile away, were supposed to be in such dangerous proximity to Beauregard's victorious army, the advance outposts of which reached Centreville some time the next day, that our wise general deemed it prudent to sacrifice our camp, if necessary, but to save the fort at all hazards. That was the grandest display of military sagacity that came under my notice during the war.

About a hundred yards distant from Fort Corcoran there stood an old barn from which the weatherboarding had been stripped, but the frame and roof were still intact. As the shades of evening began to gather over the hills of Virginia, the orphans of the 2d Wis. began to gather beneath the roof of that lowly asylum, which afforded not standing room for all, but even a prospect of shelter was some relief from the pelting rain. It did not seem possible that Gen. Sherman, or whoever might be in control of affairs, would keep us standing around there all night. The strategy of leaving our blankets and provisions on the banks of Bull Run was bad enough, but leaving our comfortable tents unoccupied, only a mile away, while we stood out in the rain or crowded into an old, dilapidated barn for shelter the livelong night, seemed beyond reason. Therefore, I stood outside with two of my tentmates, without making an attempt to secure shelter beneath the crowded roof, until almost dark, hoping that we would either be marched back to our camp or order our tents brought up. Finally I said to my comrades: "Boys, we must hunt cover." A few yards from where we stood the end of an old plank protruded from the barnyard filth, which lead we followed and quickly unearthed not one, but two very dirty, but sound and substantial, planks, a foot or more in width and about 16 feet long. To clean these planks was but the work of a moment, but to elevate them into the loft from beam to beam above the heads of our comrades crowded therein like sardines in a box, was not so easily accomplished. With us, however, it was no roost, no shelter; and after a vigorous push we succeeded. Then drawing up our guns, cartridge boxes and other meager belongings, we perched ourselves upon our improvised balcony in the shelter of that old roof-tree, like birds of paradise in the green branches, above and beyond the reach of the alligators and anacondas of the Amazon. Perhaps we did not enjoy that night of peaceful rest, we three who were above the clouds, so to speak. If Beauregard's army had penetrated our lines that night and had run up against us, we were in a position to fix them plenty. On the whole, our position, both for comfort and for defense, in case of an attack, was far ahead and greatly more strategic than it could possibly have been had we remained in camp.

The next morning our quartermaster hustled around and found a few boxes of hardtack and some Switzer cheeses, upon which we breakfasted. About 10 o'clock the rain ceased, and a scouting party that had been sent out to reconnoiter, returned and reported that our camp had not been captured by Beauregard during the night, but was still standing where we left it. Then a party with teams was detailed to bring up our tents, and we established camp in a position where we could protect the fort. After that, we put our camp in order and began in earnest to prepare for war.

Two days later, I think, on the 25th of July, Abraham Lincoln, in company with Secretary of State Seward, visited the army in Virginia, on which occasion I had the opportunity of seeing the president for the first time. Mr. Lincoln was then in the full strength and vigor of manhood, and although he was not what people would call a handsome man, there was stamped on his face a fresh, vigorous, healthy and courageous look that inspired confidence. We had just suffered a severe and humiliating defeat, and the discouraging fact was beginning to appear plainly that we had on our hands a great war that would require every resource of the nation to prosecute to a successful issue, and we certainly needed some encouragement. It was good to be impressed with the fact that the president on whose shoulders rested this mighty burden of war, with its vast train of results, either for weal or for woe to the people of a hemisphere, was not discouraged with the outlook.

Mr. Seward stood up in the president's carriage and made quite a speech to the soldiers, in which he gave us plenty of taffy; but Mr. Lincoln did not make a speech; he only said in a mild, gentle way, that he had confidence in the ability and patriotism of the American people and their volunteer army to meet and overcome every enemy of the republic, and to reestablish the government and flag bequeathed us by the Fathers in every part and portion of our country.

The soldiers gathered around the president's carriage, all anxious to shake hands with him, and they kept him handshaking until he must have been extremely tired. I felt like shaking hands with Mr. Lincoln myself, although not given to demonstrations of that kind in a crowd, but on second thought it seemed best not to assist in wearing the poor man's life out, so I did not offer my hand, and never had the honor of shaking hands with him.

During the years of war that followed I saw Mr. Lincoln many times, and every time I noticed that the lines of care upon his kindly face grew deeper, as the burden of war became heavier from month to month and from year to year.

Shortly after this visit from the president, Gen. Sherman went west, to assume some higher command than a brigade, and I did not see him again until years after the war. Sherman became a great commander and strategist before the war ended, as every man of his old brigade knew he would from the moment he gave us the order to dump our blankets and rations on the banks of Bull Run.

I met Gen. Sherman once after the war, some time during the early 90's, at a national encampment of the G.A.R. held in the city of Milwaukee, Wis. There was present at the time a grand gathering of people, especially ex-soldiers of the Civil War, from all over the country, who were holding reunions galore. There were reunions of armies, of corps, of divisions, or brigades, of regiments and of companies. There were reunions of the survivors of campaigns, of the survivors of battles, of the survivors of prisons and of the survivors of hospitals. So, on meeting Gen. Sherman at that encampment, I suggested to him that it was an opportune time to hold a reunion of his old brigade. That if he, as its old commander, would issue a call, surely it would enthuse every member of that grand old organization present in the city. But, really, the general seemed not at all interested nor pleased with the suggestion. He said that, "notwithstanding the fact that he himself would greatly enjoy such a reunion, he thought it quite impossible after the lapse of so many years to get a sufficient number together to make such reunion interesting." I suggested that the lapse of the years was not wider in relation to Sherman's than to any other brigade organized in 1861, but, if he feared such a reunion would be too small to be pleasant, he might make the call for a reunion of the survivors of the First Bull Run, which could not fail to draw a large attendance.

At this point the general begged that I would excuse him for an hour or two, as he had an important engagement, but he would see me later and, in the meantime, I might look around among the comrades and learn about how many Bull Run survivors I could find. Of course, I excused the general, and he left me—he also left with me a lingering suspicion that he was not very enthusiastic over the reunion idea; at least, so far as it related to Sherman's Brigade or the survivors of Bull Run; but, hoping that he honestly wanted my assistance in this matter, I inquired diligently, as he suggested, with the result that I was unable to find a man outside of my old regiment who participated at all in that "First Campaign"—that is, on the Union side. I found 75 or 80 ex-Confederates there, every one of whom laid great stress on the fact that he was a survivor of the "First Bull Run, sah."

Among the boys of my old company and regiment I found a dozen or more, who were on the sick and convalescent list, and guarded and held our camp near Fort Corcoran during the Bull Run campaign, and who remembered distinctly the fagged and forlorn appearance presented by those who returned from the battle on the forenoon of July 22, 1861; but when I suggested the propriety of holding a reunion of Sherman's Brigade, as our old commander was then with us, they replied: "Aren't you a little off? Sherman commanded in the West. We were never in his brigade." The upshot of it all was, we held no reunion of Sherman's Brigade nor of the survivors of The First Bull Run. What is more, I did not again meet Gen. Sherman, for he seemed to have other and more important business on hand. If he was ashamed of his old brigade and the part he took in "Our First Campaign," so far as I was able to discover, that feeling was reciprocated.

Since that encampment I presume I have met thousands of ex-Confederates who were survivors of the First Bull Run, and could tell me more of its glories than I dreamed it possessed. No wonder we were beaten. The Confederates were all there. But never in all these years have I met a Union soldier who was there, and am therefore convinced that they have all passed over the dark river. Now Gen. Sherman is dead also, and on the Union side I am, what I hope to remain for many years to come, the sole survivor of "Our First Campaign."

In the summer of 1861, and shortly after the first battle of Bull Run, Gen. George B. McClellan was called to Washington to reorganize the Army of the Potomac, and the following November, when Gen. Scott retired from service on account of age, McClellan was made general-in-chief of the Army of the United States. As an organizer Gen. McClellan showed marked ability and efficiency, and whatever else history may record of him, it must record this one fact in his favor, that he organized one of the best armies the world ever saw—an army that no disaster could dishearten and no defeat discourage; but as a general in the field where battles were to be lost and won he was a great disappointment to the country and to the army.

In the new organization my regiment was brigaded with the 6th and 7th Wis. and the 19th Ind., and during the campaigns of 1862 was known as Gibbon's Brigade of King's Division of McDowell's Corps, Gen. McDowell retaining command of the First Corps. In the fall of 1862 the 24th Mich. was added to the brigade, and from that time on it consisted of these five regiments.

During the fall and winter of 1861-'62 our camp was located near Fort Tillinghast, about a half-mile west of the Arlington House, where Gen. McDowell had his headquarters, and many a night I did guard duty beneath the roof of the old Lee Mansion. Down in the valley toward the Potomac, a mile or more from our camp, was situated a level field or plain, which we used for a drill ground and for the purpose of regimental and brigade drill we there assembled every day, except Sundays, unless we were ordered to Ball's Crossroads for a division drill, corps maneuver, sham battle or grand review.

Thus we drilled, paraded and reviewed continuously, but we did not disturb the peace and comfort of the enemy to any great or alarming extent. Throughout the fine weather of the fall and winter of 1861, when the roads were in splendid condition and everything apparently favorable for field operations, Beauregard was drilling his army and performing field evolutions on the plains of Manassas, holding the old Bull Run line, within two days' march of us, with his pickets extended 10 miles nearer our outposts, actually menacing, if not in fact besieging, our national capital, as it appeared in the eyes of the nations, watching from afar.

But McClellan delighted in reviews more than in battles. With the Prince de Joinville and his nephews, the sons of the Duc d'Aumale—the soldiers called them "McClellan's French ducks"—in his wake, it was the crowning glory of his ambition to ride for miles along the grand array of his army prepared for review in holiday attire. Not all the ducks and other web-footed species on McClellan's staff, for he had a host of them, were French.

During the early fall of 1861 an event occurred that interested me, personally, greatly more than parade and review. This event was nothing more nor less than an order—and its results—for the vaccination of the army. I had been vaccinated several years before the war broke out, and it broke out, that is, the vaccination did, on my arm very nicely, and, as the saying is, "worked well"; but this order included all, so I was vaccinated again with the others. Now, this particular vaccine virus must have been obtained from some mangy scrub that ran wild in the fever-stricken swamps of the Campagna di Roma, and it was true to the parent stock. In my case it did not produce kinepox, though it "worked" a work of woe and wretchedness that surpassed any case of genuine small-pox, taken naturally, on record.

In the very worst cases of smallpox the patient only dies after a few days of suffering, or recovers with his beauty somewhat marred; but in this case there was no such fortunate chance as death coming to his relief, and of what value is beauty to him who suffereth eternal torment? I do not know how extensive this inoculation of the fiery mange may have been, but I know that all my tentmates got it, not only in the neck, but in every other part of their physical being, and in about 10 days from date of vaccination we were suffering all the torments of the damned, unless the damned are afflicted more terribly than mortals ever dreamed.

For the next three months life became a burden to us. Our regimental surgeons prescribed the regulation cure-all—quinine and whisky, or brown mixture—while we continued to enjoy the humor of dis-ease. Later, when the winter storms set in and the stress of drill, review and sham battle was less urgent, we secured passes to the city by turns, and there purchased sulphur by the pound and Sand's sarsaparilla and other blood purifiers by the bottle, and by a persistent course of heroic treatment, wherein we used freely a mixture of gunpowder and sulphur, we finally, toward spring, succeeded in eradicating the flower and fruit of our vaccination, but I wore on my arms and person the honorable scars received in that campaign for many years after. No, thank you; no more vaccination for me. When I'm vaccinated for cowpox again I'll take the bull by the horns—take the smallpox naturally—take strychnine—take all three at a dose. Nevertheless, from that date I have been impervious to smallpox, having been often exposed to the dread scourge, which passed me by as the idle wind.

Of course, the Administration became dissatisfied and the people of the North extremely impatient with McClellan's slow tactics. They believed that the Army of the Potomac was organized to do a greater work than simply defending Washington; but McClellan, having frittered away the fine weather of the fall and early winter until the winter storms set in, had the best of an excuse for not moving then. The first snowstorm of the winter of any importance struck us early in February while we were in camp, which was, to us, a reminder of Wisconsin winters, and we improved the opportunity of indulging in an old-fashioned Wisconsin snowballing frolic.

We had several snowstorms later in the season, some of them occurring while we were on picket, for we were sent out beyond Falls Church every once in a while to do our share of picket duty; but during the whole winter I never once caught sight of a Confederate soldier—no, there was not much firing on the picket line that winter, except to fire brush when the weather was cold.

At last the impatience of the people became so unendurable that President Lincoln issued an order that the army should move in March, which was certainly a month earlier than was safe for any army to commence offensive operations in Virginia. Then McClellan made the great mistake of his military career. With the enemy almost in sight, so near that he might engage him in battle by a vigorous push within three days, with his whole army undivided, forming a solid wall between Beauregard and Washington, with his base of supplies always in reach and no long line of communication to keep open, he threw these advantages to the wind and adopted the plan of avoiding a battle as long as possible by moving his army by water to the peninsula, thus changing positions with Beauregard and giving the Confederates the advantages over him that he refused to use against them.

If in the month of March, 1862, McClellan could have turned his army over to a general, a leader of men and a soldier, the result of the campaign of 1862 would have been different. The army had grown very tired of the monotony of "All quiet along the Potomac," and longed to grapple with the enemy in the struggle of battle for which it was organized, but the leader that was to give us a fighting chance was not with us. Then, to cap the climax of absurdity as a military movement, while embarking a part of his army at Alexandria for his trip down the Potomac, McClellan ordered an advance on Centreville and Manassas of another part of the army, as if he expected thereby to deceive Beauregard, when as a matter of fact he knew that Beauregard had abandoned the Bull Run line and removed his army by rail to Richmond to meet him on the peninsula before he ordered that advance on Centreville.

I enjoyed the honor of serving in this latter campaign, and boldly we marched to Centreville, and just as fearlessly we marched back again, but I have yet to learn that we accomplished anything more than to wear out a goodly supply of shoe leather. This march took place about the middle of March. It was not a real pleasant march, but very glorious, and the victory won was bloodless. We were at least afforded a chance to test our new shelter tents—"dog tents" the soldiers called them—which were introduced in the army just before the campaign opened.

These tents were said to have been adopted from the French, and were all right for French soldiers and for Americans who were from four to five feet long only, but for soldiers six feet tall and upward many kinks, loops and doubles were required to sleep with the whole body under cover at once. If, perchance, the long soldier, in his dreams, found himself enjoying his bed of other days, and straightened his aching limbs out, he would go at least two feet into the cold, night air; or if, with his feet braced against the firmly driven foot post, he essayed to relieve his weariness of body by uncoiling, he would awake with a start to find himself stargazing, with head and shoulders half-buried in Virginia mud. I often wondered why our War Department hadn't enough common sense to make a shelter tent that would shelter both ends of a common soldier at once.

We remained at Centreville for a few days only, during which time we had our last snowstorm of that season. On our return trip, especially the day we reached Alexandria, it rained continuously all day long, the water coming down in torrents. This March rain was delightfully cool, but about the wettest rain I ever saw. When we reached the vicinity of Alexandria there was not a dry thread among us, and our hardtack was a mass of water-soaked mush.

We camped in a fine grove of timber, and immediately on breaking ranks each soldier made a dash for anything in sight that could in any manner mitigate his uncomfortable situation. There was a board fence extending along the edge of the grove about 100 yards away, and I ran for the fence, which I reached among the first. I jerked off one board, and lo! on either hand the fence had disappeared. No man got more than one board. I gave my board to a tentmate who was just one jump behind me, and dashed for a wheatstack that then seemed the center of attraction, of which I secured an armful. The rain was still falling in torrents, the ground was everywhere flooded, and night was gathering over us. All through the grove axes were getting in their work, trees were falling in every direction and campfires were blazing upward in various places. But my tentmate and myself pitched our tent hastily, broke our board in pieces and used them for a floor, on which we spread our wheat straw, and, supperless, retired for the night. Drawing our cool, moist blanket about and over us, we were soon warm and steaming and slept comfortably till morning.

This proved to be my first, last and only field campaign under the leadership and direction of Gen. George B. McClellan. President Lincoln would not consent to have Washington left defenseless, and so detached the First Corps from McClellan's army to defend the national capital, while with the remaining force he should capture the capital of the Confederacy. Had McClellan made the Confederate army, and not the Confederate capital, his objective point, he could have kept his army in it full strength and completeness, and defended Washington while he fought the army that opposed him, with every chance of success in his favor. The First Corps remained in camp near Alexandria for a week or two, and then marched overland to Fredericksburg, on the Rappahannock. The First Corps was afterwards reunited with the Army of the Potomac and made the Antietam campaign under McClellan's command, but the writer of these sketches was not with it.

Beecham's experiences with military hospitals convinced him that army medicine could be as dangerous as the Confederate army. The decorations in this photograph of the Armory Square General Hospital only partially mask the suffering of the patients.

TWO

"I was pretty sick"

Surviving the Military Hospitals
April 1862–December 1862

Three days before the First Corps marched for Fredericksburg, in April, 1862, I was sent to the regimental hospital with fever and ague. When the corps marched I was not able for duty, and was therefore sent to the Prince Street General Hospital at Alexandria. This was my first experience with and in a general hospital, but, sad to say, and just as sad to endure, it was not my last. I only remained in that hospital about three weeks, and was not delighted with it sufficiently to desire to serve out my term of enlistment there.

Everything about the hospital was neat, clean and orderly, and for the few days that I was flat on my back it seemed that my misfortune had really led me into pleasant lines. Dr. St. John was the surgeon in charge of the hospital, under the general supervision of Dr. Summers, the medical director of all the hospitals in the city of Alexandria. Dr. St. John soon had me on my feet again, and within a week I was pronounced "convalescent" and thereafter able to take my meals at the convalescent table, as it was called; but it was my opinion then, and since that time I have had no reason to change it, that the table was not convalescent, but sick, deathly sick. I ate at that table for about two weeks, and the fare was the same yesterday, today and forever. No, I'm not faultfinding, for it is too late for that, but as a matter of history I wish to record that bill of fare, a la Prince Street Hospital, just as it was served to the sovereign citizens of America who defended the national flag in the year of our Lord 1862.

In the first place the table was made of common, surfaced boards placed on rough supports and extending the whole length of the room in the basement that was set apart from a dining room. Beside the table was neither chair, bench nor stool, and when we ate at that table we sat upon our feet. When breakfast was announced the convalescents assembled in the hall, and as they filed through the dining room door each soldier received from the hand of a kind waiter, who stood on the outside of the door over a basket of bread cut in slices, from two to three inches in thickness, from a common 5-cent baker's loaf, one slice of bread (the bread was good). Then the soldier advanced to the table, which stood groaning under the weight of a tin cup of coffee and a teaspoonful of salt beside each tin cup, tastefully arranged all around the board, up and down on either side, about three feet apart, and there he could stand while he ate his bread and drank his coffee—using the salt for butter on his bread or sugar in his coffee, as he preferred; there was no compunction with regard to the use of the salt. This was our fare for breakfast, and the dinner was like unto it, so far as the bread and the table accommodations were concerned, but in place of the cup of coffee we were supplied, usually, with a tincupful of nice pressed vegetable soup and a tin spoon, with the usual supply of salt on the board.

Sometimes, instead of the rich, pressed vegetable soup, we were supplied with a tin plate, containing a boiled potato and a bite of meat, with knife and fork to dispose of the same, and a cup of good, cold water, but in no case were we supplied with soup and the potato and meat at the same meal.

For supper we had the same lavish supply of bread and a cup of tea, served in the same artistic style, and the pinch of salt also, that was never withheld. Such was our fare day in and day out, week in and week out, so long as I ate at that magnificent table.

O, it was fine; fit for a king—an American sovereign; but, strange to say, I did not appreciate it at the time, neither did I grow strong and robust as one would suppose a man must on such carefully arranged diet. I ate at that table in the convalescent department of Prince Street Hospital, Alexandria, Va., about two weeks—it may have been a trifle longer—time flies so rapidly where one has everything to his taste. Then the medical director came around and rubbed it into Dr. St. John for not getting his patients in fighting trim more rapidly. He told the hospital surgeon in plain words that it was all nonsense keeping a lot of able-bodied men feeding on the fat of the land in a hospital, month after month, when their services were needed in the field.

After the medical director had retired Dr. St. John called the convalescents of Prince Street Hospital together and, displaying a slice of bread such as we each received from the hand of the kind waiter at each meal, thus addressed us: "I want to know if there is any soldier here who is not satisfied with the rations he gets at this hospital. If any man here wants more at a meal than this (flourishing the slice of bread), I want to send him to his regiment." Some of the convalescents who could appreciate good living and a soft snap expressed themselves as perfectly satisfied with our fare, but it seemed a pity that the doctor should not be able to find an excuse for sending at least one man to the front; so I said: "Doctor, I am not sure but that slice of bread you hold in your hand is bread enough for a meal—in fact, as our meals are served here, I think it is; but man may not live on bread alone, at least I do not care to, and the soldier who is satisfied with the fare we get at this hospital is certainly not a hard kicker, and for one I'm ready to be returned to my regiment, where I can get a decent meal." My request was granted without argument that very day.

In rejoining my regiment, which was at Fredericksburg, I made my first trip down the Potomac River as far as Belle Plain Landing, which was Gen. McDowell's base of supplies, where I landed about sunset. That night I slept in some out-of-the-way corner, and the next day footed it across North Neck to the Rappahannock River, where I found my regiment in the full enjoyment of camp life, without an enemy in sight.

During the summer of 1862 the First Corps soldiered in the valley of the Rappahannock mostly, but we were not happy, believing that McClellan was reaping all the glory on the Chickahominy and would capture Richmond and end the war without any assistance from us; in fact, many of us hoped he would. We marched back and forth from Fredericksburg to Warrenton several times, and once we marched southward toward Richmond a day's journey. This latter movement was made just as the series of battles in front of Richmond, known as the Seven

Days' Battle, began, which ended in McClellan's retreat or flank movement, as it is sometimes called, to the James River. The First Corps was very anxious to join McClellan, and when this movement began we felt sure that the fighting line before Richmond was our destination, and were sorely disappointed when we doubled on our track and came back to Fredericksburg. However, many of us lived to see all of the fighting line we desired.

Gen. Gibbon was in command of our brigade. Gibbon was a regular army officer—captain of Battery B, 4th U.S. Art.—when the Civil War began. Having nothing else to do in the early summer of '62, he thought it an opportune time to make to make "Regulars" of his brigade. So he issued an order directing that each and every soldier should be supplied with an extra uniform, to be worn on parade, and also that each soldier should have two pairs of canvas leggins. In making his requisition for these supplies for his regiment, Col. Sol Meredith, of the 19th Ind., made also a requisition for four extra mule teams to transport the extra luggage, as a gentle reminder to Gibbon that infantry marched on foot and carried their belongings; but Meredith did not get his mule teams, though we all got our leggins and extra uniforms.

For the next few days Gibbon's Brigade was the flower of the First Corps when we appeared on parade, all dressed in bran-new uniforms and neat and clean canvas leggins, and Gen. Gibbon was greatly pleased with the success of his undertaking. Then came marching orders, and the corps moved up the valley. Of course, no volunteer soldier would pack an extra pound in June weather, much less an extra uniform and a lot of useless canvas leggins, so each soldier donned his best and abandoned all superfluous luggage. The next time we appeared on parade, Gibbon's Brigade was only a trifle better dressed than the balance of the corps, and there was not a leggin in sight; Gen. Gibbon made no further attempt to enforce regular army methods, and acknowledged that this brigade made a volunteer of him. However, Gibbon was a splendid brigade commander, quick to learn the needs of the men under his command, and careful to accord to them the rights of soldiers.

With regard to the part taken by the First Corps in the campaign of the early summer of 1862 history is wrong—or at least some histories are. I quote from Scudder's *School History of the United States,* page 395:

While Johnston was holding McClellan in check a brilliant Confederate commander, Gen. T. J. Jackson, was making a series of rapid movements against divisions of the Union army which were in the Valley of the Shenandoah. . . . In quick succession Jackson met and repulsed Gens. Fremont, Banks and McDowell, and then joined Lee.

McDowell's Corps was not in the valley of the Shenandoah, and Jackson did not meet it or any part of it until after McClellan had been driven from in front of Richmond to the James River.

Early in July, and after McClellan had been defeated in his purpose to capture Richmond, Gen. Pope was assigned to all the forces along the Rappahannock and Rapidan Rivers in the immediate front of Washington, consisting of the First Corps, under McDowell, and other Union forces commanded by Banks and Fremont, which army thus improvised was called the Army of Northern Virginia. Gen. Pope immediately issued his famous order, known in history as the "Headquarters in the Saddle Order," which was read to each regiment at dress parade and thereafter freely commented upon and discussed by the soldiers.

Gen. Pope was a fighter, and began at once to put his army in shape to meet the certain advance of Lee against Washington, and the campaign which followed was a hot number. Lee, having driven McClellan from in front of Richmond and cooped his army up at Turkey Bend, on the James River, lost no time in turning his attention to Pope's army as the only remaining obstacle blocking his way to the national capital and complete victory. Here we had a practical illustration of McClellan's lack of generalship in uncovering Washington in the outset of his campaign, which led to the segregation of the army, and also of the wisdom of President Lincoln's order retaining the First Corps for the defense of the capital.

The best that Pope could be expected to do was to hold Lee in check until McClellan could return from the field of his failure and reunite the army; but McClellan was in no hurry; he "took no note of time," not even from its loss and the loss of a campaign. The only reason that the writer of these sketches did not remain with Pope during that campaign in the saddle was that Providence would not permit it. Probably the world lost much from the fact that I was not there to chronicle the events as they occurred, but I have always found some personal consolation in believing that what was the world's loss was my gain.

A short time before headquarters were fully established in the saddle, I was sent to the regimental hospital with malarial fever. Then when the tramp of war sounded and my comrades marched away to glory and many of them to death, I was sent, with others in a like condition, to try again the peaceful rest of an Alexandria hospital. If I had been consulted in the matter I would have preferred taking my chances with my regiment; but, sick or well, a soldier must obey orders, and the orders were to send the sick to Alexandria.

This providential interference brought me again in contact with the general hospital system of the United States of America as it was practiced in those days.

From Fredericksburg we crossed the peninsula to Belle Plain Landing on the Potomac, from which point we took a boat up the river. On our arrival at Alexandria, and while attendants were carrying the helpless on stretchers from the boat to the ambulances (I was able to walk without assistance), I was accosted by a young officer who wore a lieutenant's shoulder straps and the uniform of an assistant surgeon, who inquired as to the number of sick on board, where we were from, etc., and presuming that his young heart was full of the milk of human kindness, I gave him such information as I was able, answering all his questions courteously and not once alluding to myself to attract his sympathetic ear. Then the young dude surprised me exceedingly by venturing this outspoken and very plain statement directed to me personally: "Well, sir, I don't think you are very sick, and men who are able for service should be in the field and not in the hospital." I never asked the dear little doctor if he intended that as medical advice for which he expected a fee, for I felt perfectly willing to pay him whatever his intentions were, and I said: "My dear pink-and-white friend, what's it to you? If I choose to play off and come to Alexandria on a lark, is it any of your business?" And then, in connection with full payment for his kindly suggestion, I made some remarks and used some expressive English terms, not necessary to repeat, but which the doctor could not fail to understand perfectly. The transaction of payment was all by word of mouth, and I did not occupy more than a minute of time, but I felt assured that the young doctor was perfectly satisfied that his disinterested interest in the state of my health was amply and generously rewarded. Being satisfied of that fact, I walked the gang plank and took my seat in an ambulance.

The ambulance conveyed me to and deposited me at the Mansion House Hospital. The surgeon in charge was Dr. Brinton, with the same medical director in supervision of the hospitals of the city who held that position in April when I made my first acquaintance with general hospitals. As I knew from experience what it meant to sit on one's feet at a table for convalescents, and as I was pretty sick myself, notwithstanding the opinion of the kind young doctor I met on the boat to the contrary, I stuck to my bed until I was ashamed to keep it any longer, for as long as a patient remained bedridden he could not ask for better treatment. In a week or 10 days Dr. Brinton had me up and around, and then the convalescent fun began again.

Mansion House was the place where Col. Ellsworth was killed, in the spring of 1861. It was now being used as a hospital, but as such was no improvement over Prince Street. Our table, dishes, soup, salt, potato and bite of meat, tea, coffee, water and bread were of the same order and served in the same delightful manner. In no case were we allowed soup and a bite of meat and potato at the same meal, and at no meal was the health-giving teaspoonful of salt withheld any more than at Prince Street Hospital; but at the Mansion House there was one noticeable improvement worthy of record: When our meals had been prepared with such wonderful culinary skill and the table arranged with such artistic care, it was certainly right and proper that the officials in authority at the hospital should see and commend, and for that reason the convalescents were never allowed to enter the dining room until the table, with its bountiful array of luscious fruits, choice viands and sumptuous roasts, was thoroughly inspected by the surgeon and his staff. Imagine several hundred half-starved soldiers waiting for from 15 minutes to three-quarters of an hour, as we often did, until the tea, coffee or soup was as cold as it could get in July or August for a lot of chumps to go through the farce of inspecting the diet of worms. This is no josh. The worms could always be found in the pressed vegetable soup if the inspectors cared to look closely for them. Those pressed vegetables were very nutritious and, for a convalescent, far superior to vegetables freshly gathered from a garden; for that reason they were used in the hospitals when fresh vegetables could be obtained readily, for in addition to the onions, beets, cabbage, carrots, turnips, parsnips, etc., etc., there were the sweet and delicious worms, that could not be found in the fresh, and when they were all pressed nicely together and made into a rich soup, is it a wonder that it filled the patriotic soul of the convalescent soldier with renewed ardor, as it filled his stomach with the new inspiration of health? When a little down at the heel there was really nothing to be compared to a cup of pressed vegetable soup to put him firmly on his feet, especially when he stood up to eat it; therefore no chairs, or other seats, were allowed in the dining room. I did not stand at the convalescent table in the Mansion House Hospital basement many days; in fact, only a few days were required to make any man robust and ready for duty. Besides, on the 9th of August the battle of Cedar Mountain was fought, and the wounded were sent in from the front. Then, also, many of the attendants, nurses and wardmasters, on duty in the hospital, were sent to their regiments in the field and their places filled from the convalescents.

The room wherein I sojourned was filled with wounded from this battlefield, and I was detailed as the attendant of that room. I had under my care seven or eight patients, none of them severely wounded, but while confined to their rooms and beds, had excellent appetites. I had the care of the room and was expected also to look after the needs and supply the wants of these wounded men.

The first day after assuming my new duties, when the time came for dinner, I went into a side kitchen or pantry where the head waiter or boss of the ward, who brought the food for the patients from the main kitchen in the basement, dished out or divided up the rations for the inmates of the several rooms in the ward. The supply I received was insufficient to satisfy the hunger of the men under my care, and when I returned for more it was curtly refused me. I had some unpleasant words with the boss, and, not being able to obtain the food supply that would satisfy the appetites of my patients, went below to interview the chief cook or any other person of higher authority where an appeal might lie, but was met with a flat refusal to discuss the matter at all. Nevertheless, I persisted in discussing and cussing as the occasion required until the hospital chaplain happened to come that way, to whom I referred the situation. The chaplain kindly consolidated his forces with mine and together we captured the fort. When we arrived at a settlement I got food sufficient for a dinner for the men in my room, and thereafter I was never refused anything I asked for in that kitchen, and the men in my charge got all they wanted to eat of good, wholesome food, and, besides, I did not live so very poorly myself.

While at this hospital a certain Massachusetts lady, by the name of Mrs. Waggoner, called in the interest of Massachusetts soldiers particularly and in the interest of Union soldiers in general. She had with her the usual supply and assortment of tracts, pamphlets and other reading matter for the soldiers, which the surgeons in charge always allowed to be freely distributed. Mrs. Waggoner also had, in addition, some canned goods, such as jellies and fruits, that had been contributed by the good people of the Old Bay State for the good of her soldiers and other Union soldiers in the hospitals, which she attempted to distribute; but our wise and vigilant medical director, Dr. Summers, caught on to what was being done and forthwith interposed his authority to prevent the further continuation of such malpractice, by which the health and the lives of the soldiers under his charge were being placed in jeopardy. The old doctor worked himself into a frightful passion and fumed and raged like a madman, ordering Mrs. Waggoner to take her trash out of the hospital, saying that the patients therein were supplied with an abundance of wholesome food, and that such stuff would serve no other purpose than to make them sick and keep them away from the front, where they were needed.

I think perhaps no other officials in the service of the United States possessed the spirit of self-sacrifice in such a remarkable degree as our hospital surgeons. Dr. Summers was an average specimen of the fraternity, and there was no doubt of his perfect willingness to run the risk of the loss of health and life by devouring jellies and canned fruit by the wholesale, if thereby he could only keep the stomachs of the soldiers free from such contaminating trash. Many a devoted surgeon lost his valuable life in that way. It was most remarkable how careful our hospital surgeons were that the patients confided to their care should not destroy their health by overeating. I noticed that many times.

I rather enjoyed my sojourn in Mansion House Hospital, especially the latter part of it, when I stood no more by the convalescent table three times a day, but—as I wrote my sweetheart in Wisconsin—I did not enlist to do hospital duty, and when Pope finished his campaign in the saddle and brought his army back to the defenses of Washington on

Sept. 1, I asked to be discharged from the hospital and allowed to return to my regiment.

When I left Mansion House Hospital, about the 1st of September, if I had been discharged—that is, set at liberty and allowed to return to my regiment, as I requested and expected—I could have found my regiment within three or four hours, for at that time the whole army was west of the Potomac. I was not so dealt with, however. I was sent, with other soldiers from the various hospitals in Alexandria, under guard, to a place called "Convalescent Camp," situated perhaps a mile and a half from the city, and there we were all retained for three days and until the army had crossed the Potomac and was well on its way toward the Antietam battlefield.

This transaction on the part of the authorities, and another like unto it, which followed, I always believed to be the meanest, most outrageous and uncalled for trick ever played on a loyal soldier of the republic. The convalescent tables in the hospitals were bad enough, but though the value of the daily ration per soldier did not exceed 10 cents, he had a roof over him and a clean, comfortable cot whereon to sleep. In that Convalescent Camp, the rations were not only too miserably poor to mention, but we were obliged to sleep in the dirt under an old tent, without bed or blanket, unless a man happened to have a blanket of his own, which very few of us possessed. Why such a disgraceful institution was maintained or allowed to exist in sight of Washington I never could imagine; but there it was, the equal of which I never saw in the shape of a camp outside of a Southern prison pen.

After the army had gotten well out of our reach we were all sent, under guard, to Washington and quartered for the night at the Soldiers' Home. The next morning we were turned loose, without blankets, tents or provisions, to subsist as best we could until we should find our commands in the wake of an army that was two days' march in advance of us. There were several hundred of us, I could not tell how many, but certainly enough to form a fair-sized regiment. Shortly after we started, a double spring wagon, containing a man and woman, passed us, and getting ahead of our column kept along just in advance until noon, when it halted and the woman passed out a sandwich to each soldier as he marched by. This was the only food of any kind that I received, except what I begged or stole, until I arrived in Baltimore—for I did not succeed in reaching my regiment—some two weeks later, about as near dead as a man cold be, and certainly in the worst situation I ever found myself during my whole life.

The first night out we camped—with or near the 36th Mass.—a new regiment just going to the front, and from some of the soldiers I begged a few hardtack. After that night we lived on green corn, green apples and potatoes, that we stole when we could get a chance, for we had no money to buy with. One night, three or four of us being together, we found a deserted shack with a potato patch attachment, from which we gathered sufficient for our supper, and making a fire in the fireplace of the shack of which we had taken peaceful possession, were engaged in roasting our potatoes, when we were disturbed by an old man, who claimed ownership of the premises and ordered us away, calling us stragglers and other pet names. I tried to explain our situation, but the old man would listen to no explanation, and I finally told him to go to Halifax, and we would stay in the shack. The old man went, but soon returned with an officer of the provost guard, who ordered us out, and as he evidently had the wherewith to enforce his order, and would not listen to any explanation of our situation, we obeyed the order and camped in the woods that night.

After about a week I became sick. I dragged myself along about half a mile to a wayside hotel, where my comrades left me and pushed on in the hope of overtaking their regiments. When I recovered my taste for bread, I begged food of an old Negro, who kindly supplied my needs, and as soon as I was able to walk to the station, about a mile away, I did so, intending to take the first train that came along, without regard to where it might be going. After waiting at the depot about three hours, a train drew up, which I boarded. I had not a cent with which to pay for a ride, but Providence assisted me. The car was full to overflowing of paroled Union soldiers captured by Jackson at Harper's Ferry, and in that crowd the conductor overlooked me. That train in due time landed me in Baltimore.

I do not remember the date that I reached Baltimore. It must have been after some of the battles of the Antietam campaign had taken place, for while I was lingering around the depot—which lingering lasted several days—a train loaded with Confederate prisoners of war halted for half an hour on the track, during which time many things in the shape of eatables were passed to the Confederates by the sympathetic, without any objection being made by their guards. I speak of this from the fact that I afterward saw the situation reversed and the Confederate guards over the Union prisoners of war were not so humanely disposed.

The reason I lingered around the depot in Baltimore was because for a time I could do no better. In my whole life I was never, before or since, placed in such a trying and discouraging situation. I was alone in a great city, without a cent in my pocket, and with nothing to show where I belonged or where I came from except a descriptive list which I had taken from my regimental hospital when I was sent to Alexandria, upon which the surgeon had endorsed the date of my discharge from that hospital. I was sick, and needed medical care, but how was I to obtain it without a friend or a living soul in the city to whom I might apply for assistance? For two or three days I lay around the depot, sleeping at night wherever I could find an empty bench or unoccupied space.

The Sanitary Commission had a room in connection with the depot where any soldier could obtain food when hungry, and there was no danger of starvation, but I needed and felt that I was entitled to all the comforts and conveniences that a United States general hospital could afford. Finally a white-haired old man, who seemed to have some influence, if not authority, and certainly possessed some humanity as well as common sense, came around and kindly inquired into my situation. To him I told my story and requested him to find an army surgeon if possible, and assist me in getting into a hospital, which he readily consented to do, and leaving me, soon returned with a surgeon. The doctor said I was certainly a fit subject for the hospital, and when the old gentleman insisted upon it, he wrote me a certificate to that effect. Then the old man asked: "Now, doctor, will you send an ambulance and take this man to the hospital?" But the surgeon had some excuse—there was no ambulance at his command just then, but after a while he would see to it. Then the old gentleman said in a tone of impatience, "I see, doctor, that it is not your intention to attend to this matter promptly as it deserves, so I will attend to it myself." Then turning to me he said, "I'll send my grandson around with a carriage after you in a few minutes." I did not learn the old man's name, and never saw him again, but within 15 minutes the boy came with the carriage, and I rode like a laird up to

"Stewart's Mansion," situated on a hill, probably two miles from the depot, and was then being occupied and used for a hospital.

On reporting at Stewart's Mansion the surgeon in charge was at first inclined to refuse me admittance, saying that the hospital was already full; but when I told him in plain words that as a United States soldier I was entitled to care and medical treatment, and would not leave that hospital until I was able for duty and properly discharged from it as a soldier was entitled to be, he concluded to find room and allowed me to stay.

I remained in that hospital something over three months, during which time I had several ups and downs. It seemed an easy matter to get down, but not so easy to get up, for the convalescent table at Stewart's Mansion would not put a man on his feet as quickly as at Alexandria, for here we had seats upon which to sit at table. This hospital, so far as convalescents were concerned, was a great improvement over those where I had formerly sojourned. The bread was cut into respectable slices and placed upon the table in dishes, and every soldier was allowed to eat as much as he pleased. We had coffee for breakfast and dinner and tea for supper. The pressed vegetable soup and diet of worms had no place in Stewart's Mansion Hospital. We usually had a potato and small piece of meat for dinner in addition to our bread and coffee, and during one whole week we had butter for supper, not in lavish quantity, but enough to spread one slice of bread, and if used with economy it could be made to veneer two slices. It was along in December that this butter experiment was tried, which was brought about from the fact that the ladies of Baltimore living in the vicinity of Stewart's Mansion had requested the hospital authorities to allow them to furnish the inmates thereof with a Christmas dinner, and in order to learn whether or not the soldiers could endure thus to be pampered, butter was ordered served once a day until its effect on the health of the soldiers was ascertained. After using butter for supper every day for a whole week without any serious injury to the health of the convalescents, the ladies were authorized to proceed in their preparations for an old-time Christmas dinner for the inmates of the hospital.

I have every reason to believe that the value of a soldier's daily ration at Stewart's Mansion Hospital did not exceed 15 cents, but it was such an improvement on what I had previously experienced that, comparatively, it seemed little short of a paradise. I have no means of knowing what it cost the government per soldier, but presume the Government paid enough to ensure at least army rations for the inmates of hospitals. The rations actually furnished fell far short of camp or field rations, and some greedy contractor made a handsome profit off the stomachs of Uncle Sam's soldiers in every one of these hospital deals. While at Stewart's Mansion I accidentally got a peep into a kind of storeroom in connection with the hospital, where canned goods, contributed by the people for the use and benefit of the soldiers, were stored. There was wagon loads of it—enough to furnish the table at every meal with some delicacy, but nothing of the kind ever found its way to the convalescent table. As the medical director of Alexandria said, such trash would make the soldiers sick, and out of regard for the health of the dear soldier, the medical fraternity and their hangers-on in the various hospitals disposed of that trash themselves.

Shortly after taking up quarters at Stewart's Mansion I wrote home for money, and as soon as I was able to get out, I went every day to a restaurant and indulged in an extra meal or dish of oysters, which seemed not to throw me into convulsions any more than the butter did when served for supper.

When Christmas arrived the ladies of Baltimore had their dinner in readiness, and such a dinner! There was roast beef, roast turkey, chicken pie, cranberry sauce—in short, everything that goes to make up an American Christmas banquet. There was an abundance of everything and nothing lacking, and for once the inmates of Stewart's Mansion Hospital enjoyed a feast fit for a hundred kings. It would have been better if the generous supply of food furnished on that occasion could have been used for the benefit of the inmates of the hospital by increasing their daily rations for a month instead of stuffing themselves for one meal only and then going back to their old meager fare, but probably not one of the ladies who participated in supplying that feast knew that they were furnishing a dinner for the hospital inmates as far above their everyday fare as heaven is above the lowest depths.

That dinner if served in an Alexandria hospital would without doubt have made a fat graveyard, but in Baltimore its effects were not bad. I know I stood the pressure all right, and did not learn of a single death resulting therefrom. The next day I informed the surgeon in charge that any man who could eat the dinner I ate on Christmas without a relapse must be out of immediate danger, and, therefore, I was ready to go to the front. The surgeon seemed to agree with me, and the following day I returned to the Army of the Potomac by way of Washington and the Potomac River, finding my regiment in winter quarters about a mile and a half from Belle Plain Landing.

Members of the Second Wisconsin Volunteer Infantry Band, who sought to inspire Beecham and other men of the division.

THREE

"A campaign of adventure"

From the Mud March to Chancellorsville
January 1863–June 1863

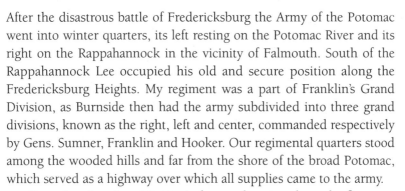

After the disastrous battle of Fredericksburg the Army of the Potomac went into winter quarters, its left resting on the Potomac River and its right on the Rappahannock in the vicinity of Falmouth. South of the Rappahannock Lee occupied his old and secure position along the Fredericksburg Heights. My regiment was a part of Franklin's Grand Division, as Burnside then had the army subdivided into three grand divisions, known as the right, left and center, commanded respectively by Gens. Sumner, Franklin and Hooker. Our regimental quarters stood among the wooded hills and far from the shore of the broad Potomac, which served as a highway over which all supplies came to the army.

From Jan. 1 to Jan. 20, 1863, the weather was about the finest we ever experienced in Virginia during the winter months. No rain fell. There was hardly a frosty night. The roads were dry and hard, and soon became nearly as dusty as in midsummer. Gladly the army would have enjoyed such superb weather all winter, while it rested and recuperated its wasted energies after the wearisome and discouraging campaigns of 1862; but very soon it became evident to the vision of every soldier that preparations were going on for another forward movement, and that nothing short of Divine interposition, to compass a change in the weather or in the knowledge and military sagacity of the commanding general, would save us from taking upon our shoulders the heavy burdens of a winter campaign.

Gen. Burnside had been terribly defeated and humiliated at the battle of Fredericksburg in December, and in his great anxiety to retrieve his waning fame he seemed incapable of realizing the fact, so plain to every private soldier in his army, that, situated as he was, with a river in his front and the opposite side guarded by a skillfully posted, victorious army, under the eye of a vigilant and war-wise general, always ready and determined to dispute his passage, a winter campaign could not be a success. Even if he won a battle, he could not hope to gather the full fruition of victory, but could do no more than winter his army south of the Rappahannock, with a river at his back instead of in front of him, thus increasing the danger of his position and depriving his army of much needed rest.

Many, therefore, were the silent prayers, as soldiers pray, offered up to the God of Battles and disposer of the destinies of nations, that the winter storms, which never fail in Virginia, might come speedily; or, if not, that Burnside might be made content to utilize the winter months— which were really a Godsend to him and his greatly demoralized army— and the strong and secure defensive position which he occupied, in thoroughly resting, reorganizing and reinforcing his army. But prayers were of no avail, so far as they related to Gen. Burnside's ideas; nevertheless, God controlled the elements and interposed the hand of His power in due season, whether in answer to our prayers or of His own good pleasure it really does not matter.

Our marching orders, which we had been expecting for several days, finally came on the afternoon of Jan. 19. At daylight on the following morning we broke camp and the long-to-be-remembered winter campaign began.

The position of rear guard of the Left Grand Division of the army had been assigned to our brigade, and after moving out from our camp on the main highway about half a mile, we formed a line near the road, stacked arms and waited for the Grand Division to pass. Jan. 20, 1863, dawned beautifully upon us, without so much as a cloud in all the heavens; but as we waited by the wayside for the troops to pass we noticed a gathering haze in the east, which gradually thickened and ere long obscured the sun. Then a gentle mist began to fall, which rapidly increased in volume and dampness, and by 10 o'clock a.m. a regular old-fashioned Virginia rain had set in in dead earnest. As the day advanced the downpour became heavier. Still we waited and still the troops marched by, the artillery plowing up the highway, the long trains of baggage wagons mixing the roads into endless mortar beds, through which the infantry waded and wallowed; and still the rain poured down.

The afternoon was far spent ere the last of the Grand Division had passed; then we of the rear guard fell in and followed in their wake. Night closed in early, and by 5 o'clock p.m. it was dark as Egypt in the days of the plague. Then the floodgates of heaven seemed to open upon our heads, but still we plodded and floundered forward in the darkness and mud, drenched to the skin, chilled to the very marrow in our bones by that icy winter rain. It was a night to be remembered, a march that could not be forgotten.

About 4 o'clock the next morning we halted and went into camp, where we could find neither stick, hummock nor solid ground, but literally a wide sea of mud. There we pitched our tents, using our muskets for tent poles and our bayonets for tent stakes, and spreading our cool blankets on the soft ooze found a peaceful repose.

When morning dawned we moved our position to a place where we could obtain wood for our campfires, and proceeded to make our coffee. About noon the shower let up and we improved the balance of the day in getting our camp in shape. The forward movement had been brought to a standstill. The army was "stuck in the mud" and unable to proceed farther upon this winter campaign, the glory of which was revealed in dreams only to no living man except Gen. Burnside, whose mighty military mind conceived it and wherein it faded and perished.

Thus was Gen. Burnside frustrated in his last effort to hurl his defeated and demoralized army into the jaws of destruction. There is no shadow of doubt that this storm saved the Army of the Potomac from a worse defeat than it ever experienced.

After a few days, when the sky had cleared and the roads had settled somewhat, we moved slowly back to our former winter quarters near the Potomac, and soon thereafter Burnside resigned, and Joseph Hooker became our commanding general instead, for which change we had great reason to be thankful. Burnside did not retire from the army, however, and although this was his last campaign as commander of the Army of the Potomac, the following year he commanded the Ninth Corps, and took an active part in Grant's campaign against Richmond. Burnside lacked the genius of a great general, which mark the distinction he shared fully with many of his brother generals, but in all probability did the best he could.

When Gen. Hooker took command of the Army of the Potomac, about Feb. 1, 1863, he found it in the most demoralized condition of all its history. Many of the soldiers had lost faith in the ability and patriotism of our leaders, believing, from sad experience, that they were no good, and desertions had become alarmingly frequent.

Gen. Hooker was, above all else, an organizer, and although he never won a victory in the field while in command of the army, the victory he won in camp over the forces of demoralization was signal and of lasting duration. The country owes an eternal debt of gratitude to Gen. Joseph Hooker for the mighty work he accomplished within the next three months. When the Army of the Potomac started on its spring campaign of 1863, it could suffer defeat without losing heart, or win a victory without losing its head. No army, carrying within its heart of hearts a nobler ambition of patriotism, a higher resolve to accomplish a stupendous duty, ever took the field.

Gen. Hooker put more faith in the ability of a well-fed, well-clothed and thoroughly disciplined, than in a weary, dispirited and poorly supplied army, to win victories and accomplish the great work that war alone could fulfill, and he went about the work of reorganization with a will. In the first place, he arranged to supply the army with soft bread to replace the everlasting hardtack as an article of daily diet, of which the soldiers had become extremely tired, and within a week ovens were constructed and bakeries running in every division of the army, and fresh bread was thereafter issued daily. Fresh vegetables were also supplied, and other improvements made in the army commissariat whereby the common soldier recognized the fact that his interests were acknowledged and respected, which policy quickly reduced desertions to a minimum.

Gen. Hooker gave his soldiers a season of rest and better food, both of which they greatly needed, but at the same time no part of the activity of military drill, discipline, and preparation for the struggle that must surely come with the return of spring was neglected. Whenever an opportunity offered to steal a march on the enemy, to disturb his comfortable repose, to harass his communications or invade his field of supplies, thus reminding Lee that the Army of the Potomac was out of the mud, such opportunity was not neglected.

One of the expeditions within the lines of the enemy's source of supplies, in which the writer of these sketches took part, proved to be quite a campaign of adventure and furnished a variety of entertainment. The troops comprising this expedition were three battalions, one each from the 2d, 6th, and 7th Wis., about 300 in all, under the command of Col. Fairchild, of the 2d Wis. The expedition left Belle Plain Landing on the morning of March 25, 1863, going down the Potomac on a small river steamboat. I have a distinct recollection not only of the year, but of the day of the month also, for on that day I was just 25 years old. Possibly the excursion was planned in honor of my birthday. At all events, I was there to receive all the honors offered and enjoy all the diversion such as excursion could afford, just as much as though I were actually the central figure.

As we steamed down the broad Potomac the wind blew chill from the northwest, and we high privates (that was before I had received my first promotion to a corporality) and noncoms found a deck passage the place of all others for an enjoyable birthday picnic. The cabin was small and fully occupied by the officers of the expedition, who kept well within shelter.

When the noon hour arrived and we began preparations for our picnic dinner, we found close picking. There was no kitchen range on that steamboat deck, and the only comfortable spot was within range of the warm side of the smokestack, which was a position in great demand. As master of ceremonies, it being my birthday, it was my especial duty to devise some means whereby my guests of the upper deck could be provided with a cup of hot coffee, so I bestirred myself as a man can only under the weight of great responsibility. Ah, as I looked upon the little waste pipe, the top of which stood about five feet above our cabin floor, wasting, in frantic puffs, its mellow, delicious breath on the cold Virginia wind, at once an idea struck me, and immediately I put that idea into practical use. Taking my army camp kettle, which held about a quart, I placed within the cold ingredients for a cup of coffee and attaching to the pail thereof about three feet of string, I lowered away the pail into the hot throat of the exhaust pipe. Within five minutes I drew it forth, and lo! there was a dish of coffee fit for the general of the army.

It was not necessary to invite my guests to participate. It is wonderful how prone are all mankind to follow a good example, and especially is this true of soldiers. They are also firm believers in the truth of the old proverb, "God helps him who helps himself," and in this instance I had only to set the example; the boys helped themselves. That is to say, I had no sooner withdrawn my pail from the steam pipe, when it was replaced by not one, but by several pails. Then the activity of the picnic began in earnest. The new process of cooking by steam was noised abroad to the farthest corners of our encampment, and the invention appropriated by each and every soldier that could reach the steam pipe as an inherent right, coequal with life, liberty and the pursuit of happiness—for here, indeed, was happiness itself. Every soldier who could muster a tin pail and string was happy, and some who had no tin pail attached strings to pieces of meat and gave them a steam-pipe baptism.

Within 15 minutes after the discovery we were all more interested in the new process of cooking than we were in the scenery along the banks of the Potomac. Long strings, short strings, and strings of medium length were in use, and the little exhaust pipe was loaded from the muzzle far downward within close proximity of its powerful lungs, that began ere long to indicate a stuffed-up condition, as if suffering from influenza. Then something startling happened, for a time throwing the gay party of picnickers into a state of wild confusion. The patient engineer, poor man, striving to do his duty in the lower regions, and all unconscious of the discovery of the new process and the peace and contentment that reigned up stairs, surmised that the steam had become waterlogged in his exhaust pipe, and in order to make its action more perfect and clear its throat of the impediments to exhalation, at that moment blew off steam. Great Scott! But didn't he clear out the pipe? The way tin pails, cold water, hot coffee and stray pieces of meat deluged that steamboat deck and disturbed the complacency of my birthday picnickers was laughable to the onlooker who had received his coffee and given place to a comrade at the busy steam pipe; but for the boys who had not withdrawn their investments, it was not so funny, they being unable to see just where the laugh came in. In fact, not a few of them jumped to the conclusion that the engineer had intentionally played them a vile and shabby trick, and in the heat of their indignation were preparing to pull the steam pipe out by the roots as a useless appendage; but the storm blew over in a minute, for the engineer, on learning the ruin he had wrought, came personally upon deck and took it all back, as far as he could. That is to say, he apologized, and protested that the mishap was unintentional on his part, and that he had no desire to interfere with our inalienable rights in the new process. He also requested that we would use care in the future, and not overcrowd the capacity of the steam pipe.

This explanation from the engineer, together with the fact that there was no use crying for spilt coffee, and that the pipe would be of more service to us all, standing where its hot breath could be utilized in the new process than it would be if lying at the bottom of the Potomac, appeased all the wrathful, and again the merry picnicking went on as before. I shall never forget that birthday dinner out on the bosom of the Potomac. To the end of the trip and on our return that little steam pipe did splendid duty, never once going back on us, but giving its breath freely for our comfort and convenience.

When well down the Potomac toward the point of the peninsula formed by the Potomac and Rappahannock Rivers, called the Northern Neck, our steamboat turned to the right and entered a narrow but deep stream or channel, which, if my memory serves, was called Pope's Creek, up which we made our way perhaps four or five miles until the stream became so narrow that we might almost reach shore on either side at one jump. Then we tied up to a tree on the north bank, or right hand of the stream going upward, and there we landed, about sunset; in the heart of Westmoreland County, Va.—the very county, as well as state, in which George Washington was born, and where little Georgie, when about six years old, tried his little hatchet on his father's favorite cherry tree, which stood by the old rail fence just back of the barn—at least, there is where it stood when I saw it, and as a matter of course it was just as dead as it was the year after little Georgie peeled its bark, but there it still stood, an everlasting monument to the honor of "the boy who could not tell a lie."

In my whole life I never enjoyed a higher privilege, a prouder honor, than the visit to the county of Washington's nativity—to the very homestead and orchard wherein, with his little hatchet, the "Father of His Country" accomplished his first great historical work. Many people of this day and generation are of the opinion that the story of Georgie and the cherry tree is myth. They say that it was not like Washington—that the mischievous prank did not foreshadow the man; that a man of

Washington's wisdom must have possessed a little sense when a boy, and if he had been on mischief bent and peeled the cherry tree out of pure cussedness, as boys sometimes do, he would have tried, smart-boy fashion, to lie out of it. But I have unbounded confidence in the truth of that cherry tree story for two good and sufficient reasons, either of which should convince any reasonable person. In the first place, Washington was a born peeler, and, like good poets, peelers are born, not made. This act of his boyhood was symbolic of the manhood the future held in store for him. It was necessary for him to begin early in life in order to become proficient in his calling, when his call came. The peeling of the cherry tree by Washington the boy was the harbinger of the peeling of King George III by Washington the man. Here is proof that the boy is father to the man. No one, not even a Canadian, can deny or doubt that Washington was a peeler from his boyhood.

My second reason is even more convincing. When I made that visit to Westmoreland County in the spring of 1863, I took great pains to investigate this whole cherry tree question. If the proof of the pudding is in chewing the string, then why should not the proof of the cherry tree be in gathering and chewing the fruit of its bearing? And surely it was the fruit of that old cherry tree, and luscious fruit it was, that we gathered. Do not misjudge me, kind reader. This may at first glance seem apocryphal, but wait till I finish. I can tell a lie when hard pressed, but here there is no need, and I assure you this is a true story.

My visit to the county of Washington's nativity was a twofold honor, from the fact that James Monroe as well as George Washington first saw the light of day in Westmoreland County, Va. Monroe, like Washington, was something of a peeler himself, and closely followed in the footsteps of his great predecessor. It is not recorded of James that he peeled his old man's cherry tree, and possibly his early education was neglected, but it is recorded that in 1819 he peeled Florida, with all its cherry trees, orange trees, and cypress trees, from Spain; just as beautifully as Washington peeled his colonial possessions from King George; then, a little later, he peeled Spain again by acknowledging the independence of the Spanish-American republics, which, taken together, was the most complete peeling she ever received until 1898, when this Yankee nation gave her a final and everlasting peeling.

It is also recorded of James that in 1823 he pealed forth the "Monroe Doctrine," loud and clear, so all the nations heard and still they hear. That doctrine so dear to the heart of every American citizen, has never been and never will be repealed while the United States of America holds life dear and liberty worth maintaining. Surely it was a grand privilege to visit the county wherein two such eminent American peelers were born.

Immediately after selecting a convenient and safe camping ground and establishing guard and picket lines, we broke ranks and leisurely proceeded to investigate the condition of Westmoreland County, Va., in the year of Our Lord 1863. In order that this investigation should be made in a thoroughly satisfactory manner, we who were particularly interested in the history of George Washington and his cherry tree— and most of us were—found it necessary to go outside our picket lines in small detachments; and never during the great Civil War was it my fortune to find another such field, so perfectly provided with all the comforts and conveniences so dear to the heart of the forager.

Westmoreland County had escaped the ravages of both raiding Reb and foraging Yank until this advent of the Badger boys upon her sacred soil. As we journeyed forth upon the highways and byways our souls were delighted with the fair prospect. Every smokehouse sent forth the rich aroma of well-cured ham and bacon, every farmyard resounded to the merry cackle of the festive hen, and as "silently the shades of evening gathered around each cottage door," with glad and thankful hearts we observed that the sleek and well-fed poultry of Westmoreland County were all unsuspicious of danger, and gathered in perfect confidence to their accustomed roosting places around the barns, in their cozy coops, in the branches of the orchard trees and on the convenient rail fences.

Our little detachment or squad of four had proceeded about a mile from camp when we came suddenly upon the old Washington homestead. We recognized it at a glance, for there, sure enough, just behind the barn, and close up to the old rail fence, stood the cherry tree, little Georgie's dead cherry tree, beautiful in death, still beautiful and fair to look upon after all these years, for although its body was bare, worm-eaten and decayed, its branches were full of luscious fruit, the very sight of which could not fail to fill the heart of a soldier with delight. Corp'l McIntosh, our leader, who was well posted in history and philosophy, called our attention at once to the sacred precinct whereon we stood, and to our duty as American soldiers. In a voice half choked with sorrow, yet echoing with a patriotic ring that reached the ear of every man in his command, he said: "Look there, boys; there's a sight to make angels weep! See those unpatriotic Virginia roosters perched in high glee on George Washington's cherry tree? Now, I'll be eternally Scotched if any fowl miscreant of treason can thus desecrate the memory of the Father of His Country and live."

Corp. McIntosh was a man of his word, and we saw by the fiery gleam of his red hair through the gathering shades of twilight, that he was in dead earnest. Corp. McIntosh was also a tall man—the tallest in Co. H. In short, he was so tall that the boys of Co. H said he never asked a blessing, but when he wanted one he reached up and took it, and on this occasion, after leading his command forward until it stood beneath the overhanging branches of the old cherry tree, and stepping up on the convenient rail fence, he reached up and took one, two, or three, or four, and perhaps more—in fact, he took every last blessing in sight, and passed them down to us who stood bravely on the ground floor below, and when we took our departure from the dear old homestead where Washington's boyhood was spent we felt that we had not lived in vain, but that kind Providence had shaped our destinies to a noble purpose in guiding our wandering feet to this sacred spot, and as we looked our last on little Georgie's cherry tree, even the dead cherry tree seemed to rejoice with us that by our hands the fowl despoilers of its fair fame had received their long-merited decapitation.

We remained in Westmoreland County two nights and one day, during which time we lived very well, and seemed to enjoy life, while we gathered in many hams and much bacon from the well-filled smokehouses; storing the same in the hold of our good ship for future use, of which I shall have occasion to speak later. We also gathered bountiful quantities of eggs, chickens, milk, butter and honey. In time of peace such acts would be called robbery, but in time of war it was called foraging. It was rough on the people, but war is all that and more. Gen. Sherman's definition of war is the most truthful as well as the most concise ever given.

When it became noised abroad through the enslaved Negroes of the vicinity that "de Lincum sogers had cum, suah," and that a Yankee steamboat lay moored at the landing in their well-known river, they deserted by scores and by hundreds the old plantations where they were born

and raised, and which had been left to their care and under their protection by their liberty-loving masters, who had gone forth to war for the
right to keep them and their children in everlasting servitude. O, they
were a thankless and unfaithful lot, those Westmoreland County darkies.
I saw many a highbred Virginia lady in sorrow and in tears entreat her
Dinah in vain to return to the old homestead and take care of her kind
and helpless mistress in the hour of her need. Old men and old women,
young men and young women, children and pickaninnies came flocking
to our boat with whatever they could catch in their haste, or came with
nothing but the rags on their backs to take passage to the land of liberty.
Who could blame them? They were foolish, of course. People always are
who want a greater degree of liberty than they are enjoying, in the eyes
of those who deny them such rights, and the man or woman who has
once tasted liberty is never wise enough to go back to slavery voluntarily. Liberty is sweet to all mankind, and the darkies of Westmoreland
County were not an exception. Our colonel in command dared not turn
them away, even if he would, but he soon discovered that if he would
retain room on his boat for his soldiers, he could not prolong his stay a
moment beyond the time necessary to accomplish the object of the expedition. So, on the second morning, about sunrise, our boat cast off
her moorings and we started on our return; but, early as it was, as we
steamed down the narrow channel and out into the broad Potomac,
with our deck so thickly crowded with Afric's sable sons and daughters
that there was barely standing room for us all, we could see them coming from every direction, and as they saw their messenger of liberty
departing, they halted where they stood, and as we passed out of their
sight they were still standing there, the pictures of sorrow and despair.
Had we remained at the landing an hour longer, and attempted to carry
all who would have applied for passage, I am inclined to the belief that
our overloaded craft would have gone to the bottom of the Potomac.

The Potomac River is a noble stream and wide at points below the
capital, while from Belle Plain Landing, at the mouth of Aquia Creek, to
its confluence with the Chesapeake, it is more like an estuary than a
river, being from three to eight miles in width. Along the sunny shore of
this historic stream it is said that Washington, in the days of his young
manhood, was wont to pass his leisure hours in throwing dollars (not
bills but coin) across its wide expanse. This was before the days of the

Revolution, when he was getting in practice to make the great throw of his life. Washington was not only a peeler, but he was a thrower also of no mean repute, whose sinewy arm eclipsed the fame of the most renowned athlete of olden time. Even David with his sling—who, later, became the great warrior-king of his time—could not compare with our George, who became the great warrior-president of all time. The most vigorous throw on record, to David's credit, is where he threw a stone across the valley of Elah, in his set to with Goliath of Gath—not nearly as far as George often threw a dollar for fun, and when he made the effort of his life, in his great contest with George of England and strove, in the earnestness of his soul, as David did, he threw a sovereign across the Atlantic Ocean. That was a demonstration for all time of the superiority of presidents over kings.

It may be contended that David was handicapped, as a dollar, very naturally, will go farther than a stone; but if David had no dollar or sovereign to throw, Saul would have gladly supplied him with a silver talent had he desired it, which ought to go farther than either. David was not compelled to throw stones nor restricted in his choice of projectiles. In this respect he stood on an equal footing with George.

Probably a dollar would go farther in colonial times than it will in our day, and a sovereign always would go farther than a dollar, but, just the same, it required nerve and a soul wherein burned the fire of sublime patriotism to throw the one across the Potomac or the other across the sea, even in the days of Washington.

This great historical fact that Washington could and did throw a sovereign across the Atlantic with the same or greater ease than he threw a dollar across the Potomac serves to furnish the gold bugs with their best argument in demonstration of the superiority of gold over silver coin as a circulating medium. On the other hand, the silver bugs find in the fact that the Father of His Country threw his last sovereign so far away beyond the sea positive proof that he intended thereby to discard forever the gold standard on the American continent. We rejoice, however, that both parties and all parties agree that Washington, when he made that godlike throw, intended that all the world should know that he and his America had no use for that or any other sovereign coined in the European mint.

Yea, verily, the Potomac is a noble stream, and as we steamed away to the northward upon her majestic bosom, she impressed me as a type of the nation founded and established by Washington and his compatriots, whose existence we were even then banded together to maintain, but which should finally, with irresistible power sweep onward to victory as the Potomac sweeps onward to the Chesapeake.

It was Sunday, but we seemed to have forgotten it. I remember it now after these many years, from the fact that we were reminded of it in a manner to fix it forever in my memory. The wind blew fierce and cold from the northwest, compelling us to seek shelter on the leeward of the little cabin and smokestack, thus by our united weight careening the craft until she was in actual danger of sinking, when the captain rushed on deck, shouting: "Go round to windward, some of you, quick; you'll sink the boat in less than 10 minutes at this rate;" but the boys replied in reckless soldier fashion: "Oh, let her sink; the old tub is of no account; who cares if she does go to the bottom."

Then the captain rushed to the colonel's quarters and begged him to go on deck and equalize the ballast, as the soldiers would not regard his orders, even if the ship were to sink the next minute. Then Col. Fairchild appeared on deck and quietly gave the command: "Soldiers, right up the ship. We are too far out to wade ashore." On the instant half the men passed around to windward and the ship righted.

It was a cold day anywhere on deck and especially cold where the wind had full sweep, and in order to keep our blood in circulation we jumped, hopped and danced around that steamboat deck with utter disregard of the Sabbath. Now, there was among the contrabands an old white-haired plantation Negro, who had not forgotten that it was Sunday, and he reminded us of the wickedness of our ways with tears in his eyes—there were tears in our eyes also, for the northwestern was built just right to touch our sympathetic hearts. Then we invited the old man to preach us a sermon, which invitation he seemed desirous of accepting, but expressed fear that "de Cap'n" would object. Thereupon one of the boys hunted up the sergeant of the Pioneer Corps, whom he introduced to our colored friend and brother as "the Captain," and, the sergeant having stated to him that there was no objection whatever to a sermon, the old man bared his gray head to the stinging northwestern and taking for his text, "the wickedness of Sunday dancing," he talked to us for probably half an hour, in an earnest, humble and God-fearing

spirit. He did not object to dancing, but drew the line at Sunday dancing and the desecration of "de Lord's day." Never was robed priest, mi-
tered cardinal, or pompous pope listened to with more respectful
attention than was that poor and humble plantation Negro just escaped
from slavery. When the "amen" was spoken, however, and the preacher
had donned his hat, the wild antics which the poor, simple-minded
black man misinterpreted as a wanton desecration of the holy Sabbath,
went on again, just the same, or probably a little livelier than before, for
standing at attention for half an hour on a steamboat deck in mid-stream
had so lowered the temperature of our blood that increased exercise was
necessary to quicken its circulation.

In storing the meats, we had gathered from the Westmoreland County
smokehouses within the hold of our ship, the hams were separated from
the bacon and piled by themselves. These were designated the "colonel's
hams," from the fact that we all knew that not a ham of them was intended for the use of any enlisted man, but were regarded as the especial
property of the colonel and other officers. We did not reach Belle Plain
Landing on our homeward journey until after dark. The high wind of
the early part of the day had fallen, and was succeeded by a gentle Virginia mist. It had been a cold, dreary day out on the wide Potomac, but
it must be an awful cold day when the American volunteer soldier gets
left. Now, this gentle drizzle and the thick darkness that came with it at
an early hour of the evening was exactly what we needed in our business, for among the deck passengers a plan of campaign had been carefully matured, whereby the private soldier might for once share equally
with his superior officers, or perhaps a trifle better. A vigilant and faithful guard had been stationed at the door leading to the storeroom below,
where the colonel's hams and the bacon were so carefully stored; but in
military life it so happens that all faithful guards are drawn from among
the enlisted men—a regulation of which private soldiers sometimes take
advantage. In this instance it was necessary for the success of our campaign that the guard should be selected with exceeding care and thoroughly instructed in his duties. All this was accomplished in perfect
order, and the countersign, "the colonel's hams," spoken in a whisper in
the ear of the faithful sentinel, when the darkness became so intense
that he could not distinguish one's features, was to admit the fortunate
possessor thereof within the well-filled storeroom. The darkness did not
fail us, neither the countersign, nor the sentinel. One by one, as the

locusts entered the storehouse of the king in the Far East, by a chink in the wall, and extracted therefrom, each, his grain of corn, so we private soldiers and noncoms, after giving the countersign at the door to the vigilant guard, stole—no, that's not the term, our soldiers never stole— they marched in one after another in perfect time, without haste or confusion, and, when he could not find a piece of bacon to suit him, he selected one of the colonel's hams, and vice versa. The result thereof was that when the excursion broke up and the soldiers had departed from the steamboat, each to his own tent, the colonel's hams were scattered— not to the four winds, but to the three Badger State regiments.

We made our landing at Belle Plain about 8 o'clock p.m., by which time it was very dark and the rain was falling. The trail up the hill to our camp was steep and slippery, and every slip the wrong way, but we got there O.K., the colonel's hams and all. There was one soldier, in his 26th year, who had two hams to tote—small ones, the large and beautiful having been selected before his turn came to give the countersign. I can vouch for the truth of the statement he made later, in my hearing, that "the man who carried two of the colonel's hams, though ever so small, up that slippery trail that night, earned them."

My tentmates were anxiously awaiting my return, for I, being the only one from our tent honored with an invitation to attend the excursion, had promised, on my honor as a soldier, not to forget them, but to bring back some memorial of the expedition worthy of one honored with so grand a birthday picnic. On reaching our quarters, I found the boys up and dressed, waiting to receive me or anything I might bring, worth receiving. I remarked laconically: "Make ready the camp kettle. Cook these hams, slice up the meat nicely, and burn the bones—tonight; for no man knoweth what the coming day may bring forth." The boys asked no questions, but obeyed orders to the letter. Imperial Caesar never had his orders obeyed with greater alacrity.

The next day Col. Fairchild ordered the baggage wagons (one would have been sufficient) down to the landing to bring up the fruits of the expedition. When the wagons returned the colonel seemed somewhat disappointed in the amount of hams produced, and at first waxed hot, expressing his discouragement in words wild and incoherent, but finally came to the sage conclusion that the division of the captured meats had been adjusted as nearly right as he could have adjusted it himself.

Thereafter, when certain shoulder-strapped gentlemen, who were on equal and familiar terms with our colonel, were inclined to joke him concerning the outcome of his Westmoreland County supplies, the colonel replied philosophically: "My hams are all right; they are guarded by Wisconsin volunteers."

In the month of April, 1863, we were visited at our camp in Virginia by some of the great men of their day and generation. Among these visitors were two governors of states—Gov. Morton, of Indiana, and Gov. Salomon, of Wisconsin. As one brigade contained one Indiana regiment—the 19th—and three Wisconsin regiments—the 2d, 6th and 7th— these gubernatorial visits were intended as, and probably were, an especial honor to our brigade, but I don't think we appreciated it. The 24th Mich. was also a part of the brigade, but we were not honored by a visit from the governor of Michigan, which slight did not in the least offend us, for soldiers always regard these official visits as "a custom more honored in the breach than the observance."

When Gov. Morton visited us, the brigade was ordered out, and forming in a hollow square, listened attentively to his address, and the incident passed from our memory, although Gov. Morton was one of the great war governors, and one of Abraham Lincoln's ablest supporters. Probably the following day not a man in the brigade could recall a single sentence of Gov. Morton's address. With Gov. Salomon and his address it was different. No man of the brigade present on that occasion and who heard that address ever forgot it while he lived. That speech furnished more fun in our camp than any other one incident during the civil war. Gov. Salomon was a German by birth, and, judging by his sweet German accent, it was plain that he had not been many years over from the "Fatherland." He had been elected lieutenant governor of Wisconsin on the ticket with Gov. Harvey, in order to hold the large German population of Wisconsin in line for a vigorous support and prosecution of the war, and after the death of Gov. Harvey, who was drowned at Pittsburg Landing, Salomon became the governor of the state. Gov. Salomon was an upright citizen and a patriotic governor, who did the best he could to sustain the government and the administration, so far as I know, but the way he handled Uncle Sam's English was great medicine for the blues. Probably no state, in or out of the Union at that time, could compare with Wisconsin in her ability to furnish her soldiers in the field with amusement.

During the Antietam campaign our brigade had received the honor of being designated "The Iron Brigade" by no less a person than Gen. McClellan himself, and although McClellan had gone where the woodbine twineth, still we proudly wore the title he gave us, which every man in the brigade tried to retain, and the brigade did retain, ever after. His honor the governor knew of this fact, and was proud of it, as he said himself; but in his effort to do us honor by spreading the honorable title over us in his little speech, his German accent played the very mischief with us and our grand title.

On the day of the governor's visit a damp Virginia rain was falling freely, and his excellency was comically attired in gum boots with leggin attachments, and cloak and cap of the same material, which added zest to his Germanized English oration. After we were properly arranged in the hollow square, the governor was introduced by our brigade commander, Gen. Sol Meredith, when he proceeded to address us, about as follows:

"Soltgers off der I run Prigate: I am glat to mage your agguaintance. I am brout to meed you today and I am brout always dat I am der ghief egsegutive off der Stade dat has der honor off sending to der var dhree regaments off der vamus I run Prigate. Venever, in der gabacity off der ghief egsegutive off der grade State off Vinconsin, I address der officers und der men off a new regament vat ist going to der vrondt, I alvays say to dhem, 'dhere ist a pride egsample in der East vordhy off your broutest emulation.'

"Now, soltgers off der I run Prigate, I dhank you in der name und in pehalf off der beople off Visconsin vor your courage in der past. You haf done soom bretty goot viding alrety und ve eggsbects you vill do a goot deal more, vor der var ist nod ofer und dhere ist hart viding to pe done pefore you gan redurn pack to your homes in der grade Vest. I vould lige to tage efery vone off you py der hant pud dhere are zo many, I vill shage mit der ovficers vor eagh soltger off der I run Prigate."

No, the governor did not weary the flesh with a long speech. We could have stood the rain a half hour longer without weariness, but short as it was, that speech had a long run in the "I run" Brigade. We learned afterward that Gov. Salomon knew what he was talking about, and was a prophet of no mean order. The war was not over. After that came Chancellorsville, Gettysburg, Wilderness, Spotsylvania, Cold Harbor, Petersburg, a long and wearisome siege of the Confederate capital, and finally the campaign that ended at Appomattox about two years later. Many of the boys who laughed over the governor's speech did their share in the "good fighting" and maintained the honor of the old flag and the old brigade with their lives. After the good fighting was over I returned to Wisconsin, but Gov. Salomon was out of office and I never met him again, but I am willing to go on record as affirming that he could make the best speech of any governor that Wisconsin ever had.

Gen. Hooker undertook the Chancellorsville campaign with perfect confidence in his army, and in his own ability to cope with Lee's generalship. There is no doubt of his expectation to defeat Lee and capture Richmond within 60 days, and with the army that followed him he should not have turned back. The fault was in Gen. Hooker himself. His strategy in the beginning of the campaign, whereby he crossed the Rappahannock and secured a position on the southern side, was superb, but he did not accomplish what he hoped and what we all hoped, and in the long run was outgeneraled and defeated.

Burnside's Grand Division organization had been discontinued and McClellan's Corps organization readopted. The First Corps, commanded by Gen. Reynolds, in which I had the honor of serving, and the Sixth Corps, commanded by Gen. Sedgwick, moved toward the Rappahannock below Fredericksburg on April 28 and during the night secured a position nearly opposite and just below the Fitzhugh House, which stood on the southern shore of the Rappahannock.

The Iron Brigade was selected to make the charge across the river and capture the Confederate rifle pits that commanded the crossing, and for that purpose we waited behind a stone wall, all stripped for the charge, while other troops slipped the pontoon boats, wherein we were to cross the river, into the water a short distance above and floated them down the current, mooring them in our front. In this work they were invisible to the Confederates, on account of the darkness and the thick fog that obscured the river during the early morning of April 29 and were defended from the Confederate fire by another brigade just to our right, which opened on their position the moment the Confederates discovered the movement of the pontoon boats down the river in their front. This fire kept the Confederates busy and took their attention from those engaged in the work of getting the pontoon boats into position.

We who were to make the charge lay perfectly quiet behind the stone wall, not firing a shot. We had discarded knapsacks and haversacks, carrying nothing but our guns, ammunition and the ever necessary canteen of water. When it became light enough for us to see fairly well, the pontoon boats being all in position, we received the order: "Forward, double-quick, march!" At the top of our speed we swept over the space from the stone wall to the river bank, probably 75 yards, scrambled down the embankment and into the boats in a jiffy, dashed across the river, about 50 yards in width, in less time than it takes to write it, then up the opposite bank, and the rifle pits were ours.

It was a wild charge, but all over in a very few minutes, and the Iron Brigade with flying colors held the southern bank of the Rappahannock. We captured many prisoners in the rifle pits, while our loss was light. The Confederates did not put up the fight at this point that their position would seem to warrant.

We held this position until May 2, but did not advance our line. This movement was intended as a feint, for during our operations below Fredericksburg the Second, Third, Fifth, Eleventh and Twelfth Corps moved up the river, crossing the Rappahannock at the upper fords, thus securing an advantageous position without a battle, which Gen. Hooker believed assured him the victory, and he issued a kind of congratulatory order, which was read to us while we occupied our position at the Fitzhugh Crossing, in which he stated that the right, consisting of the before mentioned corps, "had secured a strong position south of the Rappahannock which would compel the enemy to give battle on equal ground, where sure and certain defeat awaited him, or retreat in ignominy and with precipitation."

This order was a flash in the pan, issued before he had discovered the intentions of the enemy, for, as it soon proved, Lee neither retreated nor gave battle on equal ground, but he gave battle all the same.

Hooker really became the victim of overconfidence. He knew that a column of troops was moving off to his right, but imagined they were in retreat. This column was Jackson's Corps making a forced march to get on Hooker's right flank, which he succeeded in doing. Hooker's right was held by the Eleventh Corps, under Howard, with its right flank in the air and Jackson's attack came like a thunderbolt from a clear sky, striking Howard on the flank and rear. The Eleventh Corps, taken by surprise and at such tremendous disadvantage, had no earthly show and was rolled up and badly demoralized. The fault was not in the troops, but in the generalship that could not provide against such a surprise. This disaster occurred on May 2 and seemed to knock Hooker clear off his feet, and thereafter he was unable to regain his equilibrium. It was claimed that he was injured by the concussion of a shell, which may be true. At all events, he lost his head completely.

On May 2, if my memory serves me, the First Corps was withdrawn from its position at Fitzhugh Crossing and marched rapidly to the right, making a night march and reaching the extreme right sometime during the next day, but after the defeat of the Eleventh Corps, of course. Hooker still had an army of sufficient strength and fighting force to defeat Lee and continue his movement. The defeat of the Eleventh Corps was a severe reverse, but not sufficient to upset the whole campaign. Here, however, Hooker capped the climax of bad generalship by leaving the Sixth Corps still at Fredericksburg with orders to capture the heights and from that point push on toward Lee's right flank. This movement, if made at all, should have been by the Sixth and First Corps combined. When the First Corps was withdrawn from below Fredericksburg to reinforce the right, the Sixth Corps should have moved with it. Such a movement would have reunited Hooker's army and placed him in a position to continue the campaign with every chance of success. The consequence of Sedgwick's advance on Lee's right was that on the evening of May 4 Lee attacked Sedgwick in force, defeating and compelling him to recross the Rappahannock for safety. While this battle was going on within our hearing on the right, the balance of Hooker's army lay in the trenches and did nothing. At least the First Corps made no movement—never fired a shot.

By good generalship and rapid movements Lee had thus succeeded in knocking two corps of Hooker's army clear out of the box, and then Hooker concluded to abandon the campaign. So, on the night of May 5, we retreated from our position and the early morning of May 6 found the Army of the Potomac once more on the north side of the Rappahannock. Hooker's army lost about 17,000 men, killed, wounded and missing, during the campaign, against a loss of about 13,000 on the

Confederate side. They also lost Lee's most active and reliable general, Stonewall Jackson, which was the greatest loss sustained by either army in the loss of one man up to that time, and was never equaled but once during the whole war, which was the loss of Gen. Reynolds at Gettysburg. The Chancellorsville campaign pretty thoroughly demonstrated the fact that as a general in the field at the head of an army, Gen. Joseph Hooker was no match for Gen. R. E. Lee.

Dr. Andrew J. Ward, Major Thomas S. Allen, Lieutenant Colonel Lucius Fairchild, and Colonel Edgar O'Conner of the Second Wisconsin Infantry in 1862. During the subsequent two years, Allen was wounded, Fairchild lost an arm, and O'Conner was killed in action.

FOUR

"We were all boys then"

*The First Day at Gettysburg
July 1, 1863*

In the winter and spring of 1863, the Hooker Tribe dwelt on the northern shore of the Rappahannock River, mostly, in the state of old Virginia. The Hookers were a powerful and warlike tribe. Their wigwams extended for many miles up and down the Rappahannock's sunny slopes, and eastward across the Peninsula known as the Northern Neck, even to the shore of the broad Potomac, where the tribe received its supplies of meat, flour, groceries, ammunition, guns and blankets from the government. I was a member of the Hooker Tribe.

The Lee Tribe were our neighbors, but we could hardly call them our friends. The Lees dwelt south of the Rappahannock, and we could see their tents and watch their war dances in the distance. The Lees were also a warlike tribe, and boasted of the many scalps they had taken in battle. While we were not on very friendly terms, the Hookers and the Lees, we always had a great deal of respect for each other, using great care when we encroached upon each other's hunting grounds. Sometimes the Hookers crossed the river and joined with the Lees in a war dance or grand powwow, but we always came back to the north side in a few days if we could.

Sometimes the Lees visited us, and we went a-gunning with or for each other among our pleasant hills; but they always seemed to tire quickly of our society, and were glad when their Great Sachem called them to return to their happy hunting grounds south of the river.

In the early summer of that year, however, the whole Lee Tribe, without consulting us or giving any notice of their intentions, packed up their belongings, rolled up their blankets and departed for parts unknown; but rumor reported quickly that they had gone northward beyond the Potomac, even into "Maryland, My Maryland," and that possibly they might fish in the purling streams and hunt among the picturesque mountains of Pennsylvania ere they returned. Immediately the Hookers became ambitious also to enjoy a summer outing with the Lees, in the same delightful resorts and health-giving sports that they were enjoying, and forthwith we packed our grips, and on the morning of the 12th of June turned our faces toward the fair land of the North. A picnic surely it was. Most of us traveled on foot, carrying our beds and our grips the whole distance of 158 miles before reaching the picnic grounds proper; but we were all young and full of enthusiasm. We always ate our dinners under the shade of the trees, when we could, and at night we camped in the most beautiful and romantic places. Sometimes, of course, the drenching rains descended upon us and the mountain breezes overturned our hastily constructed tents, but when such slight misfortunes overtook us, we crept in between the mountains and the river for protection, until the daystar arose in the East and the sun of the morning shone forth in his warmth and glory.

On June 25 we crossed the Potomac River, and on the afternoon of June 30 crossed the Maryland line into the old Keystone State and encamped for the night at Marsh Creek. Then on the morning of July 1, as we continued our march northward, we met our old neighbors the Lees, with whom we had parted company on the Rappahannock in the early days of June, near the quiet and peaceful village of Gettysburg. Lo! here had the Great Spirit selected, it would seem, the grand picnic ground destined to become the culminating point of the summer outing of the tribes from the Rappahannock in the year 1863.

We were all boys then, or young men—so were the Lees, and on meeting each other we waited not for the glorious Fourth—so near and yet so far to many of either tribe—to begin our renowned celebration, but immediately we began discharging our toy pistols and exploding our cannon crackers with all the wild enthusiasm characteristic of young

Americans; keeping the air filled with smoke and the hills vibrant with tumult during the long hours of the 1st, 2d and 3d days of July; but on the 4th of July we rested, for the picnic was over.

Thirty-seven years had passed away. It was in the delightful month of May, 1900, that I revisited the far-famed city of Gettysburg and the old battlefield, where as a boy of 25 years I had marched and fought in one of the greatest battles of the world's greatest war. Wonderful were the changes wrought by those short years.

In 1863 the United States of America was looked upon by the nations of Europe as in the last throes of national dissolution, and "Bull Run Russell's" statement, made through the *London Times,* "The foundation stones of the young American Republic are falling to pieces," was taken as literally true. There were then within and without the American Union 35 states, including West Virginia, which had just previously been admitted; but of these 35 states, 11 had seceded and were then in open rebellion against the authority of the United States, waging a war of awful bitterness for what they termed their freedom from oppression, and by all that was good and great they had vowed that neither force nor favor could induce or compel them to return to or become again a part of the old American Union. There were, also, three or four other states very anxious to follow the example of their wayward sisters, and were only held within the Union by the force of arms, and we, who had fought beneath the Stars and Stripes of Gettysburg 37 years before, contended for and defended the very life of the United States of America.

In 1900, when I revisited the old battlefield, I started from the shore of Puget Sound, that wonderful inland sea of the great Northwest, scarcely known or heard of in the days of the Civil War, and, not on foot, but as a nabob in his chariot, although only a common old soldier, I rode in state across Washington, Idaho, Montana, North Dakota, Minnesota, Wisconsin, Illinois, Indiana, Ohio, West Virginia, Maryland and into Pennsylvania, 12 of the 45 states that in 1900 comprised our great and matchless American Union. Then, too, was the nation at peace throughout her borders, and not a single one of the 45 states wanted to secede from the Union, but all were contented and prosperous.

In making that flying trip, in a little less than five days, I crossed the great mountain ranges of a continent, traversed plains where millions of cattle pasture and fatten, threaded forests dark and deep and apparently without limit in extent, rode over and among fields that produce the bread of the nations of the earth, and visited cities that swell and rejoice with the arts of peace and onward rush of civilization.

In my path were the rivers of America—the Snohomish, the Spokane, the Columbia, the Missouri, the Red, the Mississippi, the Wisconsin, the Ohio, the Potomac; and rivers, cities, fields, forests, plains and mountains were all a part and only a part of "Our Country." For 2,000 miles I coursed along the northern rim and then dashed downward for another thousand miles toward the far-eastern center this broad national dish or platter that we proudly call, "The Land of the Free," which contains more of the blessings of liberty and the comforts of life than can be found in any other country upon which the light of the sun descends. Surely the men who died at Gettysburg gave not their lives in vain, for by the blood of the brave was preserved this imperial heritage. The village also, and the battlefields around it, upon them what a change the years had wrought. The town that was founded by James Gettys in 1780, after whom it was named, and which became the county seat of Adams County, Pennsylvania, in 1800, was only a village still in 1863, with a population of about 1,500 people. In 1900 it had grown to be a beautiful city of from 4,000 to 5,000 inhabitants. The picturesque hills that served as positions of attack and defense, and which blazed and thundered with the lightnings of death and the volleys of destruction during those fierce July days in 1863, were traced throughout their length in 1900 with smooth and beautifully macadamized avenues, adorned on either hand with memorial stones, that mark and designate the positions held by the grim lines of battle in the days of war.

Beautiful for situation is Gettysburg, fairest and most glorious among the battlefields of the earth; city of monuments, adorned in the garments of peace, environed with the memorials of war, where heroism and patriotism have written their mighty deeds of valor and endurance in lines so deep, so everlasting that time himself may not efface their memory.

A half mile to the east, the sparkling waters of Rock Creek meander away to the southeastward, until lost in the overshadowing woods that darken the rocky slopes of bold Culp's Hill.

Northward the fair, undulating valley, with its wealth of garden, field, orchard and meadow, stretches far and far away.

To the west, 700 yards distant, the Lutheran Theological Seminary crowns the summit of Seminary Ridge, which extends in a north and south direction far as the eye can reach. From Seminary Ridge westward for 1,000 yards the country slopes away in undulating swells to Willoughby Run.

South of the city, like the hanging gardens of Babylon of old, rises Cemetery Hill, which is prolonged to the east and southeastward for more than a mile by that rugged and rocky ridge known as Culp's Hill. Cemetery Hill is also prolonged to the southwestward by the Emmitsburg Road Ridge until it intersects the Seminary Ridge two and a half miles away, and southward by an interior ridge which terminates two and a half miles distant in Round Top, the glory of the hills, overlooking all the surrounding landscape. Southward from Round Top the valley of Rock Creek spreads out and away beyond the ken of human vision.

A dozen highways lead into and converge at Gettysburg, and they were all there in 1863. Across the streams, along the ridges, threading the valleys, over the hills they came, from the north, from the south, from the east and from the west, and it was owing to the fact that Gettysburg stood in 1863 as she stands today, at the meeting of the ways, that she was destined to become the pivotal point in America's grandest battle.

Beginning at the northwest, where the battle began, there is, first, the Chambersburg Pike, which crosses Willoughby Run a mile and a quarter and Seminary Ridge 700 yards northwest of the city; second, the Mummasburg Road, more directly from the northward, crossing the same run and the same ridge at a greater distance away; third, the Carlisle and Newville Roads, which unite about a mile north of and enters the city as the Carlisle Road; fourth, the Harrisburg Road, approaching the city from east of north, crossing Rock Creek about a mile out in that direction; fifth, the York Pike and Hunterstown Road, which unite just before crossing Rock Creek, about three-fourths of a mile northeast of, and enters the city under the name of the York Pike. Upon these seven roads the various corps, divisions and brigades of Lee's army of invasion concentrated at Gettysburg to meet the Army of the Potomac.

Then from the east there is the Hanover Road, not used by either army until July 3, when Stuart's Confederate cavalry was met and defeated by Pleasonton's Union cavalry, about three miles east of Rock Creek, on this road. The Hanover Road crosses Rock Creek a half mile east of Gettysburg.

From the southward there is, first, the Baltimore Pike, which crosses Rock Creek three miles to the southeastward of and enters the city over the eastern slope of Cemetery Hill; second, the Taneytown Road, directly from the south, the western slope of Cemetery Hill; third, the Emmitsburg Road, from the southwest, following the crest of the Emmitsburg Road Ridge crossing the Taneytown Road and intersecting the Baltimore Pike in the outskirts of the city, thus forming her main street north and south, called Baltimore Street. Upon the aforesaid three roads the various corps, divisions and brigades of the Union army concentrated for battle.

Then from the west by south there is the Hagerstown or Fairfield Road, which crosses Willoughby Run something like a mile and half south of west, and Seminary Ridge a half mile directly west of Gettysburg. This road was not used by either army before or during the battle, but after the battle was over Lee found this road a convenient gateway through which to lead his defeated army back to the shelter of his friendly Virginia hills beyond the Potomac River, and he did not neglect to make good use of it for that purpose.

Gen. Meade, in his testimony before the Congressional Committee on the Conduct of the War, stated the strength of his army at "A little under 100,000—probably 95,000 men."

That estimate was very nearly correct, as the returns of June 30, 1863, of the Army of the Potomac, "present for duty, equipped," show as follows, viz:

	Infantry	Artillery	Total Strength of Corps
First Corps	9,403	619	10,022
Second Corps	12,363	551	12,904
Third Corps	11,247	677	11,924
Fifth Corps	11,954	555	12,509
Sixth Corps	14,516	1,039	15,555
Eleventh Corps	9,197	644	9,841
Twelfth Corps	8,193	396	8,589

Reserve Artillery   335   2,211   2,546

Total infantry, 77,208; total artillery, 6,692.

Total infantry and artillery	83,900
Total strength of Cavalry Corps	10,800
Grand total of Army of the Potomac	94,700

It is an easy matter to verify these figures. They are of record in the War Department of the United States. We know to a certainty the strength of the Army of the Potomac.

In making his arrangements for the invasion of Pennsylvania in the spring of 1863, Gen. Lee made every effort in his power to enable him to lead an invincible army to victory. He did not invade the North to be beaten in his first battle across the line, if he could help it. We are absolutely certain about that.

On May 30, Lee issued an order reorganizing his army, which at that time consisted of two corps, commanded by Longstreet and Hill, respectively. According to his field returns of May 31 (the last field returns of record from Lee's army previous to the battle of Gettysburg) the total strength of these two corps was as follows, viz:

Longstreet's Corps	30,732
Hill's Corps	32,588
Total infantry and artillery	63,320
Stuart's Cavalry Corps	10,292
Total strength of Lee's army May 31	73,612

To these two corps Gen. Lee added a third—Ewell's, not for the purpose of having three corps in his army instead of two, just for buncombe. Oh, no, Lee was not built that way; he reorganized his army into three corps for the purpose of adding to its numerical strength, and he then and there added every man that the Confederate government would give him, and the Confederacy gladly gave him every man that could be obtained. Lee was about to undertake a great enterprise—nothing less than the invasion of the North, which he hoped and the Confederate government confidently expected would result in victory and the acknowledgment of the independence of the Confederacy by the nations of Europe. Is it at all reasonable to suppose that Lee would undertake such a stupendous work without first obtaining what he considered adequate reinforcements? It is fair to presume that in adding to his army a third corps he thereby and at the same time added to the strength of his army in the same proportion. This would give him 94,980 infantry and artillery, which, with the cavalry he already had, swelled his army to the grand aggregate of 105,272 men of all arms. Whatever the full strength of Lee's army may have been, Lee himself was extremely careful that the world should not know what it was, and to this day it remains a sealed book. Still, we do know of a certainty that the corps, divisions and brigades of Lee's army as reorganized for the Gettysburg campaign were each and all stronger than the corresponding organizations in the Army of the Potomac. While Lee's army was composed of three corps, ours was composed of seven corps. While Lee's army had 39 infantry brigades, the Army of the Potomac had 52.

These facts present the opportunity of making a comparative estimate of Lee's army that cannot be far from correct. In our army we had 52 infantry brigades and a total strength of 77,208 infantry, or an average of 1,485 men to the brigade. In Lee's army there were 39 infantry brigades, and as these brigades were all numerically stronger than ours, we have but to average them at 515 more to the brigade, which is 2,000 men to each, and less than many of Lee's brigades contained, and we find thereby Lee's total infantry strength to be 78,000.

We therefore conclude that the contending armies, commanded respectively by Gens. Meade and Lee, which struggled and fought so heroically at Gettysburg in 1863, were numerically about equal.

Many people do not readily understand why it was that in the concentration of the opposing armies for battle, the Army of Northern Virginia, commanded by Gen. Lee, which was the army of invasion, advanced from the north toward Gettysburg, while the Army of the Potomac, commanded by Gen. Meade, which was the repelling army, moved up from the south to meet and give it battle. This can only be explained by a brief outline of the previous movements of the said armies.

Lee's army crossed the Potomac River into Maryland at Williamsport on the 24th and 25th days of June, 1863, with the exception of his cavalry corps, under the command of Stuart. Lee had instructed Stuart to cover his movements—to deceive Hooker as long as possible with regard to Lee's whereabouts, and to prevent the Army of the Potomac from crossing the river in pursuit.

On crossing the Potomac, Lee immediately concentrated his army at Hagerstown, six miles north of the river and 74 miles southwest of Harrisburg, the capital of Pennsylvania, which city Lee proposed to make his first objective point. There was no army in his front, nothing to interfere with his onward march, and taking advantage of this, to him, most favorable situation, he lost not a moment, but dashed through the Cumberland Valley, intending to raise all the ready money he could by assessing the towns along his route, also to replenish his supply of mules and draft horses from the farmers of that region, and on reaching the Susquehanna River, to cross the same and capture Harrisburg.

When Lee reached Marion Station, six miles south of Chambersburg, he detached and sent Early, with his division, eastwardly across the mountains by the Chambersburg Pike, into the Susquehanna Valley, with instructions to assess the cities through which he might pass for all in sight, and, finally, to cross the Susquehanna by the Columbia Bridge and reunite with his main army at Harrisburg.

Early marched with great rapidity, reaching Gettysburg on the afternoon of June 26, which town he assessed to the tune of $10,000, which little amount he failed to collect. From this point Early marched northeast on the York Pike to the town of York, where he succeeded in raising some money, assessing that city at the snug sum of $100,000. From York he marched to Wrightsville, and was preparing to cross the Susquehanna when he received orders from Lee to return with all possible haste by way of York to Gettysburg.

While Lee's main army was stretched along the Cumberland Valley from Chambersburg to the Susquehanna River, a scout brought the news to Lee that Hooker had outgeneraled Stuart, and with his whole army had crossed the Potomac at Point of Rocks and Edward's Ferry on the 25th and 26th days of June, and was then in hot pursuit.

These tidings from out of the South troubled Lee, for he saw and clearly comprehended the fact that the Army of the Potomac must be taken into immediate consideration. He therefore abandoned his attack on Harrisburg, and leaving the Cumberland Valley, marched eastward across the mountains into the Valley of the Susquehanna, and on the night of June 30 his army was located about as follows:

Early's Division on the York Pike 15 miles northeast of Gettysburg, Rodes' Division 10 miles north of Gettysburg, on the Carlisle Road; Johnson's Division 18 miles northeast, on the Harrisburg Road; Pender's Division 10 miles northwest, on the Mummasburg Road; Heth's Division five miles northwest, on the Chambersburg Pike, and from that point to Chambersburg in a continuous line west for 25 miles lay the balance of Lee's army, thus covering the whole country and every highway for the distance of about 40 miles east and west, and each and every one of these highways converging at Gettysburg.

On the other hand, the Union army, which had crossed the Potomac River one day later than Lee's army, and fully 50 miles south and east, with a mountain range between, had marched northward, spreading out like a fan to the eastward between Lee's army and our national capital.

On June 27 Gen. Hooker, with headquarters then established at Frederick, Md., resigned his command of the Army of the Potomac, and on June 28 Gen. Meade, then commander of the Fifth Corps, was assigned to the command of the army. On assuming command, Gen. Meade continued our line of march to the northward, and on the night of June 30 Buford's Cavalry Division occupied a position northwest of Gettysburg, with headquarters at the Lutheran Seminary, on Seminary Ridge, his troops picketing the Chambersburg Pike and the Mummasburg Road, and guarding the crossings of Willoughby Run, within an hour's march of Heth's outposts of Lee's foremost division. The First Corps, commanded by Doubleday, was at Marsh Creek, on the Emmitsburg Road, six miles from Buford. Howard's Eleventh Corps was at Emmitsburg, 13 miles away, and from that point the Army of the Potomac lay stretched away to the southeastward along the Taneytown Road and the Baltimore Pike for a distance of 30 or 40 miles. Gen. Meade had established his headquarters at Taneytown, and was superintending the survey of a position on Pipe Clay Creek, two miles south of Taneytown, that seemed to him a choice position for a battle, and he hoped to await Lee's advance and attack at that point. His army was scattered from Dan to Beersheba, so to speak, his idea being to concentrate at some point when Lee found him.

Such was the comparative positions and dispositions of the opposing armies and their commanding generals on the evening before the
great battle, which explains why the Southern army advanced from the
northward while the Northern army advanced from the southward as
they met in a death grapple at Gettysburg.

Sometimes contending armies do not form in battle array and wait
for each other until everything is in readiness, and then, at an agreed
signal, join issue all along the line.

At Gettysburg, for instance, two armies, each nearly 100,000 strong,
confronted each other; but they were not drawn up in line, 100,000 on
either side. When the battle opened on the morning of July 1 between
the heads of the leading columns, the main portions of the armies were
from 20 to 50 miles apart.

The advantages were greatly in Lee's favor. He had his army well in
hand. He had seven highways at his service, all converging at his ren-
dezvous, to facilitate the movement of his troops. He had issued his
orders of concentration to his divisions and each was marching by the
shortest route to the point designated. When the head of his leading
division, under Heth, encountered Buford's little band on the banks of
Willoughby Run, the rear of his outermost column was not to exceed 20
miles away.

For Gen. Meade the situation was most unfavorable. While Buford
occupied the vantage ground of camping on the field and awaiting the
advance of Lee upon his lines, he could not hope for support from the
main army in that position. Gen. Meade had not ordered the advance of
his army toward this point, but with headquarters at Taneytown, 15
miles away, was waiting for Lee to come and see him. Nevertheless, Gen.
Lee was not master of the situation. The God of battles, who overrules
all human events, seemed favorable to our cause, especially throughout
the first three days of July, 1863.

Gen. Reynolds, who commanded the left wing of the Army of the
Potomac, was the leader for the occasion, the man with a sublime purpose. He saw before him the awful chessboard of war, with the champion player of the hour arranging his combinations for a winning game,
and forthwith he boldly planned a checkmate. Gen. Reynolds had sent
Buford forward to his advanced position and had ordered the First Corps
at Marsh Creek, and the Eleventh Corps, at Emmitsburg, to move in the

same direction at an early hour on the morning of July 1. When Buford was attacked, Reynolds hurried forward the First and Eleventh Corps to his support, and also sent a dispatch to Gen. Meade telling him that Lee's forces were in front of him; that he would hold the key to the situation till the main army arrived, and that the heights of Gettysburg was the place to fight the battle.

About 20 minutes before 9 o'clock a.m., July 1, Heth's Division encountered Buford's and opened the battle. An hour later the First Corps began to arrive, reinforcing Buford. Another hour and Pender's Division reinforces Heth, while Rodes' Division arrives from the north and extends Heth's lines eastward. Still another hour passes, and Howard's Eleventh Corps arrives reinforcing Doubleday and Buford. A little later, perhaps half an hour, Early's Division reinforced Rodes. All this time the battle is in progress. We receive no more reinforcements, but Lee's divisions continue to arrive.

At 4 o'clock p.m. Howard and Doubleday withdrew their shattered columns to Cemetery Hill, where at about 5 o'clock they are reinforced by Slocum's Twelfth Corps, and about the same time Gen. Hancock arrives on the field, Meade having received Reynolds's dispatch, and sending Hancock forward to view and report the situation.

Night declares a truce to the fighting, but not to the marching. Ere morning dawns Lee's army is all in line except Pickett's Division and Stuart's Cavalry, while Lee has established his headquarters at or near the Lutheran Seminary. Hancock has reported to Meade his approval of the position then being held for the continuation of the battle. Meade has accepted Hancock's report as final, has ordered his whole army to Gettysburg, and established his headquarters just in rear, or south, of Cemetery Hill arriving in person about midnight. The Second Corps (Hancock's) has reached the field and prolonged our line to the left. Sickles's Third Corps is also on the ground ready to assume position in the line. Still the Fifth and Sixth Corps, numbering 28,000 men, or about one-third of Meade's army, are absent.

With the coming of day the battle reopens. Late in the afternoon Meade is reinforced by the Fifth Corps, and the third division of the Sixth Corps. Again night puts an end to the carnage. During the night of July 2, Pickett's Division and Stuart's Cavalry reinforce Lee's army, while the First and Second Divisions of the Sixth Corps make the Army of the Potomac complete.

When the morning of July 3 dawns the two armies face each other in their entirety, all that is left of them. Gen. Meade has at last concentrated his army. Such was the order of going into battle.

When the morning dawns July 1 we find Gen. Buford occupying this unique position. With one small division of cavalry, numbering about 3,000 men, he is guarding the crossings of Willoughby Run on two highways leading into Gettysburg from a mile and a fourth to a mile and three-fourths northwest of the town, with Lee's whole army from four to 25 miles away, every division of which is marching steadily and rapidly toward him; with only two Union corps in position to support him, one of them, numbering 8,500 men (Stannard's Brigade not being with the First Corps in the first day's battle), being six miles away and the other, 10,000 strong, 13 miles distant, while the balance of the Union army and the commanding general thereof were far out of reach and in blissful ignorance of his situation. But Buford never quailed, and Heth's Division found him at his post.

The First Corps was early astir, and as we marched along the Emmitsburg Road in the direction of Gettysburg our ears were saluted with the first cannon shots of the opening battle. When we arrived within about a mile of Gettysburg we met Gen. Reynolds, who had returned to urge us forward with all possible speed to the support of Buford. This was about 9:30 o'clock. Gen. Reynolds sat upon his horse on the west side of the highway, facing us, and as I marched near the head of our column I had a fair view of his features. The general looked careworn, sad and stern, but the high purpose of his patriotic spirit was stamped upon every lineament. It was the last time I saw him. He directed the turning of the head of our column to the westward and then rode forward to confer with Buford. Within a short half-hour later he had given his life for his country.

As we turned from the Emmitsburg Road westward, scattering solid shot tore through the tree tops above our heads, reminding us that the battle was nearer than we had supposed. Then Col. Fairchild sprang from his horse, which he gave to his hostler as he shouted: "Noncombatants to the rear." We marched rapidly, loading our pieces as we advanced. Five hundred yards from the point where our colonel dismounted brought us to the crest of Seminary Ridge. Five hundred yards further, and we entered the edge of McPherson's Woods, on the crest of a second ridge where Buford's thin line, which was holding Archer's Brigade of Heth's Division in check, passed to our rear. Immediately we charged into the woods down the slope, receiving a galling fire from Archer's men. Before we had advanced 30 yards within the woods Col. Fairchild received a severe wound, from which he lost his arm. My regiment (the 2d Wis.) was in the advance. The other regiments of the old "Iron Brigade" formed to our right and left. We held our fire until within 10 yards of Archer's line, and then gave them a volley that counted. From this point Archer's line fell back, retreating slowly and stubbornly through the woods and finally across Willoughby Run. We followed close upon their heels, and crossing the Run but a moment later, captured Gen. Archer and about 300 of his men, partially sheltered behind a clump of willows. As Archer surrendered his sword to Lieut. Daily, of Co. B, and it became certain that we had won the first heat, one of my comrades, Jonathan Bryan by name, and by birth a Pennsylvanian, one of the best and bravest among the soldiers of the 2d Wis., while waving his hat in the air as he cheered for victory won, fell dead at my feet, shot through the heart by a Confederate from the edge of the woods beyond the field in our front. Comrade Bryan was the only man of our regiment, I believe, killed west of Willoughby Run. We then recrossed the run with our prisoners.

When I visited this field in 1900 I found no stone marking the spot where the brave common soldier fell, nor yet a monument on the west side of Willoughby Run showing where we captured Archer, neither a line on our regimental monument, which stands just east of the run, telling to the world the important fact in connection with the history of the 2d Wis., that it crossed Willoughby Run on the 1st day of July and there captured Archer. This oversight relative to our regimental monument arises from the fact that when our Wisconsin monuments were erected, 25 years after the battle, Col. Fairchild and his hostler were the two men appointed by Gen. Rusk, of Wisconsin, to represent the 2d Wis. in locating the position that said monument should occupy, neither of whom were on this part of the field during the battle, the colonel having been wounded in the commencement of the action and his hostler having been sent to the rear with the colonel's horse (both of which I personally witnessed), and was not in the action at any time. I was living near Madison at the time, and tried to obtain the appointment, but my application was never even noticed.

After this sharp skirmish, which lasted about half an hour, there was a lull in the battle. We reformed our line in a position to command the run, threw out a strong skirmish line and proceeded to call the rolls of companies and take an inventory of our losses. We had lost from my regiment 116 men killed and wounded out of a total of 302 that went into the action, including both our colonel and lieutenant colonel; but it was only a skirmish.

While we lay in line awaiting the renewal of the battle I noticed a soldier of my company, by the name of E. S. Williams, who had been wounded some distance to rearward, in the woods. He had secured two muskets, which he was using for crutches, and when I last saw him he was far up the slope, making his way off the field without assistance, though so severely wounded that his leg was afterward amputated above the knee.

Before the battle reopened word was passed along our line informing us of the death of Gen. Reynolds. He was killed a few moments after we went into action, a little to the right and 50 yards in front of the point where we entered the woods, a granite monument marking (in 1900), the spot where he fell. This woods is now called Reynolds's Grove.

Our Second Brigade of the First Division, commanded by Gen. Cutler, had relieved Buford's men and defeated Davis's Brigade about the same time our brigade defeated and captured Archer. The Second and Third Divisions of the First Corps extended our lines to the right and left, making the whole battle line of the First Corps over a mile in length. Buford moved his troops still farther to the right and to the north of Gettysburg. We had then in line of battle all of the First Corps (except Stannard's Brigade), numbering 8,500 and Buford's Division, numbering 3,000 or 11,500 in all, making no allowance for losses up to this time, which must have been fully 500.

Heth was soon reinforced by Pender's Division, which gave the Confederates 15,000 making no allowance for previous losses, when the battle reopened along our whole line. In the immediate front of the position where I was stationed in Reynolds's Grove, Willoughby Run ran in and out among the woods and willow clumps, and as the Confederates moved across the run we tried to make it interesting for them, and I believe we partially succeeded, as it took them a full hour to force the passage. Then Anderson's Division reinforced the Confederate line, giving Gen. Hill the full strength of his corps, and we were obliged to concede them the privilege of crossing the creek but we did not surrender the grove until hours later, and after a desperate effort to hold it.

From Willoughby Run to Seminary Ridge the distance is not great. It is 475 yards from the creek to the ridge at the edge of the woods where our skirmish with Archer began in the morning, and 500 yards from the edge of the woods to the crest of Seminary Ridge. I measured this ground carefully in 1900, because I remembered the ground as a good, long two miles. The whole distance was less than 1,000 yards, but it took Hill's Confederates five weary hours to travel it, and then they did not quite reach it. Many of them never got out of the woods.

A little before noon Gen. Howard arrived on the field in advance of his corps (the Eleventh), and assumed command of the field. From the cupola of the Lutheran Seminary Gen. Howard viewed the field and the situation. He saw at a glance the wonderful strategic conformation of the country south of Gettysburg, with its bold ridges and commanding hills, that impressed Reynolds when he sent the dispatch to Meade, "The heights of Gettysburg is the place for the battle," and he resolved at once to do his utmost in fighting the mighty game to a successful finish that Reynolds and Buford had so heroically begun. He therefore directed the First and Third Division of the Eleventh Corps as they came up to extend our right north of Gettysburg to Rock Creek, placing his Second Division in reserve on Cemetery Hill, knowing that it would be necessary to retire to that position ere reinforcements could arrive. This was a wise and soldierlike movement on the part of Howard, as was afterwards demonstrated.

Howard's two divisions gave us an additional strength of 6,300 men, making our aggregate battle strength on July 1, 17,866.

In the meantime Rodes's Division from the north and a little later Early's Division from the northeast strengthened Hill's lines, giving him an aggregate force of 30,000.

Lee's strategy consisted in getting the most men to a given point and getting them there first. In this instance he was successful, and, as a matter of course, it worked greatly to his advantage. Meade's strategy consisted in waiting for Lee to find him and assail his position, and in this instance, but for the interposition of Providence, Howard's foresight and splendid fighting all along the line, it would have worked us untold disaster.

So we fought on. It was well for the Union cause that day that the men of the First and Eleventh Corps did not know that Gen. Meade was monkeying around Double Pipe Creek, waiting for something to turn up. Every man on the fighting line supposed there was unity in this action and that Gen. Meade with his whole army would soon be with us.

Out on the west front we had at last been driven from Reynolds's Grove, about 3:30 p.m., and the lines to our right and left seemed to be giving way. After abandoning the woods, there was but one other position short of Seminary Ridge that we attempted to hold. It was in the hollow between the two ridges, 250 yards from either. This position we held for a short time, giving the Confederates a hot reception as they came out of the woods. Behind us, on the ridge, was our artillery, but not sufficiently elevated to fire over us with safety—besides, the hollow soon became too hot to hold us. Then we made a dash for the crest of the hill, where the artillery could assist us. If my recollection is not at fault, we passed over that last 250 yards much more rapidly than over any other portion of the journey from Willoughby Run to Seminary Ridge.

The Confederates were moving down the opposite slope when we started, and immediately divined our intention. They seemed to think it would be nice to run in under the cover of our batteries with us, and they made a lively effort in that direction. It became at once a life-and-death race for all of us. Any man left on the face of that hill when the artillery opened with canister would fight no more. It was certain death to any comrade disabled in that wild rush; a wound, a slip of the foot, a misstep were fatal. We must get inside the range of those gaping mouths ere they belch their fire, or we are doomed. How many of my comrades were left behind in that awful race, God only knows! I only know that I got in and had time to take one hasty glance behind. Our boys seemed safe; there were a few in a kind of fringe hanging between the battery sections that the gunners were swerving their pieces to avoid, but further down—two-thirds the way of the hill—came the Confederates, yell-ing like demons, in a mad charge for our guns.

We had struck the crest just north of a small building which stood near the north end of the seminary and about 40 yards south of the Chambersburg Pike. Here was stationed one section of Stevens's 5th Me. Battery, the other sections being stationed one north and the other south of the seminary building. Across the Chambersburg Pike were stationed three guns of Battery B, 4th U.S. Art., in half battery, the other half bat-tery being stationed 100 yards further north and beyond the railroad. These 12 guns, all of them 12-pounders, were brimmed with shell or triple-shotted with canister; they were carefully posted by the best field artillerymen in the army; every man was at his station; they were await-ing this very opportunity. The charging Confederates were brave men, in fact, no braver ever faced death in any cause and none ever faced more certain death than these.

Almost of the same moment, as if every lanyard was pulled by the same hand, this line of artillery opened, and Seminary Ridge blazed with a solid sheet of flame and the missiles of death that swept her west-ern slopes no human beings could endure. At the first belching of the guns the blinding smoke shut out the view. We fell into line between the artillery sections and assisted with our musketry, keeping up the fire till our pieces grew hot and the darkness as of night settled upon us. Not a Confederate reached our line. After we ceased firing, and the smoke had lifted, I looked again, but the charging masses were not there. Only the dead and the dying remained on the bloody slopes of Seminary Ridge.

We had repulsed the enemy with terrible slaughter along our west front; but a moment later some one shouted "Look there! What troops are those?" pointing to the northward. We looked, and the valley north of the village seemed alive with advancing troops bearing above them triumphantly the saucy battle flags of the Confederacy, and we knew that our north front had been turned and that the Eleventh Corps had been swept from its position. For us there was but one thing to do, and we must do it quickly. From our position Gettysburg was 700 yards southeast of us (I have since measured the distance). The Chambersburg Pike was wide and smooth and down hill all the way, and we made good use of it. The artillery had the right of way by virtue of the power to possess it, and they drove their horses at a pace that would have sur-prised John the mad driver of old. The retreat must have been going on for some time while we were repulsing the last charge of the Confederates on Seminary Ridge, for Gen. Doubleday, who commanded our First Corps, in a little book that he wrote on this subject a few years after the war says:

> I waited until the artillery had gone, and then rode back to the town with my staff. As we passed through the streets, pale and frightened women came out and offered us coffee and food and implored us not to abandon them. . . . The First Corps was broken and defeated, but not dismayed. There were but few left, but they showed the true spirit of soldiers. They walked leisurely from the Seminary to the town, and did not run.

It would be interesting to one old soldier to know where Gen. Doubleday "waited until the artillery had gone." I did not wait a second, but dashed down the Chambersburg Pike, and while running my best the artillery passed me, but I did not see Gen. Doubleday and his staff waiting along the pike. Of course, it stirs the heart of an old soldier to have his general speak in words of commendation of himself and comrades; nevertheless, I must conclude that some of us left Seminary Ridge sometime after our general, for when we arrived in the town, there were no "pale and frightened women on the streets," with coffee and cookies for us. They had exhausted their supply before our arrival and had gone into their houses, as any sensible "pale and frightened" lady would have done under the same circumstances, to prepare a fresh supply. In fact, the streets were no places for women then.

It was all right, and a good thing for the First Corps and the army, that Gen. Doubleday did not remain too long, for he was a good soldier, and the country needed his services, and is one of the facts of history that we lost in prisoners taken by the enemy that 1st day of July from the First and Eleventh Corps about 2,000 men, most of them captured in the town after Doubleday had ridden through and out of it.

The boys said they got tangled up in the names of the brigade commanders of the Third Division of the Eleventh Corps—Gen. Von Schimmelfennig and Col. Krzyzanowski; but that was a soldier's joke. We became badly tangled up, all the same, and many a brave man went to Richmond and to his death on account thereof.

When we reached the town the Confederates were already in possession of the northern and eastern portions. Gens. Howard and Doubleday were then on Cemetery Hill, where they should have been, reforming their shattered lines to meet Lee's expected attack on their position there; but had they, or either of them, taken the precaution to plant a few pieces of artillery in positions to sweep the streets of Gettysburg, supported by detachments of infantry, under officers with staying qualities, to cover our retreat, many of our men might have been saved from captivity, who, conditions being otherwise, were lost. When I reached the town the Confederates were having everything their own way. Those of us who could get through rejoined our commands on Cemetery Hill, and those who were headed off and picked up by the Confederates went to Richmond. It was 4:30 o'clock p.m., and the battle of July 1 was over.

Lee was a man of genius, a great man. Great men are apt to make great mistakes. The pages of history are replete with illustrations of this fact, and the great Confederate commander was no exception to the rule. Honored by the people, educated at the expense of the government, made great by the republic, he had drawn his sword against her in the hour of her peril and had become her greatest adversary. This was the great mistake of his life. A man who could thus desert a nation dedicated to liberty, foremost in progressive civilization and leader of the world in the arts of peace, to swear allegiance to decrepit old Virginia, the mother of the abomination of the age and the breeding ground of human chattels for the marts and shambles of the cotton states, in her mad effort to become the cornerstone in an edifice of state to be erected on the foundation of slavery and oppression, must have possessed a large supply of human weakness and imperfection somewhere in his make-up. Such a man can never take his place in the pages of history as one free from guile and perfect in thought and in deed.

Lee was a great general. He was the idol of his army and the inspiration of the slave holders' rebellion; but when he abandoned his defensive policy and carried the war into the North he made his great military mistake. This mistake, however, was in the line of action and in conformity with his ambition and his genius.

"There is a tide in the affairs of men
Which, taken at the flood, leads on to fortune."

Lee had made every preparation to ride the flood tide of fortune. Behind the Rappahannock's protecting hills he had marshaled an army that was the pride of his ambitious heart and the hope renewed of the Southern Confederacy. He was playing a bold game for a stupendous stake. His lieutenants were generals of marked ability, tested and tempered in the fiery ordeal of battle. To him and to his cause they were known to be true as refined steel. His officers were brave and efficient, and every man in his mighty army was ready to do and dare every hardship of march, every danger of battle that their great chieftain thought necessary to order. No army in the world since the days of Alexander the Great was ever held more completely in the power of one directing hand. No leader of men except Alexander ever stood among his generals so supremely their leader and their chieftain.

In every movement he had handled his divisions with consummate skill. He had outgeneraled Hooker and invaded Pennsylvania without a battle. He had outgeneraled Meade and his corps commanders by keeping his own army well in hand, while he separated the Union commanders widely one from the other. He would meet and defeat the corps of the Union army in detail, and sweeping the last opposition from his path, swoop down upon our national capital and, laying the archives of the republic in ruins, dictate terms of peace to a nation humiliated and overthrown, thereby establishing the supremacy and independence of the Confederacy.

Such was the dream of victory that swelled the proud heart of Robert E. Lee and inspired his warriors for battle as he met our thin columns—a fourth of our army—at Gettysburg.

Up to 5 o'clock p.m. July 1, Lee had everything his own way, except that the first detail from the Army of the Potomac had put up a fight that surprised him. Nevertheless, they had been driven from their first position, and fully expected to be attacked in their second, but he established his headquarters on the Chambersburg Pike, just over Seminary Ridge, and for the time being seemed perfectly satisfied with what his army had accomplished. This was Lee's great mistake of the campaign. Why he did not follow up the advantage gained with his wonted vigor is beyond the comprehension of everyone familiar with the conditions. It would seem that the finger of God had paralyzed his brain in the very moment of victory.

It may be said that Lee's army was weary with its long march, and with the battle that had been so stubbornly contested; but what was the condition of Howard's and Doubleday's forces on the opposing line at the same hour? In the battle just ended they had lost nearly half their number. Buford's Division had lost 400, the First Corps 5,500, the Eleventh Corps 2,600, or an aggregate of 8,500, and after suffering the discouragement of defeat, they awaited the renewed onset of their victorious opponents, while they prayed that Lee would do exactly what he did do—give us a rest until Meade arrived with the remainder of the Army of the Potomac. In line on Cemetery Hill, there were Buford's Division, 2,500 strong; the First Corps, 3,000, and the Eleventh Corps, 7,200, the remnants of the divisions that bore the brunt of battle on the 1st; in all, 12,700 men. To these may be added Slocum's Twelfth Corps, numbering 8,589, which arrived on the ground about the time of our retreat to Cemetery Hill, and extended our line to the right along Culp's Hill to Rock Creek. This gave an entire force, counting Buford's Cavalry Division, of 21,289, and there was not another regiment of Union troops within eight hours' march of our position.

At 5 o'clock p.m. there still remained between three and four hours of daylight. Lee had in line of battle at that moment not less than 50,000 men. What his losses were during the day's fighting we have no means of knowing, but one of his division commanders ever having made a report. Gen. Heth, whose division opened the battle with Buford and was afterward met by the First Division (Wadsworth's) of the First Corps, says in his report of the battle: "In less than 25 minutes my division lost in killed and wounded over 2,700 men." From this we may assume that Lee's loss was equally as severe as ours, for he had five divisions engaged, but his troops were inspired by victory, while ours were depressed with defeat. His army was nearly all on the ground, while only one-third of ours was there to meet him.

He failed to renew the attack, and we are willing to give God the glory.

Gen. Reynolds's dispatch, sent before 10 o'clock July 1, stating that the heights of Gettysburg was the place for the battle, reached Gen. Meade at Taneytown just as soon as a good horse could carry it to him, probably by 1 o'clock. Did Gen. Meade order his army to Gettysburg? No; he expected Lee would attack him at Double Pipe Creek, if he would give him time; so, instead of making an effort to support Reynolds in his position there, he concluded Reynolds would support him in his chosen position after Reynolds was beaten. That was Meade's strategy. But he did one thing that brought about a salutary result; he ordered Gen. Hancock to ride to Gettysburg, view the situation, and report.

Meade was not a great general. He had been in command of the Army of the Potomac less than four days; in fact, he was then only nominally in command. He did not know his army, and the army, outside of the Fifth Corps, knew but very little of him. Each corps commander seemed to have a general idea of the situation and what he was expected to do or what he ought to do in the premises, and he acted according to the light he possessed. It was Providence more than anything else that brought Slocum to Howard's support at Gettysburg on July 1, and in this instance Slocum was not so very slow, but the swiftest of all, and the first to come to our assistance.

We had a splendid army, but no leader, and the danger was that Lee, by his superior generalship, would defeat us in detail. With the Army of the Potomac united, we were able to defeat Lee's army without a leader, but would Meade display sufficient generalship to unite his army? That was the all-important question. Gen. Meade lacked confidence in his own ability. In plain English, he was afraid of Lee. Very likely he had good and sufficient reasons to fear Lee's soldierly qualities. Probably every prominent general in the Army of the Potomac considered Lee superior as a general to Meade or to himself, but that fact did not deter Reynolds from letting him know that he was on earth and doing his best to put up a winning fight. It did not deter Howard from taking up the battle where Reynolds laid it down with his life and making every effort toward a soldierly disposition of his small force to hold Cemetery Hill as long as good fighting could hold it. It did not deter Slocum from marching his corps to the assistance of those already there on the field. It did not deter Hancock from riding to Gettysburg in response to Reynolds's dispatch and Meade's order, and reporting forthwith to Meade by another dispatch to the effect that Reynolds was right.

Probably there was no time in the history of the Army of the Potomac when it stood in greater need of a direct interposition of the hand of God in its behalf than at 5 o'clock in the afternoon of July 1, and Lee's inaction at that time, a weakness so foreign to his character, seems to have been in answer to that trying need. He waited, and while he waited our army concentrated.

Gen. Hancock arrived at Gettysburg a little before 5 o'clock. He assisted Gen. Howard in forming his lines of defense and sent a dispatch to Gen. Meade to order the army forward. Here Gen. Hancock became for the time being the commanding general. Gen. Meade had no choice in the matter. He had left the situation to Hancock's judgment, hoping, no doubt, that he would decide against Gettysburg for the battleground, but when he decided in its favor Meade was compelled to reinforce him.

When Meade received Hancock's dispatch, about 8 o'clock in the evening, Hancock was then at Gettysburg actively making preparations for the battle of the coming day; so Meade issued the order for every absent corps to advance with all possible haste.

Gen. Meade and staff reached Gettysburg about midnight, when he established his headquarters in a little old frame building on the west side of the Taneytown Road, 300 yards east of the crest of the southern prolongation of Cemetery Hill and about 400 yards south of the west gate of the cemetery. The same old house, or shack, stood there in 1900.

After the arrival of Gen. Meade on the field a council of war was held by the Union generals then present; at which council Meade gave it as his opinion that Gettysburg was not the place to fight a battle. His generals, however, without a dissenting voice, favored no retreat from the position they then held to Double Pipe, Single Pipe or any other Pipe without a fight, and Gen. Meade was compelled to give his consent and assistance to the battles that followed.

During the night of July 1 the soldiers in battle line of both armies rested on their arms, while their absent comrades, under urgent orders to reach the field, rested on their feet. There is no other march so severe and so trying to the soldier as a night march, but this was an occasion for the greatest of human efforts, and throughout the silent hours of the night they plodded on.

Before the morning dawned Lee's whole army, with the exception of Pickett's Division and Stuart's Cavalry, had arrived on the field, and it might be presumed that he was ready for battle. His left rested on Rock Creek, and was commanded by Ewell. His center ran through the village, and along Seminary Ridge, and was commanded by Hill. His right was commanded by Longstreet, whose troops were the last to arrive and, for some unaccountable reason, were a long time in getting into position. It was the continuation of Lee's mistake of the afternoon before. Hour after hour passed with only an occasional picket shot or the solitary boom of a heavy gun, and every hour's delay added to Meade's advantage. From 5 o'clock p.m. of July 1 until 4 o'clock p.m. of July 2 Lee waited, and by that 23 hours of inaction his "tide" had ebbed; the dream of his ambition could never be realized.

The Second Wisconsin suffered an extremely high rate of casualties at Gettysburg, losing more than three quarters of its men.

FIVE

"The living prepared for the morrow"

The Second Day at Gettysburg
July 2, 1863

When the morning dawned of July 2, the condition of Meade's army had greatly improved. Not only had the troops in line at sunset rested and recuperated their strength and courage, but the Second Corps (Hancock's), 13,000 strong, had arrived on the field and extended Howard's line to the left, southward, along the interior ridge toward Round Top.

The Second Corps came upon the field along the Taneytown Road, from 300 to 400 yards in rear of the ridge upon which Gen. Hancock, with Meade's approval, had selected his position, so that as each subdivision arrived opposite its place in line, it moved forward to the ridge and point selected and the tired soldiers dropped to repose, ready for battle at any moment when the signal sounded. The Second Corps made our line of battle 34,000 strong, extending from Rock Creek in a continuous line to the west gate of the cemetery on the Taneytown Road and thence southward half way to Round Top.

The Third Corps, commanded by Sickles, 12,000 strong, was also on the ground, but not in position in the morning. This gave Meade a force with which to meet Lee's army of 46,000 men, all told. The Fifth Corps (Sykes's), 12,500 strong, and the Sixth Corps (Sedgwick's), 15,500 strong, were many weary hours' march away. Would Lee take advantage of the fact that a third of Meade's army, 28,000 men, were still absent? If he intended to pursue his tactics of the previous day and previous battles, and defeat us in detail, here was his opportunity, but fortunately for the Army of the Potomac and the progress of liberty and civilization, Lee waited.

Between the southern prolongation of Cemetery Hill, which terminates in Round Top two and a half miles to the southward, and the Seminary Ridge opposite, there lies an irregular valley, about two and a half miles in length by from a mile to a mile and a quarter in width. This valley is divided into two irregular triangles by the Emmitsburg Road, which follows a well-defined ridge from the western slope of Cemetery Hill in a southwesterly direction, until said ridge merges into and said road crosses the Seminary Ridge, about a mile almost due west from Little Round Top. The eastern triangle has its apex toward the north, its base from Seminary Ridge to Little Round Top, and its perpendicular extending northward along the easternmost of these three ridges, from Little Round Top to Cemetery Hill. The western triangle is the reverse of the former—its base extending from Cemetery Hill about a mile west to Seminary Ridge, its perpendicular running southward along said ridge for the distance of two and a half miles, the juncture of the seminary with the Emmitsburg Road Ridge forming its apex. The Emmitsburg Road, therefore, forms the hypothenuse of both the aforesaid triangles.

The eastern of the aforementioned ridges, occupied by Hancock's Corps from Cemetery Hill half way to Little Round Top, is the least prominent of the three. In fact, for more than half the distance, and throughout the whole left wing of Hancock's line, the ridge is nothing more than a gentle elevation. The Emmitsburg Road Ridge is more prominent, and west of Hancock's left and the unoccupied space between his left and Little Round Top shuts off the view of the Seminary Ridge beyond. The Seminary is the most commanding ridge of the three, and from the point opposite Hancock's center southward to its juncture with the Emmitsburg Road, it becomes abrupt, rocky and heavily wooded.

Gen. Sickles, with his Third Corps, marched to the field along the Emmitsburg Road. At the time he crossed the Seminary Ridge, two and a half miles southwest of Cemetery Hill, Longstreet, with his Confederates, held the same ridge further north, and west of Hancock's right. Sickles noticed the splendid formation of the Emmitsburg Road Ridge both for defensive and offensive operations, with a broad highway running along its whole length, to facilitate the movement of troops, and especially artillery, from one point to another in the line, and, very naturally, desired to avail himself of such a grand strategic position. Gen. Meade, however, seemed to think the interior, or eastern, ridge a stronger and more secure position, and he instructed Sickles to form his corps on Hancock's left, extending his line southward to Little Round Top; at least, Gen. Meade so claimed afterward. Sickles construed the order as giving him discretionary authority in selecting his position. This blunder, or want of understanding between Gens. Meade and Sickles cost us dear and came very near leading up to incalculable disaster.

Gen. Meade was extremely cautious—too cautious to win a great victory like the capture or annihilation of an army opposed to him, and in this instance he had every reason to be cautious, from the fact that a third of his infantry was absent from the field. Meade reasoned that as Lee had marched his army far from his base with the intention of assuming the offensive, it would be well to give him a chance to fight a truly offensive battle, and certainly he did not wish to take any position that would bring on a renewal of the contest before the arrival of the Fifth and Sixth Corps. The longer Lee delayed his attack the more advantageously to Meade the situation became. By extending Hancock's line southward to Round Top would give him a strong, compact position, with his left absolutely secure. The Fifth Corps was approaching by the Taneytown Road, and would arrive on the field in the exact position to readily reinforce any part of his west front, as the Taneytown Road runs the whole length of the position and only 300 or 400 yards in rear of it. Sickles's Corps, nearly 12,000 strong, was ample to form an invincible line of battle from Hancock's left to that impregnable bastion to the southward.

From the absence of the Fifth and Sixth Corps, but for no other reason, was Meade justified in placing his army in such a purely defensive position, for, to abandon the Emmitsburg Road to Longstreet was in itself a victory for Lee. The Emmitsburg and Hagerstown Roads both lead to the Potomac, and with these roads in his possession Lee could readily retreat in absolute safety in case of defeat.

Sickles was a man of action—a fighter, and his idea—notwithstanding his judgement was at fault in one very important particular—of holding an offensive position to be taken advantage of the moment it became practicable, was the correct one; provided, of course, that the army was strong enough to assume it. Every soldier must admit Sickles's courage, while deploring his lack of soldierly sagacity.

The distance from Cemetery Hill along the Emmitsburg Road Ridge to Seminary Ridge is only a trifle, if any, farther than from the same point southward along the interior ridge to Round Top. Clearly the Emmitsburg Road Ridge was the line that should have been selected for our battle line, had the whole army been on the field and ready to assume the position on the morning of July 2. To assume this position would have necessitated the moving of Hancock's Corps forward or westward to the Emmitsburg Road, which would have swung his left westward a half or three-fourths of a mile, while his right would still have been pivoted on the west gate of the cemetery, thus giving him a line of battle about a mile and a quarter in length, or the same length of the interior line held by him, with his left on the Emmitsburg Road about 400 yards north of the point where it is crossed by the Wheatfield Road. Such formation would have carried Sickles's right 500 yards farther southwest on the Emmitsburg Road than the point at which he placed it, from which point his battle line would have followed the Emmitsburg Road to the Seminary Ridge, a mile and a quarter farther toward the southwest. Then, with the fifth Corps to hold the left on Seminary Ridge, and the Sixth Corps in reserve, Meade could have fought Lee to a finish at any point and every point along his line and followed up his success by sweeping northward with his left along the crest of Seminary Ridge until, gaining possession of the Hagerstown Road, he would have cut off Lee's retreat and turned his defeat into a rout. But the Fifth and Sixth Corps were not there, and in the absence of 28,000 infantry, and until they should arrive on the field, it was a good generalship on Meade's part to assume the strongest defensive position possible and maneuver to delay rather than to facilitate and invite attack.

Here, then, was the situation. There were two lines open for occupation. The inner was superior for a defensive, the outer for an offensive position. The army was not ready for battle, much less to assume the offensive. Meade was the commanding general, and had only to say to Sickles in plain English: "Form your corps on Gen. Hancock's left and continue his line southward along the ridge to Little Round Top, Gen. Sickles," and surely Gen. Sickles would have followed such instructions. The misunderstanding on the part of the generals was most unaccountable. At the very time of all others, when harmony in council and unity in action was necessary to insure success, harmony and unity were lacking. Neither position was selected. Hancock occupied one position in part, Sickles, in part only, occupied the other. There was, seemingly, no head to the formation, no harmony in the relation of the Second and Third Corps toward each other, no unity in their action as a whole, and the result was almost a disaster.

Hancock's Corps remained in its old position, while Sickles formed his corps according to his own discretion, which he claims was the import of the orders given him by Meade. A military eye can hardly be impressed with the stupendous weight of Gen. Sickles's discretion in following his old battle line. Placing his right on the Emmitsburg Road at a point about 300 yards southwest of the Codori House, which point was fully 500 yards in advance of Hancock's line and overlapping it about a half mile, he extended his line along the Emmitsburg Road for the distance of 900 yards, crossing the Wheatfield Road and going about 100 yards beyond to the southwest corner of the Peach Orchard. At this point Sickles seemed to weaken in his determination to make the Emmitsburg Road Ridge his line of battle, and turned abruptly to the rear or eastward, running thence at a right angle with his former line in the direction of Little Round Top, which is distant from this point one mile in a direct line. This was "Sickles's Salient." The point is three-fourths of a mile from the Seminary Ridge by the Emmitsburg Road in a northeasterly direction and between a fourth and a half mile directly east of the same ridge by the Wheatfield Road.

The moment Sickles abandoned the Emmitsburg Road and ran his battle line eastwardly away from it, he surrendered to Longstreet without a struggle the very point and the only point that, in order to seize and hold, could in any manner justify him in forming his corps in such an exposed and unsupported position. Nor by this turning of his line eastward did he lessen his exposure. In fact, it was this very angle in his line that gave it the name it bears and shot the Third Corps forth into a prominent and exposed position that no soldier, much less

Longstreet, could fail to see and take advantage of Sickles's Corps was like a pair of dividers opened to a right angle, the hinge at the southwest corner of the Peach Orchard, the right leg extending northeastwardly along the Emmitsburg Road, and the left extending southeastwardly toward Little Round Top. Longstreet's batteries on Seminary Ridge, or at any point along the Emmitsburg Road between the ridge and the Peach Orchard, could rake the right limb of the dividers fore and aft, while batteries on the same ridge or at any nearer point along the Wheatfield Road could do the same service for the left limb.

Sickles's skirmishers, comprising battalions of 1st Vt., 3d Me. and 1st N.Y. Sharpshooters, who penetrated as far west as the crest of the Seminary Ridge about a half mile north of the point where it is crossed by the Wheatfield Road, developed Longstreet's forces about noon of July 2, losing a number of men in a hot skirmish at that point. Sickles's skirmishers were driven in and Longstreet continued his movement toward the south and upon Sickles's left flank. From this fact Sickles must have been aware of Longstreet's efforts and intentions to find his flank or weak spot, if he left it exposed, and as he could not discover Longstreet's movements, sheltered as he was behind Seminary Ridge, any more accurately from the point of his salient at Peach Orchard than he could were his line a mile to the rear, where it should have been, with his left protected by Round Top and his right within support of Hancock, in order to protect his left he ran this zigzag line, which formed the left limb of his dividers, from the southwest corner of Peach Orchard to Death Valley, between Devil's Den and Little Round Top. The length of that line by actual measurement, following the many turns and angles in it (I measured it very carefully in 1900) is 1,500 yards, and ends in the low ground, 500 yards west of Little Round Top, with the rocky eminence of Devil's Den in its front.

This, then, was the position of Sickles. He had cut himself loose from the balance of the army, had isolated his corps, had taken up a position that was absolutely untenable, with his right 500 yards in advance of his nearest supports, with the angle of his salient advanced three-fourths of a mile beyond his supporting line, and his left, a long, helter-skelter line of nearly a mile in extent, supported by nothing and resting nowhere.

And where was Meade? The commanding general's headquarters

were situated just 300 yards in rear of Hancock's right. In 1900 I followed Meade's Avenue directly west from Meade's headquarters on the Taneytown Road to the crest of the ridge, which was Hancock's position. One hundred yards to the right stands a steel tower of observation, erected at this point on account of its prominence. Fifty yards to the left, or south, stands a bronze equestrian statue of Gen. Meade, erected where the general commanding might be presumed to have been occasionally when the lines were forming for battle. What a pity Gen. Meade could not have ridden forward from his headquarters, 300 yards, to this sightly position some time during the early part of the second day of July, 1863, and with his field glass surveyed the landscape to the southwestward. In 1900 I stood upon this ground, just 300 steps by actual count from Meade's headquarters, and saw without a field glass, although my eyes were old, the long line of white monuments extending down the Emmitsburg Road to the old Peach Orchard at "Sickles's Salient," and thence southeastward among the hills, groves and glens, through the Loop, through the Wheatfield and away to the Devil's Den and Death Valley, which tell, in a faint measure only, the sad story of Sickles's unaccountable blunder and the awful sacrifice, and I said to myself, "Where was Meade?"

Yea, and where were the members of Meade's staff? Where was Hancock and his staff? What were they all about from sunrise until 3 o'clock p.m. of July 2, 1863, that none should inform the commanding general that Gen. Sickles was using his own discretion in forming his corps? Along in the afternoon, in some unaccountable way, Gen. Meade discovered that Sickles had disregarded his instructions and formed his corps far out of the line that he intended him to occupy, and immediately he ordered Sickles to withdraw his corps to the inner line at Hancock's left, but it was too late—Longstreet had to be reckoned with in any further movement on those lines that day.

After the battle Gen. Meade talked in harsh terms of Sickles, and even essayed to prefer charges against him for disobedience of orders, but Sickles had lost a leg in the battle and fought like a hero, and we had really won a great victory, considering the chances against us in the outset, although at tremendous cost; therefore Abraham Lincoln squelched the court-martial. Perhaps he thought if Sickles deserved punishment for disobedience of orders, in forming his corps in such an exposed position, which no doubt he did, the commanding general also deserved punishment in a greater degree for not knowing what his subordinate was doing at such a time, in season to prevent such disastrous results, and that if courts-martial were commenced it would be hard telling where they might end.

There is no doubt but Lincoln was right.

Sickles's Corps comprised 11,924 men, in two divisions of three brigades each. Humphreys's Division extended along the Emmitsburg Road, facing the northwest. His position was a strong one, so far as a front defense was concerned, but his right was in the air, having no support nearer than Hancock's line, 500 yards to the rear, while his left was open to an enfilading fire from any artillery stationed along the Emmitsburg Road at any point between Peach Orchard and Seminary Ridge. Birney's Division faced the southwest and extended from the Peach Orchard to Death Valley, following no regular line, the country being diversified with hills, valleys, rocks and woods. His line was long and irregular, and, although facing generally to the southwestward, it made so many angles, loops and twists in trying to conform to the lay of the land and to select the most advantageous defensive positions that if faced nearly every point of the compass in one place or another along the line.

Longstreet had not been idle. From early morn he had been pushing his divisions southward and eastward under cover of Seminary Ridge and the sheltering hills and woods that intervene between said ridge and the Round Tops. His corps consisted of three divisions, one of which (Pickett's) was absent from the field, so that he had two divisions of four brigades each, commanded by Hood and McLaws, for active operations against Sickles. Longstreet therefore made his attack with 16,000 men. His orders from Lee were, "Strike the enemy on his left flank and roll him up like a blanket," and there is no doubt that Longstreet did his best to carry out those instructions. He had massed Hood's four brigades against Birney's long, crooked line, defended by three brigades, and at 4 o'clock p.m. of July 2 the battle of Peach Orchard opened.

Hood's Division struck Sickles's left like a cyclone from out the south, but the Third Corps did not roll up according to Lee's program worth a cent. Sickles was a fighter to be proud of, and no better soldiers ever lived than the men in his salient; they were placed at a terrible disadvantage; they had been led like lambs to the place of slaughter, but when the signal rang out for the slaughter to begin they were lambs no longer, and there was more or less slaughtering done on both sides. The McLaws's Division charged Humphreys's front along the Emmitsburg Road, doubling back his right flank, while the battle to the left soon extended along the entire length of Birney's line from the Peach Orchard eastward through the Wheatfield to Devil's Den and Death Valley.

Hancock supported Sickles in every way possible. When he saw Humphreys's right turned he sent Willard's Brigade across the fields, which met and checked Barksdale, in which action both Willard and Barksdale were killed. He also sent forward his whole left division, under Caldwell, to support Sickles's left, and the Wheatfield soon became the center of a whirlpool of battle. Hancock sent to the support of Sickles before the battle ended in all about 8,000 men, or two-thirds of his corps.

Hill reinforced Longstreet with all of Anderson's and part of Heth's and Pender's Divisions, swelling Longstreet's force to 28,000 men, and the battle continued to rage with increasing fury.

While the battle was still raging at its highest—each side pushing forward every available man, the chances being in Lee's favor, from the fact that he was enabled to concentrate nearly a third more men on Sickles's left than Meade could possibly bring to bear against him—Gen. Warren, chief of engineers of the Army of the Potomac, rode far down to the left and ascended Little Round Top. He at once discovered the importance of that position and that it was, in fact, the key to our left. At the same time Warren discovered that Hood's forces were even then making a movement in the direction and for the purpose of occupying this very position. Five hundred yards in rear of this position the First Division of the Fifth Corps was at that very moment marching along the Taneytown Road toward the battlefield. Warren lost no time in detaching and ordering forward Vincent's Brigade to the summit of Little Round Top, where it met and defeated Law's Brigade on its western slope, in which action Gen. Vincent was mortally wounded. The fighting for the possession of Little Round Top was continued for some time thereafter, and was very severe, but it was permanently held by the troops of the Fifth Corps. Battery D, of the 5th U.S. Art., was dragged by hand to the summit and, supported by Berdan's sharpshooters, soon cleared the Devil's Den of Confederate sharpshooters, which point was shortly after captured by Fisher's Brigade. The battle of Peach Orchard, with the continuation thereof at the Wheatfield, Devil's Den, Death Valley and around the Round Tops, lasted from 4 o'clock until dark, or about four hours of the severest fighting recorded in history. The timely arrival of the Fifth Corps gave Meade's columns the ascendancy, or about 32,000, as opposed to Longstreet's 28,000, making no allowance for losses. The Union loss, however, was about 10,000, the Confederate loss being fully equal thereto, if not greater; but as there are no returns of record of their losses, nothing but an approximate estimate can be given. After dark Meade ordered the withdrawal of his lines from all points west to the interior ridge, extending from Cemetery Hill to Round Top, and Sickles made no objection, being content to let the "salient" go with his leg.

Before seeking his couch that night Lee offered up thanks to God on high for what he had so dearly won, and Meade returned thanks to the same wise Providence for what Lee failed to win, while the Army of the Potomac thanked God for the timely arrival of the Fifth Corps, and the people of the United States thanked Him for good fighting done all along the line.

The battles of July 2 began but did not end with Peach Orchard. Lee had determined to try the strength of the center and the right, as well as the left that day, but the fact that the left did not "roll up" as readily as he anticipated, caused him to weaken his center and somewhat changed his program. Still, he had his eye on both the other points, and while the fighting was still raging on the left, the center came in for a touch of war also.

Between Cemetery Hill and the western prolongation of Culp's Hill there is a narrow valley extending southward in a deep indentation and thence rising gradually to a grassy slope. Running along the northeastern base of Cemetery Hill from Baltimore street a narrow lane leads up this valley to the point where Slocum Avenue crosses the valley from hill to hill. That lane was there on July 2, and along its southern side were posted Howard's Eleventh Corps, troops consisting of Ames's and Von Gilsa's Brigades. Above and behind them Cemetery Hill fairly gleamed with guns whose gaping mouths commanded this valley and from West Culp's Hill Stevens's 5th Me. Battery, which did such splendid service on Seminary Ridge on July 1, looked savagely down from its commanding position. At the foot of Culp's Hill, and about a dozen yards northwest from the lane, is a large spring, from which a ravine trends northeasterly to Rock Creek. Both the lane and the ravine afforded protection to advancing troops until well within this valley, and here Early had massed his division for a desperate effort to capture Cemetery Hill. Just before sunset of July 2 the crash of musketry in the valley below announced to the men at their guns on both Cemetery and Culp's Hills that the battle was on.

Early's Division had crept up the lane and ravine as far as possible without attracting the attention of Howard's men, and then, with Hays's Brigade of Louisiana Tigers in the lead, charged straight for Howard's line of infantry, yelling and firing as they came on. Howard's men seem to have been caught napping. To my mind their line was too near the foot of the hill, and Early's men were almost on them before they were discovered. Howard's men returned the fire, but soon gave way before the celebrated "Tigers," who paid no heed to musketry or canister for a time; they dashed through all opposition, and swarming over the wall and up the slope, captured two guns of Rickett's Battery and fought hand to hand with the gunners for the others. Finally they advanced so far up the hill that their left flank was turned for a moment in the direction of the guns of the 5th Me., on Culp's Hill, which raked them fore and aft with canister. At the same moment Battery B, 4th U.S. Art., gave them canister in front at short range. Nothing human could withstand such a reception, and they fell back to shelter. A moment later the infantry line was reinforced by Carroll's Brigade of the Second Corps, which dashed down the slope of Cemetery Hill, clearing both lane and ravine.

This was Early's only attempt to climb Cemetery Hill, and there many of his brave followers found a cemetery. Of the Tigers who led the charge less than 300 returned to their lines, and the organization was wiped from existence. It was a bold and desperate effort, but, for the Confederates, a most discouraging failure. This battle was of short duration, but exceedingly sharp while it lasted. Carroll's Brigade lost 211 men, while the Eleventh Corps lost 800 or 900; or from 1,000 to 1,100 in all. The Confederate loss was very severe, the Tigers alone losing about 1,200, or more than our entire loss.

Simultaneously with Early's attempt to carry Cemetery Hill—just before sunset of July 2—Johnson's Second Division of Ewell's Corps, which held the extreme left of Lee's line, made a vigorous, determined and, for a time, successful attack on Meade's extreme right on Culp's Hill, held by Slocum's Twelfth Corps.

Culp's Hill was the strongest natural position along our whole line. It is a high, rocky ridge extending southeastward from its point of highest elevation to Rock Creek, a distance from the valley separating it from Cemetery Hill of about a mile. The west prolongation adjoining the Eleventh Corps was held by my old division (Wadsworth's), the First Division of the First Corps. This was joined on the right by Slocum's Corps, which extended our line to and beyond Rock Creek. The face of the hill and ridge to the north and east is abrupt and easily defended, but as it nears Rock Creek it slopes away more gradually, ending in a level meadow 300 yards wide, through which winds the creek. Back of this ridge a small branch heads in the valley west of the Baltimore pike, runs eastwardly, crossing the pike, and empties into Rock Creek east of the termination of Culp's Hill. Spangler's Spring, of which I shall speak later, is situated just back of the easternmost prolongation of the ridge and about 50 yards north of the branch, with which it is connected by an outlet. These valleys uniting at this point make a wide, open space that lay at Slocum's right, penetrating far to rearward, which had to be guarded carefully.

While the battle of Peach Orchard was in progress and Sickles was being hotly pressed, Slocum was ordered to reinforce the left with every man he could spare from his line. Slocum had in his Corps 8,589 men to hold a line a mile long and guard the valley and creek on his right. Of these he sent nearly all except Green's Brigade to Sickles's aid, and when Johnson attacked the right on Culp's Hill at sunset he found it very weak. Green's Brigade, however, held the hill and the main portion of the ridge, but Johnson swept in along the creek and carried the ridge northward for a space of about 300 yards. The 2d Md. (Confederate) infantry penetrated up the ridge to the farthest point occupied by any of Johnson's troops, and in 1900 their monument stood on the crest with monuments of the Union regiments, showing the exact spot which marked the division of the contending forces. Johnson then moved the main portion of his troops up the valley of the branch in rear of Culp's

Hill as far as the Baltimore pike without meeting any opposition. Four hundred yards farther, just north of Power's Hill, was parked Meade's whole ammunition and supply train, but Johnson did not know it. It was after dark. The battle was over, not a shot was being fired, and Johnson really became alarmed. To his staff he said: "This is too easy; I believe the Yanks have set a trap for us." So he marched his division back to the vacant line on Culp's Hill, and waited for morning. The Twelfth Corps troops did not get into the engagement on the left, and were even then returning. They followed Johnson as far as the branch in rear of the ridge, where they also waited for daylight, and during the night both Johnson's troops and Slocum's forces drew their supply of water in peace from Spangler's Spring, that was thus placed between the lines.

Again merciful night spread his mantle over the battlefield. The dead slept in peace, the wounded suffered and endured, and the living prepared for the morrow and the renewal of the sanguinary struggle.

The Sixth Corps (Sedgwick's) arrived, 15,555 strong, thus at last concentrating and reuniting the Army of the Potomac in its full strength and completeness, and from that moment Lee's last chance for the realization of his ambitious dream was at an end.

While the Army of the Potomac had lost 20,000 men during the previous two days, it would confront Lee on the morrow with an unbroken front four miles long, with 63,000 men in line and on reserve, with our left buttressed upon Round Top and our right upon Culp's Hill; but the leader for the hour and the occasion was not there. Defensively our position was impregnable, for the temporary lodgment of Johnson on the southeastern spur of Culp's Hill could be readily overcome, and on our flanks were our cavalry, active and watchful, ready to grapple with and turn back Stuart on his approaching from either direction. Offensively, Meade had already abandoned the idea, if he ever entertained it. Lee held the Hagerstown and the Emmitsburg Roads, with a wide-open door for retreat the moment the necessity arrived, and Meade would never attempt to cut his army in two or crush his right in order to get possession of that back door. The man who was to fight Lee to a finish and bar the door behind him was yet to be found.

So Gen. Meade prepared to stay, and in that he did well, but the idea of capturing or destroying Lee's army never entered his head. He strengthened his lines from Culp's Hill to Round Top, throwing up entrenchments that were still there in 1900, and planting batteries in every available position.

It was now Lee's turn to call a council of war. It had been wiser to call a council of retreat, but that came also in due season. At the council Lee was still the master spirit, the same indomitable and courageous leader; in fact, at this council more than at any other time in his life Lee laid himself open to the charge of pigheadedness. He there told his corps commanders and his staff that on the next day he would assault Meade's center. To this Longstreet objected. He said: "Gen. Lee, we have failed today in a mighty effort to break Meade's front. I give it as my opinion that another effort will not succeed. I would advise moving southward by the Emmitsburg Road, which we hold, toward Washington, thus compelling Meade to abandon his stronghold and give us battle on more favorable ground." Lee replied: "No, gentlemen, no! I will strike them between the eyes. I have tonight been reinforced by Pickett's Division, the flower of my army, and by Stuart's Cavalry." Here it becomes necessary to diverge from the proceedings of the council and explain the whereabouts of Stuart, and how he came there. When Lee crossed the Potomac he left Stuart behind to befog and delay Hooker, but Stuart was outgeneraled and completely cut off from Lee's army. He then set out on a raid around the Union army to the eastward, and on June 30 he encountered Kilpatrick's Division of Union cavalry in the town of Hanover, 14 miles east of Gettysburg. Knowing that Lee's original destination was Harrisburg, Stuart retreated from Hanover toward Carlisle, which point he reached on the evening of July 1, where he learned that Lee had abandoned his contemplated attack on Harrisburg, left the Cumberland Valley, crossed to the east side of the South Mountain, and that there had already been one day's fighting between him and the Army of the Potomac at Gettysburg. From Carlisle Stuart moved southward and reached Gettysburg on the night of July 2.

Therefore, in that council of war, Lee said: "I have been reinforced by Pickett's Division of infantry and Stuart's Cavalry. Tomorrow I will mass Pickett's Division in the woods on the west slope of Seminary Ridge, in front of Meade's left center, well supported to the right and to the left. I will dispatch Stuart around Meade's right flank to make a rear attack in conjunction with Pickett's front attack; then let every battery and every gun along our line open and concentrate their fire upon that point in Meade's line, the center of which is designated by that umbrella-shaped clump of trees that shall be Pickett's objective point, and when the bombardment shall cease, then shall Stuart and Pickett charge, and I will cut Meade's army in two and destroy it in detail." Too late! too late!

After the war, veterans returned to Gettysburg to reflect on the battle and honor the dead. These commissioners from Wisconsin visited the battlefield in 1887 to locate sites for monuments to the state's regiments.

SIX

"Into the fiercest hell of battle"

The Third Day at Gettysburg
July 3, 1863

The morning of July 3 dawned bright and beautiful. At 4 o'clock Johnson was reinforced by Smith's Brigade of Early's, and Daniel's and O'Neal's Brigades of Rodes's Divisions, and all were formed in line ready for the attack on Slocum's position. Then Slocum's batteries on Power's Hill opened fire upon them, throwing them into temporary confusion and compelling their retirement for reformation. Soon, however, they advanced again, when Geary's whole division met them with a withering fire of musketry, and for hours the battle raged furiously. About 9 o'clock a.m. Shaler's Brigade of the Third Division of the Sixth Corps reinforced Geary. A little later Ruger's Division moved around to the right so as to enfilade Johnson's left flank, from which point they advanced up the southeastern slope of the ridge.

Johnson made a heroic effort to retain what he so easily won the night before, but Ruger's charge was too impetuous, and he abandoned the works, with a loss of 500 prisoners and many killed and wounded, retreating helter-skelter through the woods to the shelter of the valley below. The 2d Md., that held the highest point attained, made the attempt to storm the ridge above them, but was repulsed with heavy loss. Their colonel was severely wounded and captured, and the regiment lost more than half its members.

By 10 o'clock Slocum had won a complete victory, reestablishing his lines where he had planted them on the evening of July 1, the Confederates thereafter making no further demonstrations on our right flank.

In this battle, which was distinctly separate from any other and a continuation of the battle of Culp's Hill of July 2, Slocum had, including Shaler's Brigade, a force of 10,400 men, and his total loss was 1,157.

Johnson's Division went into the battle 6,000 strong, and was reinforced on the morning of July 3 by three brigades, or 4,500 men, making a total strength of 10,500, and losing, all told, 2,350.

In this battle the forces opposed were numerically about equal. Slocum had the advantage of position, except when winning back the extreme right, and the comparative losses are a fair representation of that advantage.

Lee seemed to have perfect confidence in his plan of battle for July 3, as previously portrayed to his generals in their council of war, by which he expected to cut Meade's army in two and defeat it utterly.

The supposition, as expressed by some writers, that Lee ordered Pickett's charge not with the expectation of breaking our line, but simply to "gain time"—as a kind of bluff to deter Meade from making an offensive or counter movement on his lines while his army was preparing to retreat—is at variance with every known fact and movement in connection with his army during July 3.

There was no bluff about it, and no necessity for a bluff. Lee well knew that there would be nothing "offensive" about Meade, whatever the result of his final effort to break his lines; otherwise he never would have taken the desperate risk of sending Stuart's jaded cavalry on another wide circuit and wild dash where he was expected to try titles with a line of securely posted infantry, nor of putting his only division of infantry that had not been war hammered and terribly battered within the previous two days, on which he could rely as a reserve in an emergency, into the fiercest hell of battle, where, if it failed of success, it could not be otherwise than the certain and complete destruction of the whole division.

Lee still hoped that God or good luck was on his side, and would at last give him the victory. In this he was mistaken, but he knew of a certainty that the gate back of him was always open for his retreat, and that Meade would make no effort worthy of the name to close the gate against him or wrench it from his possession, even if Stuart and all his band rode beyond the shadow of everlasting night and the last man of Pickett's Division lay stark and cold on the death-haunted field.

So Lee issued his orders for the day's operations, and early in the morning Stuart was in the saddle, leading his daring riders in a wide detour around the right flank of the Army of the Potomac.

Three and a half miles east of Gettysburg, where certain crossroads leading southward beyond Wolf Hill toward the Baltimore pike intersect the Hanover Road, Stuart encountered Gregg's Second Division and Custer's Brigade of the Third Division of Union cavalry, and then and there was fought one of the sharpest cavalry battles of the war, known in history as "The Saber Fight." Stuart was at a disadvantage; his men were weary with long and continuous riding, his horses were jaded and spiritless; while Gregg's and Custer's men and horses were comparatively fresh and vigorous and ready for action. Stuart was overcome in every charge. His lines were broken, his troopers scattered. He was defeated, and returned in haste to the rear of Lee's infantry—not Meade's as ordered—and so it came to pass that Stuart did not charge in conjunction with Pickett when the thunder of the artillery ceased.

The second act in Lee's program for July 3 began at 1:15 p.m. Lee's orders had been obeyed to the letter, and every battery in his army of sufficient range to reach Meade's lines had been carefully posted and trained upon his left center. At 1:15 the silence which had for an hour or more brooded over the field was broken by a signal gun fired by the Washington Artillery of New Orleans, which was posted in the edge of the woods on Seminary Ridge opposite the Union left center, and then the whole ridge up and down for the distance of a mile and a half lighted up with one continuous blaze, as gun after gun and battery after battery opened their belching throats and vomited forth fire and the messengers of destruction. It was a grand demonstration of military buncombe; but it demonstrated only one fact, which is, that Lee was not so weak in men and material, and the Confederacy was not so destitute of the sinews of war as many people, both North and South, would have us believe. Lee was a long way from home, yet he developed a strength of artillery in this cannonade that surprised Meade. If Lee was putting up a bluff for Meade's benefit or consideration, it should have ended there. It cannot be claimed for an army that it is inferior in numbers and war material to its adversary when it is able to concentrate on a given point from 120 to 150 pieces of long-range, heavy field artillery, while that adversary is only able to reply with 80 guns, and that was the situation at Gettysburg on the 3d of July.

Of course there was immense damage done on both sides during the great military duel, which lasted about two hours, or until 3 o'clock. Caissons were blown up, guns dismounted and disabled, batteries silenced, trees splintered, rocks riven, horses and men killed and wounded, and all that; but it had no effect whatever on the general result of the charge in contemplation.

If Lee expected to retreat—as he afterward did, and was burdened with an overweight of ammunition that he was anxious to get rid of, which is not likely—then this grand cannonade was a display of wisdom on his part, for the only possible advantage he could have gained was that by expending more ammunition than Meade did, his limber-chests, caissons and ammunition wagons were lighter for the retreat.

On the other hand, if Lee expected to have any use for ammunition on the retreat, or ever after, or if it was a fact that the Confederate government was sore pressed to procure the very stores that he so lavishly threw away, then it was another of the great blunders of a great general. For my own part, I cannot help believing, that not only in the Gettysburg campaign, but in the whole war, we were on God's side and Lee was not.

While Lee had the advantage in the number of guns engaged, and possibly in their positions, as it was his funeral, so to speak, and if it were possible to find any advantageous position, he would not scruple to avail himself of them; Meade had the advantage in reserves with which to replace his crippled and exhausted batteries, and a decided advantage in the fact that his chief of artillery, Gen. Hunt, foresaw that his cannonade was the prelude to some act that was being prepared behind the scenes. Very naturally he mistrusted a charge on the point designated by the concentration of Lee's artillery fire, and knowing that the cannonade could not continue much longer, he ordered the Union guns all along the line to cease firing and then immediately put the artillery in the best shape possible for the next demonstration. That Lee was deceived by this timely precaution on the part of Hunt there is grave doubt. Lee might have hoped that the grand artillery effort of his life had accomplished more than it really did, but he was not the fool to suppose for a moment that Meade was out of ammunition, or all the guns along his line disabled.

Shortly after the Confederate artillery also ceased firing. The short-range guns—brass 12-pounders, Napoleons and howitzers—were quickly gotten into position with the Parrotts and Rodmans. The Union line was intact; the infantry had not been shaken; the artillery was in readiness for the last act of the great drama.

Pickett's Division of Longstreet's Corps numbered 6,114 present for duty equipped, on June 20, 1863, the last return of which we have record made by Pickett previous to the battle of Gettysburg, and it could not have fallen far short of 6,000 when it started on that immortal charge on the afternoon of July 3. The division comprised three brigades, known as Garnett's, Armistead's and Kemper's; each brigade numbering about 2,000 men. This was the force that Lee had selected to strike the Army of the Potomac in the center and cut it in two. Was there ever an act more foolhardy, more unworthy the genius of a great general? Lee had ordered that Pickett should be strongly supported, but it was impossible to find in his army supports who had not been there before, many of them more than once on this same field or nearby, and it was not strange that their enthusiasm was not at the white heat that seemed to burn in the hearts of Pickett's men.

Pickett's Division was formed in the woods on the western slope of Seminary Ridge in column of brigades, three brigades deep, Garnett's, Armistead's and Kemper's, about 100 yards space between each brigade, the front or width of the column being the length of a brigade, or about a quarter of a mile, supported on the left by two brigades of Heth's Division, on the right by Wilcox's and Perry's Brigades, and in the rear by Wright's, Mahone's and Posey's Brigades of Anderson's Division of Hill's Corps; but these supports really did nothing more than to come out of the woods far enough to show that they were there, and retired to cover again very soon after Meade's artillery opened upon them. Pickett's Division charged the Army of the Potomac, and history must chronicle the decree that sent it to its doom as the act of a madman.

From the edge of the woods on Seminary Ridge to the umbrella-shaped copse on the ridge beyond the valley is little short of a mile. The course crosses the valley and the Emmitsburg Road north of the Codori House, where the ridge at the Emmitsburg Road is only a gentle elevation. Cemetery Hill presented one continuous front of artillery, and the ridge southward and every knoll behind it was studded with cannon, while several lines of gleaming steel along the tawny earthworks told where patiently the infantry bided its time.

When Longstreet, who foresaw the slaughter and opposed the charge, looked out over the wide field and beheld the far side thereof with its frowning ridges and glimmering labyrinths where death and destruction watched and waited, what wonder that his voice failed him, and as one struck dumb with sorrow for the useless sacrifice of his brave soldiers answered only with a nod of assent when Pickett saluted him and asked: "Shall I lead my command forward?"

Twenty minutes after the artillery ceased firing Pickett's brave Virginians marched out of the woods with their guns at a right-shoulder-shift and, with steady and measured tread, as if on parade, headed down the eastern slope of Seminary Ridge and straight for the "jaws of death." When the rear line of Pickett's column was well out of the woods, presenting a splendid mark thus silhouetted against the face of the ridge, Cemetery Hill and all the ridge southward blazed and thundered anew, concentrating an appalling fire on the advancing forces, but on they came. When they reached the Emmitsburg Road they entered the very "mouth of hell," for then the 12-pounders and light field guns loaded with canister, which they doubled and trebled as the column advanced, came into action. In the face of it all Pickett's men reach the foot of the ridge. Now they are climbing the slope; Lee shall not think—the world shall never say—that the fault was theirs. Two hundred yards farther is the copse on the crest of the ridge—a hundred yards only to Hancock's waiting lines of infantry. Then the crash of musketry becomes as the sound of falling forests, and Pickett's lines melt away as snow before the breath of the Chinook. Garnett falls just outside our lines. Armistead leaps the outer wall and dies within. Kemper falls wounded close up to the trenches. The force of the charge is spent; they are at the end of their journey; they cannot return; they throw down their arms and surrender, all that is left of them. Pickett's charge is over.

This was the last act in the great drama among the picturesque hills of Gettysburg, but sometime during the afternoon Hood's Division of Longstreet's Corps made a demonstration on Meade's left flank in the vicinity of Round Top, but was frustrated by Farnsworth's Cavalry Brigade, in which action Gen. Farnsworth was killed.

During the advance of Pickett's column across the valley the Confederate artillery was not idle, by any means, but gave the Union artillery the very best (or worst) that was at their command. All through the advantages were with Meade, even then the fight was not all on one side.

Gens. Hancock, Gibbon and Stannard were wounded during this

engagement, and Lieut. Cushing, commanding Battery A, 4th U.S. Art., was killed while working the last serviceable gun of his battery about 100 yards to the right and front of the umbrella-shaped copse, within a few feet of the spot where the Confederate General Armistead fell riddled with bullets. This point, called "the Bloody Angle," was so named from the fact that it was about 75 yards in advance of the line on either side, being defended in front by a stone wall over which Armistead and some of his followers leaped to their deaths. This was the only point where any of Pickett's men got within our lines, not one of whom ever got out again, and is therefore figuratively called "The high water mark of Pickett's Charge."

Pickett's Division was said to have been annihilated. Of four generals and 15 field officers only Pickett and one lieutenant colonel escaped unharmed; but Pickett himself went no farther east than to the Emmitsburg Road. By 4 o'clock p.m., or a little later, the great battle was over. Lee and Meade faced each other in battle line until the morning of July 5, but during all that time Lee was hustling his trains to the rear.

When the battle of Gettysburg was over Meade's lines were all intact, and he had a concentrated army of 70,000 men of all arms under his command. The losses sustained by the Army of the Potomac during the three days at Gettysburg are officially stated as follows:

General Headquarters	4
First Corps	6,024
Second Corps	4,350
Third Corps	4,210
Fifth Corps	2,187
Sixth Corps	242
Eleventh Corps	3,801
Twelfth Corps	1,081
Artillery Reserve	242
Total infantry and artillery	22,141
Calvary Corps	849
Total loss of all arms	22,990

These figures leave the strength of the various corps and of the army when the battle was over as follows:

First Corps	3,998
Second Corps	8,554
Third Corps	7,714
Fifth Corps	10,322
Sixth Corps	15,313
Eleventh Corps	6,040
Twelfth Corps	7,508
Artillery Reserve	2,304
Total infantry and artillery	61,753
Calvary Corps	9,951
Total of all arms	71,704

As these figures make no allowance for loss by sickness during the battle, it seems fair to assume that Meade's army after the battle of Gettysburg was finished was 70,000 strong.

It is not by any means so easy to fix the strength of Lee's army, as his losses never were and never can be ascertained with any degree of accuracy. The official figures from Confederate guesswork reports, however, are as follows:

Longstreet's Corps	7,536
Hill's Corps	5,937
Ewell's Corps	6,735
Stuart's Cavalry Corps	240
Lee's total loss at Gettysburg	20,448

These figures, if true, show that Lee retreated from Gettysburg with undue haste, for his army must have been, as compared with Meade's, better able to remain in Pennsylvania than when he invaded it; or numerically stronger than Meade's by 5,000.

In this connection I wish to review some of these official Confederate reports of losses, in comparison with certain known facts.

First. The loss of Pickett's Division is reported at 2,863, or less than 50 percent, and yet that division went through the very whirlpool of battle. Was it possible that Hancock's men were shooting for fun, and accidentally hit a few of Pickett's men? The First Corps of the Union army went into the battle of July 1 8,500 strong, and lost 5,500, or nearly 65 percent. Armistead's Brigade is reported to have lost in the charge 1,191, or about 60 percent, while my old brigade (the Iron Brigade) on July 1 went into battle with 1,883 men, losing 1,212, or about 70 per cent.

Second. The loss of Hays's Brigade (the Louisiana Tigers) of Early's Division, that led the charge on the evening of July 2 against the northeast front of Cemetery Hill, is reported, in this aforesaid Confederate report of losses, at only 313, while Hoke's Brigade, which supported Hays, is reported to have lost rather more, or 345, making a total loss to the two brigades in the battle of 658. Hays's Louisiana Tigers were never heard of after their repulse that night, and yet the whole brigade lost only 313 men; absolutely absurd on the face of it. In repelling the charge Von Gilsa's and Ames's Brigades lost more than their opponents are reported to have lost, and Carroll's Brigade of the Second Corps, that arrived after the artillery had raked Hays's Brigade and repulsed the charge, lost 211 men, or nearly as many as Hays is reported to have lost. Surely these reports are to be taken with more than one grain of allowance.

Third. Heth's Division, which opened the battle on the part of the Confederates and fought from 9 o'clock a.m. until 4 o'clock p.m. of July 1 against Wadsworth's Division of Reynolds's First Corps, is reported herein to have lost 2,827 men; yet Gen. Heth, in his official report of the battle, says: "In less than 25 minutes my division lost over 2,700 in killed and wounded." This is but 127 less than the division is now reported to have lost in the whole battle, and no prisoners included in Heth's official report. Now, I happen to know of my own knowledge that we took many prisoners from Heth that day. Archer's Brigade of Heth's Division met the Iron Brigade in our first onset. We drove them across Willoughby Run and there captured Archer and 300 of his men in one haul, while our Second Brigade (Cutler's) a little later captured the 2d Miss., of Davis's Brigade, same division, commanded by Maj. John A. Blair, the whole regiment, major and all, surrendering to Col. Dawes, of the 6th Wis., which regiment was temporarily attached to Cutler's Brigade. One of Heth's regiments, the 26th N.C., of Pettigrew's Brigade, which later in the day met the Iron Brigade, replacing Archer in Heth's line, went into the action with 800 men, losing 708, coming out of the fight with only 92 men. The 24th Mich., which was to the left of my regiment (the 2d Wis.) in our brigade line, met this 26th N.C., with 496 men, losing in the same battle 397, coming out with a force of 99 men.

Pettigrew's Brigade is reported to have lost 1,105 men, which is, after deducting the loss of the 26th N.C., a loss of 397 men for the remaining six regiments of Pettigrew's Brigade, or 66 1/2 men to the regiment. These reports are out of harmony with the known facts. If Heth's original official report is true, and I see no reason why it should not be, then his division must have lost fully 4,000 men. Heth's Division went into the battle more than 7,000 strong, and if its loss was equal in percentage with the First Corps, with which it fought, or 65 percent, instead of losing 2,827, as reported in these guesswork reports, its loss must have been 4,550.

Fourth. Stuart's Cavalry Corps is reported to have lost 240 men. That being true, his battle on the Hanover Road with Gregg and Custer must have been a small affair, and Stuart retreated immediately on finding a fighting force in his front. If he had reached the rear of our infantry and charged in conjunction with Pickett, he could not have hurt us much.

Fifth. When I visited the old battlefield in 1900 I walked along Confederate Avenue from the Chambersburg pike southward on Seminary Ridge, across the Emmitsburg Road and eastward to the foot of Round Top, where said avenue merges into Sykes Avenue. This was the Confederate artillery line during the battles of July 2 and 3, and wherever a Confederate battery stood during the cannonade or at any other time there stand two guns and a metallic tablet to commemorate the spot and the heroism of the men who stood behind these Confederate guns. I was greatly interested in reading those tablets, for they revealed the fact that the survivors of these Confederate artillery companies have forgotten a great deal about the details of the battle, if they ever knew. In the vicinity of the steel observatory that stands on this avenue about one-half mile north of the point where it crosses the Emmitsburg Road there are a number of these tablets, from which I copied the reports of losses thereon contained, verbatim et literatim, as follows: The first, "Loss, two killed, 10 wounded"; the next, "19 killed, 114 wounded, 6 missing, horses lost, 116." This was the only severe loss given on any tablet. The third tablet reads, "Losses heavy, but not reported in detail"; the fourth, "Losses serious, but not reported in detail"; the fifth, "Losses heavy, but not reported in detail"; the sixth, "One killed, six wounded"; the seventh, "Three killed, four wounded; missing, four; horses disabled, 20"; the eighth, "Two killed, eight wounded"; the ninth, "Losses heavy, but not reported in detail." It would be more satisfactory in arriving at the true aggregate loses to have the "heavy losses" reported in detail, and not guessed at in a lump sum.

Sixth. This Confederate guesswork report puts the entire number of Confederate wounded at 12,706, and missing 5,150. The record of prisoners of war in the office of the adjutant general at Washington bears the names of 12,227 wounded and unwounded Confederates captured at Gettysburg. Deducting the number of unwounded prisoners, or 5,150, from the whole number of captured, and we have 7,077 wounded prisoners, all or nearly all of whom were so severely wounded that they were abandoned by Lee and left in the hospitals around Gettysburg, but every last man among his wounded who had a chance of standing the retreat was hurried to the rear on the night of July 3. After the battle of the Wilderness, in 1864, I went with my regiment, the 23d U.S.C.T., with which I was then serving, from the rear of Grant's army to Belle Plaine Landing, on the Potomac River, as guard for Grant's supply trains, and on the outward trip every ambulance and every wagon was filled with wounded; besides, more than an equal number of slightly wounded accompanied the train on foot. Besides these there were hundreds of severe cases who could not be removed from our field hospitals. I know by actual experience, somewhat of the proportion that the slightly wounded bears to the severely wounded in battle. As at Gettysburg we captured 7,000 severely wounded Confederates, we may assume as an absolute certainty that Lee lost twice as many more who were not wounded so severely as to disable them from making the retreat. That would fix the entire number of Confederate wounded at 21,000. Their killed could not have been less than 3,500 and their missing 5,150; making Lee's aggregate loss at Gettysburg 29,650 men.

The Confederates, living and dead, have no reason to be ashamed of the battle of Gettysburg so far as the battle itself was concerned. I think they have reason to be ashamed of the cause they espoused, but the fight they put up was heroic. In every instance, except at Sickles's Salient, we held the vantage ground and repelled their assaults. At Fredericksburg Burnside assaulted Lee's position, which was hardly more secure and impregnable than Meade's was at Gettysburg, the principal difference being that Lee had his army all concentrated and in position at Fredericksburg when the battle opened. There Burnside's loss was 12,321, Lee's 5,309, or more than two to one, but the United States did not belie our losses to save Burnside's reputation. Lee made military blunders at Gettysburg that were only excelled by Burnside at Fredericksburg during the Civil War, and it seems perfectly foolish for his admirers North or South to befog and belie the truths of history in order to glorify the military genius of a man who deserted the nation that educated him in the art wherein he was gifted, and turned the strength of his genius against the sword of God and the might of his truth.

After the battle, and during the remainder of the 3d and all of the 4th of July, with an army of 70,000 men under his command, 15,000 of whom, or one-fourth of his infantry (the Sixth Corps) having scarcely pulled a trigger during the action, Meade watched Lee pull his defeated army together, which had been pounded and hammered and slaughtered and repulsed at every point, and march away with flying colors to prolong a wicked and inhuman war for another year and a half, that should have been ended then and there.

Gettysburg was Meade's first and last battle as a commanding general. He retained the supreme command of the Army of the Potomac until the next winter, and handled the army skillfully in avoiding battle. He retained the command under Grant, and until the war closed and proved himself a skillful and reliable lieutenant in executing the plans of a leader; but if the United States could have given him 500,000 men and allowed him to retain the chief command, it is doubtful if he ever would have taken Richmond or captured Lee's army.

In the month of May, 1900, I put in two weeks of hard work, for an old man, in reviewing and closely studying the battlefields as they were in 1863, as compared with their appearance and condition at the time of my later visit.

In the first place, I rode along the principal avenues that follow closely the various battle lines of the old war days. These are called Buford, Reynolds, Howard, Sickles, Slocum, Hancock, Sedgwick and Sykes Avenues, after the corps commanders of the Army of the Potomac. My guide, or rather driver, was an old man who was at Gettysburg at the time of, but not in, the battle. I found him of use in locating any point with which I was not familiar, but he seemed not to be a successful guide or driver on the field; not for the reason that he was not a soldier in the battle, as one might suppose, but rather for the reason that he was old and had some knowledge of the battle gathered from personal observation.

It was a remarkable fact, but nevertheless a fact, that on the field of Gettysburg in 1900 could not be found as a guide even one old soldier who participated in the great battle; and more than that, I soon learned that the reason of it all was that the people who visit the field have no use for one, but prefer to be guided and instructed by some pink-and-white kid. It was certainly amusing, and just a little disgusting withal, to an old soldier who fought in the battle to watch the fine and pompous airs assumed by these young sprouts as they insisted on explaining to him the intricacies of some military position or maneuver.

After my first ride over the field, which cost me a dollar, I went afoot and alone, paying no man or boy to stuff me with yarns, and there was no spot of place in connection with the battle that I neglected to visit.

The field is three miles wide by five miles long, and contains about 15 square miles of territory. The various avenues, together with Reynolds's Grove, Culp's Hill, Spangler's Spring, Cemetery Hill, the umbrella-shaped copse, the Devil's Den, Death Valley and the Round Tops are owned by the United States, and constitute one of the grandest national parks in America.

There are five steel towers of observation, ranging from 65 to 75 feet high, erected on the five most prominent points of elevation overlooking the battlefields. These towers were erected by the government at a cost of $50,000, and the grand and far-reaching views to be obtained from their summits should not be missed by any sightseer who has the good fortune to visit Gettysburg.

Standing upon the tower at the point where the Mummasburg Road crosses the Seminary Ridge, I looked southward far down Reynolds Avenue to its point of termination on the Hagerstown Road, and westward over Buford Avenue and Reynolds Grove to Willoughby run and beyond. Eastward, Howard Avenue crosses the valley from the Mummasburg Road to Rock Creek, and southeastward lies Gettysburg in beauty and in peace.

The lines held by the First Corps on July 1, 1863, and especially where I fought with my brigade from Willoughby Run through Reynolds Grove back to Seminary Ridge, where we repulsed Heth's last charge, 37 years before, were full of glorious though sad recollections of the olden time. Along those grand ridges, within that shady grove, beside those sparkling waters and on those grassy slopes, thousands of my comrades endured wounds and suffered death that other summer day which almost seems but yesterday.

Standing upon the tower on Confederate Avenue, down near the Emmitsburg Road, I look westward and behold the wooded slopes of the ridge and the rocky valley below; while to the eastward the wide, diversified landscape stretches away to the foot of the Round Tops, heavy with the verdure of spring and sweet with the odor of flowers. There battle raged in sublime fury, the old Wheatfield—reaped with the harvest of death on the 2d of July, 1863—waves with a growth renewed that shall not be trodden under the feet of men; nor shall the fruit of the young Peach Orchard, standing where the old one stood 37 years before in Sickles's Salient—a huge bouquet of loveliness now—be gathered in blood.

Standing upon the tower on the crest of Culp's Hill I see the fair city under my feet, as it were, to the northwest. Northward are woodland, field, orchard, garden and meadow; eastward is the broken gorge and the wild valley of Rock Creek; southward are innumerable picturesque hills, glens, rivulets and glades. To the west we look down upon Cemetery Hill, with its imposing statues and towering monuments, and the starry flag of freedom waving above them. Grand and inspiring is the scene, for only the memories of war remain.

Standing upon the tower on South Cemetery Hill, the center of the Union line of battle on July 3, 1863, northward is the cemetery and the city; eastward stands Culp's Hill, in all his rugged glory; southward stretches Hancock Avenue, far past the Bloody Angle and the umbrella copse, away to the rock-faced key of the left and its towering mate in the distance; southwestward the Emmitsburg Road and Sickles Avenue, with the Salient, Peach Orchard and the Wheatfield, with their many monuments, spreads out before me like a huge map unrolled. Due west is Seminary Ridge. From that point across those flowery fields came Pickett and his 6,000 braves, enveloped in the clouds of war and buffeted by the cyclones of death. But the storm has passed forever.

Standing upon the tower on the apex of the king of the rock-ribbed hills of Gettysburg, I am lifted up as on a pinnacle of heavenly light and gladness, from which I look down upon everything that is earthly. What a glory is Round Top! The pines and the rock oaks clothe him in garments of green from his base to his summit, and the pilgrim above on his tower looks down o'er the sides of a mountain of feathery branches. Northward are the old battlefields and the hills and the city; southward the groves and the orchards and meadows, but with them and among them of war no memory lingers. Here all is beauty and peace. The old soldier forgets the past, with its strife and turmoil; forgets the present, with its cares and its burdens, while within this holy temple in air he communes in spirit with the Great Master. Who shall describe Round Top, or paint the scene from his tower?

About 350 yards south of the steel tower on South Cemetery Hill stands the little umbrella-shaped grove that guided Pickett in his mad charge on Hancock's lines. The grove stands on the west side of Hancock Avenue, and consists of 40 trees—30 rock-oaks, nine red-oaks and one hickory. They stand on a rocky knoll in a thick cluster, which causes their branches to spread out in all directions like an umbrella. The clump is inclosed by an iron picket fence in a circle 60 yards in circumference.

Seven hundred and fifty yards south of this grove, on Hancock Avenue, stands the monument of the 1st Minn. Of all the regiments that participated in the battle of Gettysburg on either side this regiment deserves especial honor. Not on the field of war since the world began was ever performed a more daring and heroic deed than by the 1st Minn. in front of this point on the afternoon of July 2, 1863. At a critical moment, when Sickles's line had given way and the Confederates were advancing in strong force, in order to gain the necessary time to get an opposing line intact, Gen. Hancock ordered the 1st Minn. to charge the advancing Confederates. The regiment charged with 262 men in line, meeting a whole brigade and losing within 10 minutes 215 killed and wounded, or 83 percent of their whole number; but they checked the advance and held their ground against them until Hancock was enabled to reinforce them. This was a display of heroism that threw Pickett's charge of the following day in the shade. The charge of the 6,000 at Gettysburg July 3, 1863, and the charge of the 600 at Balaklava Oct. 25, 1854, were both outdone by the charge of the 200 on the 2d day of July, 1863; for there the brave Minnesotans accomplished what they undertook.

John L. Burns has been called "The Hero of Gettysburg," but a "hero," as well as a "prophet," is not without honor save in his own town, of which fact I was impressed when I visited Gettysburg in 1900. There I was told by men who claimed to know, that as a hero Burns was a myth and a fraud. That the true version of the matter is that Burns was something of a squirrel hunter, was out that morning hunting up his cow and gathering a few squirrels for dinner; was accidentally wounded or shot himself through fright, and ran home and hid under his bed. Then I learned another phase of the story, for the Burns story is not without two phases in Gettysburg, where everybody's father or uncle knew Burns better than he knew himself; and this is it: That Burns was wounded in battle and returned to his home in the evening; that the next day, when the Confederates seemed in a fair way of having things about as they pleased, with the city in their possession, some of the copperhead element put the Confederate authorities after Burns, so he told the other phase of the story to fool the Confederates, which proves Burns not only to have been a hero, but a diplomat as well. I feel sure the last version is the correct one, for John Burns joined the 7th Wis. early in the day in Reynolds Grove, and fought with them until wounded and was advised to retreat, which he did. I never saw John, but have seen many of the 7th boys who did, and had the story of the old man's heroism from their lips, and have every reason to believe their report true. It is 50 years too early to make a poltroon of John L. Burns of Gettysburg.

The old people who lived at Gettysburg after the battle tell some horrible stories of the sights they witnessed, which will not bear repeating here; but they tell one story upon which they all seem to agree, and as it relates to birdkind rather than to mankind we may assume that it is true, notwithstanding the fact that it places the character of the buzzard in a new light to me, and possibly to people generally. I was told that after the battle the birds of all kinds left the country round about Gettysburg, and did not return again until the next year, some species not returning until the second or third year, and that even the vultures or buzzards, which before the battle, as they are now, were quite numerous in that vicinity, and which are accredited with a great fondness for human flesh, also deserted the country, and not one darkened the sky again until the next summer. If this is a yarn, it cost me nothing. When I visited Gettysburg in 1900, buzzards and all kinds of small birds were very numerous there, and I saw with my own eyes a verification of the poet's lines:

"Beside our fierce black eagle the Dove of Peace shall rest,
And in the mouths of cannon the wild bird build her nest."

More than once I was startled by the whizzing of a bird past my ears from the mouth of a cannon where the birds were nesting.

The story is told at Gettysburg for truth that a young man by the name of Wentz, who once lived with his father near the Peach Orchard, but having gone south, when the war broke out had donned the gray, and being assigned to Lee's army, was with him at Gettysburg and stood, with his battery, in his father's yard during the battle of July 2.

Also, that a young man by the name of Culp, and a nephew of the owner of Culp's Hill, who went south before the war, joined the Confederate army, came north with Lee's invasion, and fell on Culp's Hill, near the house where he was born.

Then, too, I met at Gettysburg a native of North Carolina, who joined the Confederate army when the war began and served with it until after the battle at Gettysburg, wherein he was, and from which point he deserted after the battle was over and had lived there ever since. He told me this story himself, and I learned that he was well and favorably known by many people there. He said he "had all the war he wanted, and thought that a good place to quit."

At the time of the battle the National Cemetery was a rough and rocky hillside between the Baltimore pike and the Taneytown Road, and north of the city cemetery. The Gettysburg Cemetery Company was organized and incorporated by the state of Pennsylvania shortly after the battle, for the purpose of establishing here a soldiers' cemetery. These grounds were dedicated for that purpose Nov. 19, 1863. In 1872 they assigned it to the government of the United States. The soldiers who died at Gettysburg in defense of the flag and the Union are buried here in sections, in a large semicircular plat, each of the 18 states represented in the battle occupying a section. The states represented and the number of their soldiers are as follows:

Maine	104
New Hampshire	49
Vermont	61
Massachusetts	159
Rhode Island	12
Connecticut	22
New York	861

New Jersey	78
Delaware	15
Maryland	22
West Virginia	11
Ohio	131
Indiana	80
Illinois	6
Michigan	171
Wisconsin	73
Minnesota	52
Pennsylvania	534
U.S. Regulars	133
Unknown	979
Total	3,553

Among those here buried I found the names of Geo. H. Stevens, lieutenant colonel of the 2d Wis., and also the names of three of my company—Lieut. Wm. S. Winegar, Privates Henry R. McCollum and Edward H. Heath, also the name of Serg't Walter S. Ronse, of Co. E, all of whom were killed on July 1 between Seminary Ridge and Willoughby Run. McCollum was my tentmate, and stood beside me as we went into battle, and the others I well knew.

At the converging of this semicircular plat stands the Soldiers' National Monument. It is 60 feet high and 25 feet square at its base, crowned with a statue representing the genius of liberty. Projecting from the four corners are allegorical statues representing war, history, peace and plenty. These figures were made in Italy by Randolph Rogers. This monument was dedicated on July 1, 1869, on which occasion Gen. Meade made an address, Gov. Morton, of Indiana, delivered the oration, and Bayard Taylor contributed an ode.

It is said by the old residents who were there that this monument stands on the spot where stood Abraham Lincoln when he made this immortal address on Nov. 19, 1863:

Four score and seven years ago our fathers brought forth on this continent a new nation, conceived in liberty and dedicated to the proposition that all men are created equal. Now, we are engaged in a great Civil War, testing whether that nation, or any nation, so conceived and so dedicated, can long endure. We are met on a great battlefield of that war. We have come to dedicate a portion of that field as a final resting place for those who here gave up their lives that the nation might live. It is altogether fitting and proper that we should do this. But, in a larger sense we cannot dedicate— we cannot consecrate—we cannot hallow this ground. The brave men, living and dead, who struggled here, have consecrated it far above our power to add or detract. The world will little note or long remember what we say here, but it never can forget what they did here. It is for us, the living, rather to be dedicated here to the unfinished work which they who fought here have thus far so nobly carried on. It is rather for us to be dedicated to the great task remaining before us, that from these honored dead we take increased devotion to that cause for which they gave the last full measure of devotion; that we here highly resolve that these dead shall not have died in vain; that this nation, under God, shall have a new birth of freedom, and the government of the people, by the people, and for the people, shall not perish from the earth.

Sanitary Commission.

United States Hospital Division No 2
Ward 5
Annapolis Maryland
August 5th/63.

Dear Sister;

I arrived at this place — Annapolis — on the 3d. I was then pretty well and had no expectation of going to a hospital, but in the afternoon I was taken with severe pains and sickness to my stomach and was sent to this hospital.

I am feeling pretty comfortable now. I am able to sit up in bed and write and move about some tho' I am pretty weak.

I shall get along well

Beecham wrote to his sister soon after being released from a prisoner-of-war camp by the Confederates in August 1863.

SEVEN

"The scenes I witnessed there"

Life in a Southern Prison Camp
July–August 1863

In the month of July, 1863, I visited Richmond, Va., the capital at that time of the so-called "Confederate States of America." I did not make this visit from choice; I would have preferred visiting the capital of the United States of America, or the capital of any one of the United States north of Mason and Dixon's line, where the stars and stripes were respected and honored; but there were two circumstances that conspired about that time to make this visit to the Confederate capital a necessity.

In the spring of 1863, near the middle of the month of May, or about a week after the Chancellorsville campaign, the following orders were published in every regiment of the Army of the Potomac, viz.:

War Department, Adjutant General's Office,
Washington, Feb. 28, 1863.

General Orders No. 49.

I. The following rules in regard to paroles, established by the common law and usages of war, are published for the information of all concerned:

1. Paroling must always take place by the exchange of signed duplicates of a written document, in which the name and rank of the parties paroled are correctly stated. Any one who intentionally

misstates his rank forfeits the benefit of his parole and is liable to punishment.

2. None but commissioned officers can give the parole for themselves or their commands, and no inferior officer can give a parole without the authority of his superior, if within reach.

3. No paroling on the battlefield; no paroling of entire bodies of troops after a battle; and no dismissal of large numbers of prisoners with a general declaration that they are paroled, is permitted, or of any value.

4. An officer who gives a parole for himself or his command on the battlefield is deemed a deserter and will be punished accordingly.

5. For the officer, the pledging of his parole is an individual act, and no wholesale paroling by an officer, for a number of inferiors in rank, is permitted or valid.

6. No noncommissioned officer or private can give his parole, except through an officer. Individual paroles not given through an officer are not only void, but subject the individuals giving them to the punishment of death as deserters. The only admissible exception is where individuals, properly separated from their commands, have suffered long confinement without the possibility of being paroled through an officer.

7. No prisoner of war can be forced by the hostile government to pledge his parole, and any threat or ill treatment to force the giving of the parole is contrary to the law of war.

8. No prisoner of war can enter into engagements inconsistent with his character and duties as a citizen and a subject of his state. He can only bind himself not to bear arms against his captor for a limited period, or until he is exchanged, and this only with the stipulated or implied consent of his own government. If the engagement which he makes is not approved by his government, he is bound to return and surrender himself as a prisoner of war. His own government cannot at the same time disown his engagement and refuse his return as a prisoner.

9. No one can pledge his parole that he will never bear arms against the government of his captors, nor that he will not bear arms against any other enemy of his government, not at the time

the ally of his captors. Such agreements have reference only to the existing enemy and his existing allies, and to the existing war, and not to future belligerents.

10. While the pledging of the military parole is a voluntary act of the individual, the capturing power is not obliged to grant it, nor is the government of the individual paroled bound to approve or ratify it.

11. Paroles not authorized by the common law of war are not valid till approved by the government of the individual so pledging his parole.

12. The pledging of any unauthorized military parole is a military offense, punishable under the common law of war.

II. This order will be published at the head of every regiment in the service of the United States, and will be officially communicated by every general commanding an army in the field to the commanding general of the opposing forces, and will be hereafter strictly observed and enforced in the armies of the United States.

By order of Maj.-Gen. H. W. Halleck.
L. THOMAS, Adjutant General.

At the date of this order and long after, H. W. Halleck was general-in-chief of the armies of the United States, with headquarters in Washington. This Order No. 49 is an exact copy of the order as I received it from the war department in 1884. It can be found of record there, but probably is not mentioned in any American history. This order bears date Feb. 28, 1863, but was not published in the Army of the Potomac until nearly three months later. If the publication had been delayed another three months, or until after the battle of Gettysburg, it would have been a most fortunate delay for thousands of brave and patriotic men.

This Order No. 49 was one of the circumstances that conspired to make my visit to Richmond a necessity; the other being the fact that I was cornered in Gettysburg while retreating through said city on the evening of July 1, 1863, and, strange though it may seem, this Order No. 49 was the cause of the death of in the neighborhood of 2,000 Union soldiers, as brave and heroic as any who during the world's existence upheld the cause of their country through the perils of war.

Our entire loss of prisoners at Gettysburg is officially reported as 5,535 men. Fully one-half of this loss, or 2,767, was sustained during the first day of the battle, and these only were sent to Richmond.

About 9 o'clock a.m. of July 2 a Confederate colonel called upon the prisoners captured the previous day, with authority to parole us then and there, and it was right there and then that Gen. Halleck's Order No. 49 got in its deadly work. I call the reader's especial attention to paragraphs 2, 4 and 6 of said order.

Every soldier was familiar with these requirements of Order No. 49, and we therefore requested the colonel to allow us to communicate with our officers, who were under a separate guard, in relation to this question; which was granted; but our officers refused to take the responsibility of the parole, and united with us in a message to Gen. Meade, asking his consent and approval. The colonel readily agreed to carry our message, and in the afternoon reported that through Gen. Lee he had communicated with Gen. Meade, and that Gen. Meade had refused to give his consent, but, added the colonel, "I have the authority from Gen. Lee to parole you, and will parole you just the same without the consent of Gen. Meade. It's for you to decide: Take the parole or take a trip to Richmond."

Again we consulted among ourselves, and having learned the first duty of a soldier all too well, and believing that Gen. Meade must have a good and sufficient reason to warrant such refusal, we foolishly decided to obey Halleck's Order No. 49, which decision sealed the death warrants of 90 percent of us. We foolishly decided to obey orders. That may seem like stating it too strong, but the fate of these men, who, in opposition to their better judgment, obeyed that order, is a justification of that statement; for, while these soldiers, after exhausting every honorable means to escape the dire consequences of imprisonment, loyally, heroically obeyed the order they did not approve, and marched to Richmond as prisoners of war and most of them to their death; the other prisoners, captured on the 2d and 3d of July, ignoring Gen. Halleck's order, without deigning to ask the advice or consent of Gen. Meade, wisely disobeyed Order No. 49, by taking the parole when the opportunity was offered, thereby escaping the untold horrors of imprisonment, and, in the way of punishment, did not receive even a reprimand.

Of the utter lack of wisdom on the part of Gen. Halleck in issuing his terrible Order No. 49, it is unnecessary to speak. Gen. McClellan exhausted the subject of Halleck's competency to fill the position he occupied when he characterized Halleck as "a general without a single correct military idea."

General Order No. 49 was only a blunder made by a general in a high position who possessed a remarkable genius for blundering; but Halleck's incompetency furnished Gen. Meade with no reasonable excuse for the part he played in the matter. Gen. Meade had the authority to set aside Halleck's order in this case, but instead of doing so he played the part of a petty tyrant and thus made Order No. 49 with all its attendant consequences his own, and in this instance, as in 99 percent of military blunders, the awful consequences fell not upon the unreasonable general who made the blunder, but on the devoted heads of the rank and file—on the common soldier, who bore the burdens without receiving the honors of war.

Tennyson's lines express the whole subject in a nutshell. No other stanza in concise English verse contains a truism more frequently and terribly demonstrated in every stage of the world's history. How completely, with only a slight modification, it tells the story of the 2,000 victims of Halleck's order and Meade's inhumanity:

> Into the valley of death
> Marched the two thousand!
> Though the soldiers well knew
> That some one had blundered;
> Theirs not to make reply,
> Theirs not to reason why,
> Theirs but to do and die;
> Into the valley of death
> Marched the two thousand.

The few changes made from the original mars the rhyme slightly, but it tells the whole sad story.

As to the part taken by Gen. Meade in refusing to consent to the parole, I had the Confederate colonel's word that he so refused, and have every reason to believe the colonel acted in good faith with us, for after returning from Richmond I read these facts published in Washington and New York papers, substantially as here related, and in justification of Gen. Meade's action it was further stated that he believed Gen. Lee would be greatly hampered by having such a body of prisoners on his hands, and that he (Meade) intended to recapture them before Lee could succeed in getting them across the Potomac.

Whatever Gen. Meade's intentions were his action was not only a terrible mistake, but a piece of gross injustice and inhumanity, lacking in that generous sympathy for the men of his command that should always characterize a commanding general, and also lacking in the prompt acknowledgment of the gallant services these soldiers had just rendered their country and their general in the first great battle wherein Gen. Meade was the commanding general of the army.

These soldiers had fought as heroically as men ever fought on American soil. History fails to point out the field where any army or part of an army, ancient or modern, displayed a greater degree of devotion and soldierly endurance than was displayed by the troops that contested the field with Lee's army on July 1 at Gettysburg. By unflinching valor they held in check the bulk of Lee's army for long and weary hours, thus giving Meade a chance to secure and concentrate his army in a strong and advantageous position, and retreated only when further resistance was hopeless. These prisoners were among the last to quit the field northwest of Gettysburg, and surrendered when every avenue of escape was cut off, and when further fighting on their part would have been madness.

Did they not merit some consideration by the general commanding? One word from Gen. Meade would have given them their liberty, but that one word Gen. Meade refused to speak in their favor.

Would you know how these soldiers, or a great majority of them, were rewarded for their gallantry and obedience? Go where the zephyrs of the southland chant their sad requiems through her weird and desolate charnel fields that keep in everlasting remembrance and in eternal infamy the blackest pages of Southern history, written in horror and in blood at Belle Isle, in Libby, in Salisbury and in Andersonville, and count there the slabs that mark the lowly mounds where they lie buried!

Lee commenced the removal of his wounded from Gettysburg on the night of July 3, and on the morning of July 4 we prisoners of war were hustled off in a southwesterly direction via the Hagerstown Road toward the Potomac. It began raining the night of the 3d and continued to rain nearly all the time during the 4th. I have celebrated our great national holiday in various places, and sometimes under peculiar and discouraging surroundings, during the past 60 years, but can truly say that of all the glorious Fourths I ever enjoyed this was the most inglorious and unenjoyable.

Think of honoring the greatest day in American history by plodding along a muddy and rocky mountain roads, from early dawn to dewy eve, drenched and bedrabbled, weary and hungry, footsore and heartsore, with an armed guard surrounding you, and not a single American flag in sight. If any of my readers think they would like thus to celebrate the 4th of July just once, for the novelty of it, I hereby tender this free advice, by one who knows whereof he affirms: Don't, unless you have to, for there is not the enjoyment in it that one might suppose.

But there was one grain of comfort—one fact that we did enjoy, and that was, that Lee's army was beaten and making tracks for the Potomac. Of course, we had no absolute assurance of this, as up to this time we had seen no portion of Lee's army, except our guards, from whom we gathered various pointers indicating that fact. They would not at first admit defeat, but from time to time dropped remarks which plainly showed that they appreciated the situation; such as: "This is going a mighty long way from home to celebrate the fo'th;" and, "I wonder if old Bob Lee enjoys this fo'th of July as well as we-uns?"

In the dusk of evening we halted on or near the summit of South Mountain. The night set in dark, wet and dreary; we were in a wild and rough locality; the guards were weary with their day's march, and not overvigilant; the time, the place, the condition of the weather, the weariness of the guards united in making this a favorable opportunity to escape, and some of the prisoners improved it, but the majority were too much worn out to make the attempt. I had strength left for the effort, but among the prisoners there was one I could not leave; he was a tentmate, straight-haired and true, and the only other member of my company captured, except our captain, who was not with our crowd. This comrade had been afflicted for six months with that scourge of the camp which clings like grim death, and when we left Fredericksburg in June on the Gettysburg campaign he should have been sent to the hospital, but instead he made the march with us, was wounded in the battle, and if I deserted him then, death was surely his doom. During the day's march we had become separated, and though I searched through the crowd that night in the darkness and mud till I was ready to drop off my feet, I was unable to find him, and our only opportunity of escape passed.

On the 5th we continued our tramp, hardly halting a moment during the whole day except once, when Lee's retreating army needed the road. That was about midafternoon, and we rested, probably two hours, while a part of his army and Lee himself passed us. Then we knew for certain that Lee was defeated, and that the greatest army of the rebellion had received a blow from which it was not likely to recover, and in contemplation of that fact we almost forgot that we were prisoners of war. Standing or sitting by the wayside, we had a splendid opportunity to see a badly beaten army making a hasty but well-ordered retreat. As regiment after regiment with depleted ranks filed past; as battery after battery, each showing the marks of the terrible conflict through which it had passed, hurried by, it became evident to us, who had every chance to see and study their condition, that the Army of Northern Virginia had lost more than a battle,—it had lost that overweening confidence in its prowess and in its leader, which was a twofold defeat. I had been talking with an officer of our guard—a Virginia captain—and feeling a little jubilant, of course, while reading the book that was open before us, I said: "Captain, judging from the condition of these passing troops, it is not likely that Lee will undertake another invasion of the North this year." He replied: "I reckon you're right," and a moment after added: "I wish your government would put a million men in the field and whip us at once; for there is no question now as to the final result of the war." That was surely a great admission for a captain to make to a prisoner of war. But when Lee rode past, shortly after, this officer pointed him out and said in a tone that expressed unbounded pride in his general: "There goes the great Confederate leader."

Then the superb Confederate chieftain rode by within a few yards of me. His long, grizzled beard was neatly arranged; his clothing was clean and faultless; his horse had been groomed and saddled with care; there was nothing about his personal appearance to indicate haste, uneasiness or even weariness; he bestrode his steed apparently cool and confident, not as one who had suffered defeat, but rather as a conqueror. Then I looked from him to his shattered battalions, and read the evidence of his terrible conflict and humiliating defeat, and it was plain to see that Lee himself must have fully recognized the fact that the glorious dream of his ambition could never be realized. Nevertheless, his bearing in defeat was heroic and inspiring; had he been successful in every undertaking; had he conquered the world and was returning with his victorious army to receive a triumph at the hands of his worshipers, instead of fleeing in haste to the shelter of his friendly hills beyond the river to save the remnants of a defeated army from annihilation, his bearing could not have been more dignified and imposing. Lee was the only man of that defeated army, so far as I saw it on the retreat from Gettysburg, who did not reveal the marks of defeat; but it is fair to presume that beneath this outward show of pride and unyielding courage there was an ambitious heart that was very sore.

We reached the Potomac near Williamsport. The river was booming high, and for lack of pontoon facilities Lee was unable to cross over for several days. If Gen. Meade really intended to recapture the prisoners, here was a God-given opportunity; but, alas! it was not improved. If a single gun was fired by Meade's army it was not within my hearing. The prisoners were ferried across the river in pontoon boats during the forenoon of July 10, and as soon as we were all on the Virginia side we were pushed forward toward our destination. We reached Martinsburg before sunset, where an agreeable surprise awaited us. We did not expect to meet a loyal man or woman south of the Potomac; but as we entered Martinsburg, weary and famished, out came the people with food and water for our relief. Our guards objected, however, and seemed determined that this demonstration of loyalty and humanity should not accrue to our advantage, and instructions were given to allow nothing to be passed to the prisoners, which order was enforced so far as it could be without resorting to actual violence, and threats and bluster did not always avail. The ladies especially were persistent, as women sometimes are, and in utter disregard of orders and threats improved every opportunity to carry out their part of the program. I noticed a group of three or four who had chosen a favorable position, from which they refused to be driven, and were passing supplies to all who came within reach. Exasperated by their cool indifference, an officer of the guard whipped out his sword and, flashing it in their faces, ordered them back with an oath, but they stood their ground, like brave women true and tried, and one of them, in contempt of his authority, coming nearer, instead of retreating her cheeks glowing with the fire of indignation and her eyes flashing defiance, in clear and ringing tones replied: "Oh, you needn't think you can scare us. We are used to this, sir; we have seen rebels in Martinsburg before today." When I passed out of sight the ladies were still holding the fort, all honor to them. Our guards hurried us through the town and far beyond ere we camped for the night.

In the vicinity of Winchester we met a kind of relief corps, en route from Richmond to Lee's army. There were 30 or 40 vehicles of various kinds, each drawn by from two to four horses or mules, and carrying from four to eight men. They seemed mostly rather old men, many of them quite portly, all of them well dressed, and were probably the wealthy class of Richmond, who were too fat as well as too old to go to the war. They all wore badges on their hat crowns containing the inscription: "To care for our wounded." Many, in fact, most of them, wore high-crowned silk hats, called "plugs" for short, and they presented a comical appearance, though their mission was very praiseworthy.

This paper could hardly be complete without including one incident that illustrates in clear and vivid lines the lofty character, the high mightiness of the proud and haughty Southerner of those days, educated, as he was, in the brutalizing school of slavery, where humanity had no teacher. During Lee's Pennsylvania campaign he captured from 40 to 50 Negroes. I do not know where or in what capacity they served in the army, for at that time we had no regularly enlisted black soldiers, though we afterward had. These Negroes may not have been in our army at all. I only know that they were Lee's prisoners, and that what I am about to relate is true, although it was so utterly devoid of humanity and so unnecessary and uncalled for that its truth may be doubted. For several days these black men were kept close to us, under a separate guard, and two or three times beeves were killed by the guards, of which we received a portion of the meat, but to these black men they gave only the offal, and on such dainties rare they were obliged to subsist or starve. Was there any excuse for this? Oh, yes; the same excuse that in the "befo' the wah" days was an excuse for every act of inhumanity; a justification for every crime in the category against the black race—they were only "niggahs."

What a glorious advance in the civilization of the 19th century, if, in the name of liberty, the cause for which Davis planned, Lee fought and Jackson prayed, had succeeded, and a government had been established where justice and equity could be meted out after that manner, to the degraded sons and daughters of our late Uncle Ham, down through the countless ages.

Up to the time of our arrival at Staunton, which was about the middle of July, we had received no ill treatment from our captors. We had been allowed to retain our own property, such as tents, blankets, ponchos, haversacks and canteens, and with them to make ourselves as comfortable as possible; but at Staunton there was a change.

A field adjoining the railroad was selected, a strong guard posted around it, and as we passed between two sentinels, in the presence of an officer, and by his orders, we were robbed of every tent, blanket, poncho, knapsack, haversack and canteen in our possession, and as so many cattle were turned into pasture in the beautiful valley of the Potomac.

Even our pocketknives and everything useful or ornamental to be found about us were taken from us, and not one of these things was ever again returned, nor anything to supply their places, and while we remained in this pasture, our only shelter was such as we were able to construct out of boughs and grass that we gathered by hand, with a very limited supply in store to draw from.

On or about July 20, a train of nice freight cars was backed up beside our pasture for the purpose of conveying a portion of us to Richmond. We could see at a glance that the train would not carry more than half of us. Of our little squad of 2d Wis. men, some were in favor of remaining in pasture there, thinking we would receive worse treatment in Richmond. I said: "If we expect to serve out our terms of enlistment in prison pens and pastures, that is the correct theory; but the first to reach Richmond will be the first exchanged, and I'm on the first train." So we divided; about half of us going. I took my tentmate, Frank Wilkins, and with the others who were in favor of taking the first train we moved at once upon the railroad, where in a short time, we secured free tickets and free checks for our baggage, and the same day we rode in grand style from our clover pasture in the picturesque hill country to the great city, the capital of the Confederacy.

It was after dark when we arrived in Richmond. We were invited by those high in authority to walk up to the Hotel de Libby, and we walked.

The landlord, seemingly, was not expecting us, and had made no preparation for our reception. It was wartime, the price of provisions in the capital was high, while the provisions in our hotel larder were low; besides, the cooks had retired for the night, and the dining room girls were attending a presidential levee, for we were in the city where Jefferson Davis held his august court; it was, therefore, not convenient to furnish supper for so many guests, or, possibly, the landlord supposed we had taken supper in the dining car. Still, we were not entirely neglected; the landlord seemed aware that we had traveled far, and instructed the head clerk to show us up to our rooms. The hotel accommodations, for so large a city, were not ample. There was a lack of conveniences that hotels in smaller cities of the North afforded. Many were obliged to occupy the same room; the ventilation was imperfect, the beds needed rebedding, and above all the odor of tobacco was triumphant. We were not inclined to find fault with our accommodations, as some traveling men are, so we retired for the night, and were soon enjoying the bliss of balmy sleep.

We were not aroused suddenly at 6 o'clock in the morning by the rattle and ring of the gong, calling us to an early breakfast; no, we were allowed to rest in our luxurious couches until 9, when we were quietly aroused and requested to make our toilets, if we desired to be shown about the city. We were just aching to be shown about the city, and fearing to miss so fair an opportunity, we did not even wait for breakfast. We started about 10 o'clock a.m. The sun was shining with intense summer warmth, which was unpleasant, as we were not provided with parasols. Many became faint, and fell down in the streets as we were passing. Our guides were not particular to tell us the names of the avenues through which we passed, nor did they point out with pride the exact spot where stood the aboriginal mansion in which dwelt in peace and security the beautiful and far-famed Pocahontas, with her renowned father, the great Powhatan, between two and three centuries before, when all Virginia was a howling wilderness; neither did they show us the wigwam nor conduct us into the presence of the reigning sachem of their day and generation, Jefferson Davis, the Big Indian of the Confederacy, who had inherited all the vices and none of the virtues of Virginia's ancient ruler, and who, controlled by a spirit of cowardly cruelty and savagery unknown to the aborigines of America, disgraced the throne of Powhatan even as Nero disgraced the throne of the Caesars. In fact, we had no desire to learn more than we already knew of this Babylon of the James, and the great king who ruled over it, for the Southern atmosphere and change of diet seemed to have wrung our souls dry of the poetry of romance.

At last we reached the James River, and were conducted across a bridge to that far-famed pleasure ground of the South, sunny Belle Isle, where, according to Richmond papers, the Yankee prisoners passed their captive days in one continual round of pleasure.

As Belle Isle was our abiding place for some time, and as it soon after became in every sense of the term what it was even then fast becoming, one of the "death traps" for Union prisoners, of which the South developed several, I will endeavor to give a fair idea of how it appeared to us that July day in 1863.

The island seemed well shaded with trees and fair to look upon, but the soil was a bed of sand and the island was low and level. The prison pen was adjacent to the river, and comprised three or four acres of ground surrounded by a wide, deep ditch and an embankment, within which enclosure there was neither tree, nor shrub, nor plant, nor flower, nor blade of grass; nothing but a bed of sand. In or near one corner, where the water came close to the surface, were three of four excavations about six feet deep, with sloping sides. These were our wells of living water, and the green scum that covered the water made them very inviting. There were also a number of old tents, all badly dilapidated, pitched in a promiscuous cluster in the center of the inclosure, occupied by several hundred Union prisoners of war captured in part from Milroy's command at Winchester in June, and others at some earlier date. No extra tents were furnished for the additional prisoners, and we found shelter as best we could or went without. During our whole imprisonment I never once enjoyed the luxury of a change of clothing or the opportunity to wash a garment.

For sporting men our island had one attraction that must not be overlooked; Belle Isle abounded in small game. There was more hunting to be enjoyed to the square inch on that island than anywhere else in the wide world, and the beauty of it was that the hunter could always find his game, and if he refused to hunt the game would soon find him. The little animal was too small to be of any use in the economy of nature in supporting life, but it was a great life destroyer, and would boldly invade our camp in broad day. Very few of us were lovers of the chase, and we did not hunt them in wanton cruelty, but for the same reason that British soldiers hunt tigers in India—to free the land from a bloodthirsty enemy of mankind. These animals would never hesitate for a moment to attack a man, and frequently I have known comrades to be badly bitten by them. In short, they were death's myrmidons, the tigers of Belle Isle, and although these Southern "grabax" were not as powerful, singly and alone, as an Asiatic tiger, they were just as bloodthirsty, and through their combined efforts would kill a man just as surely, if not driven off or destroyed.

Need I say this continual round of pleasure became irksome and monotonous? That we were not content with our delightful sandlots? That the days dragged wearily by? Talk not to me of your long June days in the North—they are as but moments. The longest days ever experienced by man were those prison days of July and August in the sunny Southland, within a stone's throw of the court of Jefferson Davis.

I will not attempt to depict the scenes I witnessed there; I could not if I would; I would not if I could; but death was among us, gathering in his victims from day to day. There was not the semblance of a hospital in connection with the prison, and everything was arranged to invite disease and increase the death rate. Yet we saw only a fraction of the horrors of prison life—or prison death, as it afterward became, when all exchange of prisoners had ceased, and the doors of hope were closed. At that time the oldest prisoner on Belle Isle had not been there to exceed 60 days, for exchanges were being made at irregular intervals. We all expected to be exchanged, and hope is a wonderful invigorator.

The statement has oft been made and published that the clergy, especially the Catholic clergy and Sisters of Charity, were frequent and almost constant visitors of Southern prisons, doing all in their power for the temporal as well as the spiritual welfare of the prisoners, but during my imprisonment neither Catholic nor Protestant clergyman, or Sister of Charity ever darkened the gate. The hearts of the clergymen of the South in those days were too full of treason to leave any room for the gospel of Christ.

The cooking establishment for the prison was situated just outside of the pen, on the bank of the James River, and 20 or 25 rods above it, at the other corner of the pen, and out over the river a few feet, were situated the prison sinks. The water supply for cooking purposes was drawn from the river, and of the relative situation of our kitchen and the sinks I have no further statement to make, except that the statement of their relative positions is true.

The quality of our food was not first-rate, but fair—at least it was our fare. On this question of the fare of prisoners generally in the South, the effort has been made of late years, both in the South and in the North, to show that prisoners were treated as well as it was possible to treat them, and that any starvation of prisoners that may have occurred was unintentional and all owing to the fact that a state of destitution, akin to famine, existed all over the Southern country. Not long since an article headed "Libby Prison" went the rounds of the Northern papers, being first published in the *Cincinnati Enquirer.* I give the article here in full as published:

LIBBY PRISON

Talk with Capt. Jack Warner, Commissary of That Notorious Place. Captain Jackson Warner, quartermaster and commissary of Libby Prison during the war, was in the city during the past week and left for his home in Illinois last night. Capt. Warner is now enfeebled by age. He has nearly reached the 73d milepost, but his mind is as clear and as bright as ever. The old gentleman was a conspicuous figure in Richmond during the most exciting period of the rebellion. It is difficult to engage him in conversation about the prison, but when once started he talks freely and relates many interesting incidents which hundreds of Union prisoners will remember. From letters in his possession it is evident that Capt. Warner was as humane and considerate to unfortunate prisoners as circumstances would permit. He made scores of friends by his kindness, and is in regular correspondence with several army officers who boarded with him during the late unpleasantness. "I was commissary and quartermaster at Libby Prison from 1861 to 1864," he said, when requested to give some of his reminiscences to the Enquirer. "It was not a pleasant duty, but I have the consciousness of feeling that I never treated any man harshly or cruelly. When we had good provisions the prisoners got them.

Sometimes they fared better than the men in the Confederate army.
I have seen Lee's soldiers pick up and eat crusts of bread thrown
out by the prisoners."

That last sentence shows Capt. Jackson Warner to be unworthy of
belief. I did not make the gentleman's acquaintance while in Richmond,
and possibly his heart was full of the milk of human kindness, but when
he deliberately states that he has "seen Lee's soldiers pick up and eat
crusts of bread thrown out by the prisoners," he states what he knows,
and what every prisoner who was ever in a Southern prison knows, to
be false. Never a crust nor a crumb, nor anything that could possibly be
eaten by an Eskimo dog was thrown out by the prisoners. Starving men
do not throw away crusts of bread, and the fact, which is a matter of
history, that out of 94,072 federal prisoners who passed through or into
those horrible slaughter pens, 50,000, or 53 percent of them, died; while
out of 227,580 Confederate prisoners held by the United States during
the same period, only 30,152, or 13 1/3 percent, died, is proof positive
that 37,508 deaths were the direct result of exposure and starvation;
and in the face of such facts to talk of prisoners throwing away crusts of
bread.

The idea that there was a state of famine or anything approaching it
in the South, or that Lee's soldiers were starving, is preposterous. There
were at times, owing to lack of transportation facilities, a scarcity of
provisions in Lee's army, and in every army, for that matter. I have seen
hardtack worth a dollar apiece in greenbacks, and none to be had at that
price, in the Army of the Potomac, where it is generally supposed we
lived on soft bread and butter when we were short of shortcake and
honey; but the fact does not prove a scarcity of provisions in the North.
In the South, provisions of the substantial kind used in an army, such as
they produced in the South—beef, pork, cornmeal, rice, beans and vegetables—were just as abundant. What earthly reason can be given why
such should not have been the case? Did they not have, in the South
4,000,000 slaves, every one of whom—men, women and children—
were compelled to till the ground to produce food for their lords and
masters? While everything sold at fabulous prices in depreciated Confederate rag money, one could buy for 25 cents in silver as much food as
could be bought in the North for the same money, which fact I have seen
demonstrated more than once.

During the last year of the war Sherman marched an army of 60,000 men from Atlanta to Savannah, a distance of 300 miles, in dead of winter, subsisting upon provisions they found in the country, and Sherman's men did not starve, but came through fat, saucy and in splendid fighting condition.

This starvation of prisoners was a savage, inhuman and cowardly policy, inaugurated by a set of men better qualified by nature, and by their education, to become henchmen of the prince of darkness than the rulers of a nation which they sought to establish.

The people of the South, generally, may be exonerated from complicity in this wicked and cowardly policy, but it is useless for them to deny that such a policy existed; that it was planned after cool and deliberate consideration by Jefferson Davis and his cabinet; that it was approved by such men as Lee, Johnston and Jackson, who commanded the Confederate armies in the field; and that it was executed in cold-blooded cruelty by Winder, Ould and their minions.

On or about Aug. 5 an order came to the prison authorities to exchange or parole several hundred prisoners. First, all the sick were selected, without regard to priority, which amounted to about half the quota. Many of the sick were so far gone that they held to life by a thread, and these were the men the Confederates wanted to exchange without fail; but as many well men were trying to play the sick dodge in order to get exchanged among the first, the Confederate official, Dick Turner, I think, then in charge of the prison, took his station in the gate with a long butcher knife in his hand to keep back the surging crowd, and selected the sick from the well as they were exhibited before him.

By this time my tentmate, Frank Wilkins, was barely able to walk. He was, seemingly, nearer to death's door than any man could be and recover, and for several days previously I had expected to find him dead each morning. I was not in very robust health or strength myself, but I could take Frank under my arm and carry him as I would a child, and when I arrived at the gate the butcher-knife official thought he saw a man on whom death had set his seal and he said: "Let that man pass through." The official was mistaken. Frank Wilkins's last day of service for the old flag ended when he tottered through the prison gate, but his heroic heart and vigorous constitution tided him over, and he lived for many years after the war ended. After the sick had been selected the remainder of the quota was filled in the order of priority. The oldest prisoners were called until all were taken, and there remained only the Winchester and Gettysburg prisoners. The quota lacked then 100 or more of being full. The Winchester prisoners were the next in priority, but the rolls had been mislaid, and the rolls of the Gettysburg prisoners were substituted.

This event caused an excitement that is easier imagined than described. It was like a death knell to the hopes of the Winchester men, but it gave a new and unlooked for hope to every man from Gettysburg. After getting my tentmate through the gate I had gone back to my desolate den with no expectation of being exchanged on that day, but the moment I heard the call for the Gettysburg prisoners I joined the excited crowd and watched the result, with my heart beating like a trip hammer. We had been enrolled by regiments, but knew nothing of the priority on the rolls of our organizations. Usually there were only a few in each regiment, and we watched anxiously for the name of the next on the rolls. We held tickets in a great lottery. Our names had been shaken together, so to speak, in the box. Every name drawn out was to receive a prize, and that prize was liberty—life! Who were to be the fortunate ones? What wonder that excitement ran high—that men held their breath in suspense? Rapidly the names are read off by the clerk, to which each fortunate one responds as he runs through the gate. The quota is almost filled; there are only a few more names to be drawn. The 2d Wis. is called. How that name thrills the very marrow in my bones, for my name is among the number on that short list. Then follows a moment of suspense that no living being who has not been placed in a like situation can imagine, a few seconds of time of almost endless duration. My heart stands still in an agony of hope and dread. Will the quota hold out? Will my name ever be reached? Live a thousand years, I cannot experience another such moment. At last the spell is broken, my name is called, then my heart gives a great rebound, and I stepped out from under the "Shadow of Death."

A few more names, not to exceed half a dozen, were called after mine. They followed me through, and the gates were closed. We did not know it then, our comrades left behind did not know that so far as this world is concerned the gates of freedom had closed upon them forever.

This proved to be the last general exchange of prisoners until February, 1865, more than 18 months later. How many of the thousands we left on Belle Isle and at Staunton were alive at the end of a year and a half?

It is estimated that 90 days was the average life of prisoners confined in those places of torment during those appalling months. I was on Belle Isle about 15 days; add to that 75 more, which would have carried us up to the last days of October. No man with less than an iron constitution could have lived through it. But not in October; not until a year from the next February was there another general exchange, at which time these men were all in their graves.

When Gen. Meade refused to allow us to take the parole at Gettysburg, of course, he did not know that all exchange of prisoners was about to cease; if he had known it he would have been the blackest-hearted murderer the world ever produced. But Gen. Meade knew enough of the treatment of prisoners by the Confederate authorities to have touched the chords of sympathy and humanity in his heart, if they were there, and the lives of these men would have been saved.

On leaving Belle Isle we were conducted directly to the depot, where we boarded a train of palace box cars, and an hour later arrived at City Point, where a flag-of-truce boat—if I remember rightly, the New York— was awaiting us.

As the train pulled up to the landing there fell upon our vision a sight that to my dying day I shall never forget. There upon the placid stream lay the good ship that was to bear us away from those inhospitable shores back to "God's country." It is our Saviour, a messenger from the happy land beyond the dark "dead line."

There can be no mistake—there is no uncertainty, for at her masthead, floating grandly in the breeze—

"Now it catches the gleam of the morning's first beam,
In full glory reflected now shines in the stream."

We behold once more, after all these days of weariness, the "Star Spangled Banner" of the republic; the fair emblem of our country, for which of old our brave fathers fought and our heroic mothers suffered and prayed. The flag that we had loved in peace and cherished in war; the flag that we had followed in victory and guarded and defended in defeat; the flag for which our mothers, sisters, wives and daughters gave the crown jewels of their hearts; the flag that, during those four years of devastating war, 2,778,304 men rallied to defend and in defending, 900,000 wounds were received and 364,116 lives were sacrificed. The flag that by a thousand battles on land and sea was borne to final victory; that triumphed at last over the vile emblem of treason, slavery, starvation and death, and now guards and honors the graves of the 50,000 who languished and perished beyond the reach of hope or mercy, where the foul rebel rag held sway, with the graves of their more fortunate comrades who fell beneath the inspiring glory of her starry folds; the flag that today is the proud emblem of 75,000,000 of free and happy people; the one flag of one country extending from the Great Lakes to the Mexican Gulf, and from ocean to ocean, through 24 degrees of latitude, and 57 degrees of longitude, to say nothing of Alaska and the islands far away; which is known in every harbor in the world; is respected on every sea and honored in every land. As the face of a lost loved one seen for all time through the mist of the years of the dead, but never to be forgotten past, so engraved on the retina of the mind's unfading eye, I see as I saw it then while gazing from this last environment of a hateful imprisonment, just over the line, the flag of free America, flooded with the transcendent light of full and perfect freedom; bright, beautiful, resplendent, glorious. How every eye kindles, how every heart thrills. Then follows a cheer, a glad, ringing, wild hurrah, that echoes from over the river and among the hills and glens and re-echoes forever in the recesses of my memory.

Every comrade joins in that cheer; the young, the old, the strong, the weak, the well, the sick, the dying, all unite their voices to swell the grand chorus. But see! They are coming out from the ship with cots and stretchers to carry in the sick, and springing lightly to the ground I made my way along the train through the excited crowd until I found my old tentmate again, whom I assisted past the last gray line that intervened between us and our "angel of mercy," over the gangplank and into the hospital.

The last man was soon on board; then our ship cast off her moorings, steamed down the historic James, past the ruins of the old church where Pocahontas was married in the ancient city of Jamestown, wherein Capt. John Smith planted the first English settlement on American soil in 1607; past old Fort Monroe with its frowning batteries of heavy guns, and rounding the point turns her prow up the bay, speeding away to the northward over the blue waters of the Chesapeake, and holding her course onward until the towers and domes of Annapolis loom up before us, and a little later our good ship rests by the pier in the snug and quiet harbor of "Maryland, My Maryland." Out upon God's land we step, thankful to the giver of all good for a safe return from our visit to Richmond.

Nearly 200,000 African-American men served in the racially segregated Union army during the Civil War. The soldiers shown here are members of the Fourth U.S. Colored Troops.

EIGHT

"My first promotion"

Becoming an Officer with the U.S. Colored Troops
August– December 1863

When I enlisted at Madison, Wis., in May, 1861, as a high private in Co. H, 2d Wis., I was all unaware of the wide and almost impassable gulf that yawns between the enlisted soldier and commissioned officer. My first introduction to real official dignity, or pomposity, as it appears in military life, came a few days later, and before I was mustered into the United States service. Lieut.-Col. Peck was temporarily in command of the regiment, and having business with him, I was admitted into his quarters, where I found him with his hat on his head and his feet perched upon the table (a very dignified position), luxuriating in a fragrant Havana. I was only a country boy of 23 years and imagined that no soldier of the republic was a menial, and that I had no call to uncover while standing in his presence; but the noble colonel, knowing that such unsoldierly conduct, if not at once rebuked and eradicated, would lead to the defeat of our armies in the field and the overthrow of the republic, said to me very firmly, but with a withering sadness in his voice, which lingers in my ears even to this distant day:

"Take off your hat, sir, when you come into the presence of your superiors."

Well, Sumter had been fired upon, and the old flag that waved above the fort riddled and torn, and notwithstanding this, the first command I had ever received from a colonel in uniform was a damper to the patriotism that filled my heart. I had started out to lend a hand in righting that wrong and in avenging that insult to our national honor, and I took off my hat, but right there and then I vowed in my heart, that if I ever succeeded in crossing the gulf, I would stand on the other shore adorned with gilt buttons and shoulder straps, still retaining sufficient manhood and common sense to treat a private soldier as a gentleman and as an American citizen.

Time passed. Promotion from the ranks in the American army is always rapid and certain for all who possess military genius and natural official dignity, and in the month of March, 1863—less than two years from date of enlistment—I rose to the rank of eighth corporal! Just think of that, all ye aspiring young Americans. Think of it, ye ambitious sons of the great republic who long for military honors, and fear not to enter the service of your country as private soldiers. Be not alarmed, if you are worthy soldiers and possess military ability, your country will find you when you are needed. Did not their country "find" Grant, and Sherman, and Sheridan, and Meade, and a host of other heroes as long ago as when they attended the military academy at West Point? During the latter part of the great Civil War their country "found" tens of thousands of men who would have preferred not to have been "found."

If a private soldier can reach the rank of eighth corporal in less than two years of service, he can surely count on becoming a brevet brigadier general before the close of a long war. The first step is always the most difficult, and although a corporal is not a commissioned officer by any means, once a soldier has reached that rank he is in the line of promotion, and on the high road to honor and fame.

About that time, when I first ran up against that line of promotion, the United States conceived the idea of calling upon those people who had lived for many generations practically beneath the stripes, although it was hardly possible for them to have discerned the stars in our glorious flag, to take up arms in defense of national unity. The government needed officers to command these new regiments of black men, and just after the return of the army from the Chancellorsville campaign to our old position north of the Rappahannock, the following appeared in the *Washington Chronicle*:

A board of examination has been established in Washington, D.C., of which Maj.-Gen. Silas Casey is president, for the purpose of examining all applicants for commissions in the U.S. Colored Troops. Soldiers recommended by their company and regimental commandants shall be allowed to come before said board for examination, and any applicant rejected by said board shall not be allowed the privilege of a second examination.

This was really an official order from the war department, signed by the adjutant general of the army, and a splendid opportunity for any ambitious soldier in the line of promotion. I immediately applied to my captain, Nat. Rollins, for such recommendation, which he gave, and Gen. Fairchild, then colonel commanding the 2d Wis., approved the same, which was thereupon dispatched to the war department.

On the morning of June 12, 1863, as the Army of the Potomac was in the act of breaking camp near Fredericksburg, Va., for that long march to the northward which resulted in the battle and victory of Gettysburg, I received by mail from the war department a document of which the following is a copy:

> War Department, Adjutant General's Office,
> Washington, D. C., June 9, 1863.
>
> The following named enlisted man is hereby permitted to appear before the board of examination, of which Maj.-Gen. Silas Casey is president, at Washington, D.C.: Corporal R. K. Beecham, Co. H, 2d Wis. Vols.
>
> By order of the secretary of war.
> [Signed.] E. D. Townsend, A.A.-Gen. Vols.

Truly I was greatly elated over this early and favorable reply to my application, and, very foolishly, supposed that such a permit emanating from the secretary of war and signed personally by the adjutant general of the army, was authority sufficient to visit Washington; but I had much to learn. Red tape, a term used to designate the vexatious routine and delay in business matters as practiced by bombastic military sapheads, could not forbear a hand even in this transaction, so plain and simple to men of ordinary common sense.

I reported to my captain, expecting to take the benefit of my permit without any delay. The captain advised me to report to the colonel. I expressed the opinion that such was unnecessary, as an order from the war department covered the whole situation, and he had but to report me absent by said order; but the captain was fearful that he might overstep the bounds of military subordination, and insisted that I should report to the colonel. As an obedient soldier, I so reported, and, to my utter amazement, was informed "that this permit, from the secretary of war himself, was not sufficient to pass me to Washington, but I must make application to Gen. Reynolds, commanding the First Corps, for a leave of absence to visit Washington, and that I must attach thereto this permit from the war department, to show the corps commander that my application had merit in it, which, being approved by my captain and himself, would be forwarded by him through the regular official channel to corps headquarters for approval, where, without doubt, leave would be granted, and on the return of such leave of absence I could then go to Washington."

I firmly believed and attempted to assert that an order or permit from the war department was sufficient to govern in this case, without any monkeying with the "official channel," or "corps headquarters," but the colonel promptly and decidedly overruled my attempt at argument, saying:

"It would be impossible for you to reach Washington on that permit. You would certainly be arrested as a deserter if you made the attempt."

At first Col. Fairchild had jumped to the conclusion that I must apply for a leave of absence, and had said so. On consideration he knew better, or would have known better had he considered, but it would have lowered his official dignity in his own estimation to have said so. As the colonel would not even hear me, much less consider my opinion, my only course, without creating a rupture, was to apply for a leave of absence, and, believing that such application could pass through the "regular official channel" from regimental to corps headquarters and return in 48 hours at most, and that this unnecessary proceeding would only delay my trip for a few days, I acted on the colonel's orders, and within 10 minutes my application for a leave of absence, together with my permit from the war department, were speeding through the "regular official channel" in the direction of corps headquarters, while I, in heavy marching order, was pursuing my way, as an obedient soldier, along a hot and dusty highway in the direction of Gettysburg.

Time rolled on. So also did the Army of the Potomac. We traveled old, familiar paths, and paths that were not so familiar; we left our battlefields of previous years far in the rear as we pursued our march to the northward, and still my papers from the war department with my application for a leave of absence were pursing that mysterious "official channel." We reached and crossed the Potomac River; we marched o'er the borders of "Maryland, My Maryland;" before our eyes were the mountains, beneath our feet the valleys of the Keystone State; but from the "regular official channel" my papers had not yet returned. The morning of July 1 dawned upon us; over muddy roads, through drizzling rain we marched to the memorable field of Gettysburg, and when the battle was over, as a prisoner of war, I accompanied Lee's defeated army to the shelter of the Virginia hills beyond the Potomac, and later took a weary trip to Richmond. After basking for a season on sunny Belle Isle, I was among the fortunate who were paroled and returned to God's country, arriving in Annapolis some time in the month of August.

Immediately after my return from jail I wrote to my company in the Army of the Potomac, to learn if my papers from the war department, etc., had been as fortunate as myself, and had returned from the "regular official channel," and, lo! with the answer, which came in due season, came also my permit from the war department and a leave of absence to visit Washington, bearing date July 15, 1863, officially approved from corps to regimental headquarters, in compliance with the wishes of the secretary of war. Thus, it will be seen, these documents traveled the "regular official channel" on their upward journey from regimental to corps headquarters, in the short space of 34 days; but how long it took them to accomplish the home run I never learned. At last I held in my possession a leave of absence to visit Washington, which had passed safely through the "regular official channel," and yet it was but so much worthless paper, for I was then far removed from the power and influence of the commander of the First Corps, and if I still desired to visit Washington my only hope lay in this old permit from the war department, which was just as good, but no better, than it was on the 12th of June, the day I first received it. Although by sad experience I had learned that the secretary of war was inferior in rank to the corps commander of the Army of the Potomac, I still retained a lingering hope that he was superior in rank to the commandant of Camp Parole. However, when I presented said permit to the gallant major in command of the barracks where I was quartered, in the city, with the oral statement that I proposed visiting Washington, the major informed me that a permit of that kind from the war department was of no use there, only as a recommendation for a leave of absence, for which, if I desired, I could make application. That he, the major, holding the secretary of war in much esteem, would approve the application and forward the same, together with my paper from the war department, through the "regular official channel" to Col. Root, commandant of Camp Parole, where it would in all probability be approved, and on its return I could visit Washington.

Greatly though I admired the expeditious manner with which documents of this kind traveled the "regular official channel," my late term in jail had added an impatient recklessness to my spirit quite foreign to my naturally long-suffering disposition, and without entering into an argument with the major on the relative powers and authority of Col. Root, commandant of Camp Parole, vs. E. M. Stanton, secretary of war of the United States of America (the major would surely have gotten the best of the argument in such a case), I concluded to play "hookey," and thanking the major for his very kind information, took my departure.

The following morning I purchased a ticket to Washington, and took my seat in the car, when directly I was accosted by an official of the provost department, who asked for my pass. With beating heart but bold front, I presented my worthless permit from the war department, just as if the secretary of war and the adjutant general were persons of authority. The said official examined the document with a critical eye, and remarked with a wise and confident look:

"That won't pass you over this road, sir." I answered: "Surely you are mistaken; a permit from the war department not authority in Annapolis? It is all that is requisite anywhere in the Army of the Potomac." He replied: "The Army of the Potomac cuts no ice in my department. I tell you plainly that that permit, or whatever you call it, is of no use to you here. Why, look at its date, the 9th day of June last; if authority in the Army of the Potomac, why did you not use it while you were there?" I answered: "I had good and sufficient reasons for not using it then, as I have for using it now, all of which I have no call to explain; it is sufficient for you to know that this permit comes from the war department, and is signed by the adjutant general of the army. If it had been previously used it would not now be in my possession uncanceled. As you say, the Army of the Potomac cuts no ice in your department, but allow me to suggest, with all due respect to you and the office you hold, that the war department cuts some ice even in the city of Annapolis, and if you refuse to allow me to pass on this document, I'll try me level best to learn where you get the authority to countermand the order of the secretary of war." This little bluff proved successful, and the official quietly abandoned the field.

Arriving in Washington, I reported to the board of examination, stating the facts in my case, and why I appeared before said board at that time, on a permit issued on the 9th of June. I also exhibited my leave of absence from corps headquarters, of which I was, justly, proud, as it had passed through the "regular official channel," suggesting that the secretary of war would be pleased to learn of the great esteem in which he was held, and the promptness with which his orders were obeyed by the general officers of the First Corps.

Gen. Casey informed me that as I was then a paroled prisoner of war, nothing could be done in the matter of examination and promotion, but after being exchanged and rejoining my company in the Army of the Potomac, I would receive another permit from the war department to visit Washington, and appear before the board of examination. So it began to appear that this line of promotion was a long line, and somewhat tedious to follow; but one of the virtues that a soldier is frequently called upon to exercise is patience.

I went back to Annapolis, and, later, was exchanged and rejoined the army, finding my regiment still in the First Corps, stationed on the north bank of the Rapidan River, as far away from Washington in that direction as it had ever succeeded in getting up to that date, and that very night, about midnight, we abandoned the position, commencing a backward movement which resulted in the liveliest army race on record, between the Army of the Potomac and the Army of Northern Virginia for the heights of Centreville. The roads of old Virginia were in splendid condition; our wagon trains had been previously lightened by issuing six days rations to the soldiers in order that the trains might keep pace with us, and we made the best time ever made over that race course, and probably the best ever made by any army in the world, the Army of Northern Virginia coming in second best and close to our heels. It was a splendid race. We reached the heights of Centreville about 15 minutes before the Army of Northern Virginia would have reached the same position had not Lee discovered that he could not win the race, anyway, and halted his army at Bull Run to "rest under the shade of the trees."

We formed our line of battle along the heights of Centreville, but Lee did not try issue with us, and during the time we held that position, I wrote the war department, explaining the fate of my former permit and the outcome of my subsequent visit to Washington while a paroled prisoner of war; also Gen. Casey's assurance that another permit would be sent me on my return to the army, and that I was there and in readiness to receive the same.

In a short time the Army of the Potomac made a forward movement, rebuilding the railroad as we advanced, which the Army of Northern Virginia had destroyed, seemingly out of sheer spite because we had won the foot race. We slowly retraced the ground we had previously traveled so rapidly, and on Nov. 1, were encamped near Bristoe Station. That evening, hardly five months from date of receipt of my first permit, I received from the war department a second edition of the same article, granting me the same privilege to visit Washington and appear before Gen. Casey's examining board.

Again I reported the fact to Lieut. G. M. Humphrey, commanding my company, and, by him was directed to report to the colonel of the regiment. The following morning I so reported to Col. John Mansfield, who instructed me to make an application for a leave of absence, etc., exactly as Col. Fairchild had directed on the former occasion, and forward the same through the "regular official channel" to corps headquarters.

By this time the "regular official channel" had lost much of its charm. A man does not like to swing from the same "line" forever. Besides, this second permit which was, as printed, an exact copy of the first, had written in red ink across the face thereof in a bold and legible hand these words: "Not through the headquarters of the army." To my humble understanding it appeared evident that the secretary of war was becoming ambitious to be considered superior in rank to any corps general, and in fact to the commanding general of the army, and I called the colonel's attention to the written words, asking if such was not their import; but Col. Mansfield, like his predecessor, was very positive, and replied: "No, sir; there's no other way by which you can leave the army but by a leave of absence from corps headquarters." Well, that settled it, and I made the application, but concluded that I would not part, this time, with my permit from the war department, but go in person with my papers through the "regular official channel."

My application for leave of absence having been approved by my company commandant, I presented it in person to Col. Mansfield for his signature, which he gave, and I passed on through the "regular official channel" to brigade headquarters, where they were approved by Gen. Sol. Meredith. Onward I passed through the "regular official channel" to division headquarters, and there, too, my application was approved by Gen. Lysander Cutler. Still on I passed through the "regular official channel" up to the very tent door of the corps commander, where I was admitted for just a moment not into the presence of Gen. Newton, but into the far more magnificent presence of Capt. C. Kingsbury, Jr., Gen. Newton's adjutant general. I approached him with my hat under my arm, as becomes an obedient soldier of the great republic, when addressing his superior officer, presenting my papers and requesting, in a modest and unassuming manner, that he would procure the necessary approval of the commanding general to my leave of absence. The captain examined the papers with a disdainful touch and a glittering eye. It was plain that his official pomposity was stirred to the very bottom of his august gizzard. Immediately he turned his withering gaze upon me and spoke as becomes an officer holding a high and honorable position:

"This, sir, is not the way to conduct military business. You, a corporal, carrying official papers from one general headquarters to another? I am surprised that any such irregular proceedings should be allowed at division and brigade headquarters. Nothing of this kind will be tolerated here. Go back to your company at once, sir, and forward your application through the 'regular official channel,' and it will receive attention when it reaches these headquarters."

I was nearly paralyzed with fear, and in a voice choked with emotion, stammered, as I took from his puissant hand the papers I so greatly valued:

"I beg your pardon, captain. One of these papers is an order from the war department; for the other I have no use. You seem to understand your business, captain, and very likely the secretary of war understands his." Then I tore the application for leave of absence, in his presence, threw the pieces upon the ground, put my permit carefully in my breast pocket; saluted the captain and a.a.-g. and took my leave.

I did not return to my company, as the captain had ordered, but remembering that I had at Annapolis, Md., bluffed an official of the provost department with so simple a document as an order from the war department, concluded that my only hope of reaching Washington and receiving a commission admitting me into the fraternity of military swell heads lay in accomplishing that same exploit again, I went directly to the office of the provost marshal at the station, no more than 100 yards distant, presented my permit from the war department with the same assurance that I would have presented a leave of absence that had triumphantly passed through the "regular official channel," and asked for transportation to Washington. The provost marshal glanced at the document, and without question wrote the transportation.

Arriving in Washington, I reported promptly to Gen. Casey's board, and within a few days was called before it for examination; which proved to be one of the most interesting and enjoyable events of my whole military service, and amply repaid me for the long and arduous struggle experienced in reaching it through the entangling meshes of red tape.

The Board consisted of Maj.-Gen. Silas Casey, president; assisted by a colonel and two or three officers of minor rank, whose names I did not learn, with a medical department, or examining surgeon with the rank of major.

The colonel, who acted as a mouthpiece for the board, and conducted that part of the examination relative to the examinee's knowledge of military facts and affairs, possessed a magniloquent voice and was perfectly attired in a neatly fitting uniform which fairly blazed with gilt buttons, while gaudy straps sparkling with the silvery plumage of the emblem of his country and rank, adorned his broad shoulders. O, he was a peach of a colonel, the best dressed if not the bravest hero that I ever had the honor of meeting in military uniform.

First he examined me upon the tactics, and as the tactics then in use in the army were compiled by the same Gen. Casey who presided over the board, I was soon aware of the fact that my knowledge of the tactics was satisfactory to the presiding officer. Then the colonel branched out into general military history, but being quite familiar with the campaigns of such noted warriors as Alexander, Caesar, Hannibal, Napoleon, Powhatan, and Red Jacket, I was very much at home therein, and the satisfied expression of the old general's homely face gave assurance that my answers to the colonel's questions were about correct.

At this point our colonel seemed to realize that his bleeding country required of an officer of his magnificent parts a more exalted service than propounding questions that an enlisted man could readily answer, and turning full upon me the awe-inspiring splendor of his majestic countenance, he said: "I am sorry to say, sir, that you present a very unprepossessing personal appearance, to say the least, for a soldier who aspires to fill the dignified position of a commissioned officer in the army; in fact, you scarcely look fit for the position you already hold. Why is it that you do not wear better clothes? Can you give any reasonable excuse for coming before this board without presenting a more respectable appearance?"

People who have, all their lives, been accustomed to meeting gentlemen and receiving courteous treatment under any and all circumstances may imagine, if they can, the feelings of a freeborn American citizen who had grown to manhood in the glorious West, when addressed in such language. That colonel knew that within the five months just passed, I had marched on foot from Fredericksburg, Va., to Gettysburg, Pa., and from thence a goodly portion of the way to Richmond. He knew that, from the beginning of the war, I had been continuously in camp, on the march, in battle, and in prison. He knew that very recently Lee's army had been making it exceedingly interesting for us, having reestablished their lines, which they held for a time, in their old position at Bull Run, and from this active front I had just come, not on a holiday occasion, but as a soldier on duty, and under orders, and yet he had the brutality to taunt me with my "personal appearance." O, Swell head! thou art a dread disease, that quite unmans a man, frequently robbing him of every vestige of common sense and common decency.

Well, having met colonels before, I was not wholly unprepared for this onslaught, and, recovering my breath, answered: "Yes, colonel, I can give good and sufficient reasons, satisfactory to this or any other board. I am not a gentleman of fortune with a bank account to draw from, but a common soldier, dependent upon my salary of 13 (lately increased to 15) greenback dollars a month. As a soldier, I am expected to wear, and do wear, what the government furnishes, and what I draw in excess of the regular clothing allowance I pay for. The quartermaster's department made no arrangements to furnish me a new uniform for this occasion, and it would be unreasonable to require or expect a soldier to put up in this city for a suit of clothes in which to appear before this board. It is true that my uniform has seen hard service, but it is neither ragged nor dirty, and is not service honorable for both the soldier and his uniform? At all events, it is the best I have, and must of necessity serve with me until I receive a commission or until such time as it may become convenient for the government to furnish new uniforms to soldiers in the field. As to its respectability, it compares favorably with the uniforms worn by my comrades in the army when I came from the front the other day, and was considered quite respectable there, and a uniform that is 'respectable' any time and all the time in Gen. Meade's army ought to be 'respectable' for a few days in Washington. Furthermore, I had every reason to believe that this board was established for the purpose of examining soldiers with regard to their knowledge of military matters. It would seem like utter foolishness on the part of the war department to order soldiers from the front to Washington to have their uniforms inspected."

Gen. Casey's eye twinkled, but he said nothing. The colonel's eyes flashed as he snapped: "But a soldier is expected at all times to have some regard for his personal appearance. A collar would add greatly to your looks; now, what excuse have you for not wearing a collar?" Then, quite unexpectedly, Gen. Casey seemed to turn against me, and to champion the colonel's collar theory by remarking: "Yes, that is true; a soldier may be excused from wearing a shirt sometimes, but from appearing publicly without wearing a collar, never."

It would not do to allow the citadel to be captured at this stage of the battle, so I arranged by small force to the best advantage possible on short notice, for a countercharge. Addressing Gen. Casey, himself, I said:

"I beg your pardon, general, but as I take exceptions to the rule as you have stated it, I ask for a full and fair hearing on this question. I have served in the Army of the Potomac from the day of its organization, except when unable for duty or in jail. I have 'appeared publicly' in the presence of Gens. McDowell, McClellan, Pope, Burnside, Hooker and Meade, and on state occasions in the presence of President Lincoln, always wearing an army shirt as furnished by the quartermaster's department, with never an artificial collar attached, and never, until today, have I been reprimanded for unsoldierly appearance. Even in the winter of '61 and '62, when the army, under McClellan, just over there in Virginia, wore out tens of thousands of muskets with sandpaper, and wore white gloves on parade and review, we were not once called upon to wear, and never wore, collars, except those which were a part of the regulation army shirt. During such service I have also appeared 'publicly' several times in the presence of portions of Lee's army, when, shirt or no shirt, cartridges and not collars were the articles in demand. I therefore conclude, general, that there are occasions, and that this is one of them, when a soldier may be excused for appearing publicly without wearing a collar, and for these reasons I came before this board wearing the uniform and underclothing of a private soldier, believing that I owe no apology to any living being for wearing exactly such articles of dress furnished me by the United States of America."

The general looked serious and seemed deeply impressed with the truthfulness of my statement of facts, but the colonel was all the more intent on formulating a question that would upset me, and, quickly, he said: "You certainly might comb your hair occasionally and keep that looking respectable. It looks as if it had not been combed for a week. Is that because the government does not furnish you a comb?"

I answered: "No, sir; I have a comb of my own that I bought and paid for, but I protest against the assumption that I do not comb my hair or that it is not respectable. It is, as you can see, 'trimmed to the short warrior cut,' and I comb it every day. It is a little inclined to independent action, I admit. But if sleek hair were a sure indication of military genius, the government would not be long in finding a commander for the Army of the Potomac who would capture Richmond and end the rebellion. Probably no general in the world ever wore a more genteel head of hair than our General McDowell, but it did not win at Bull Run, as we all know. My hair is certainly not of the McDowell order; I feel encouraged from the fact that it is rather of the Jackson type, although somewhat less radical, and, surely no member of this board will contend that the hero of New Orleans did not possess great military ability, or that he might have added to his personal fame and his country's glory by giving more attention to combing and brushing his hair."

Here the old general leaned far back in his chair; his massive, square jaws parted until his mouth resembled a yawning mountain chasm, and beyond the valley his bald head shone like a smooth boulder, and his smile rippled and rumbled and reverberated through the gorge like the echo of distant artillery. The colonel fixed his mouth for another question, but it did not materialize, for when Gen. Casey ceased to smile, he said: "There, there, colonel, I think that will do. The corporal seems to have the best of it." Then, addressing me, he said: "Take a seat at the desk there, corporal, and state in writing the position that you desire or think yourself qualified to fill and sign your name thereto." I did so, and, later, received what I asked, my dread of the "swell head" preventing me from becoming a colonel.

Nevertheless, I had yet to pass one more test in this trying ordeal, and was forthwith shown into the office and presence of the examining surgeon, where, in order that a soldier who had served two and a half years as an enlisted man should not have the opportunity of defrauding the government by passing himself off as physically competent to perform the duties of a commissioned officer, if not sound of limb, or if suffering from bodily infirmities, I was required to lay aside my habiliments and appear in undress uniform. After the surgeon had examined and tested my physical make-up in any and every way he desired, he frankly informed me that: "Your personal appearance, sir, is very much against you. The worn, soiled, and generally dilapidated condition of your clothing is greatly to your discredit." In the language of Antony "this was the most unkindest cut of all," and quite unexpected, coming from the source it did. If there is anything in the world that will excite a man's heart to wrath it is to have his dearest friends abused in their absence, and I would have enjoyed telling the surgeon, in plain English, just what I thought of him, but, having stood, without flinching, the colonel's cannonading in the presence of the whole board, it would never do to get rattled at a few scattering shots from one lone doctor, and I said: "Yes, major, so the board, or rather the colonel, informed me, and it affords me much satisfaction to learn that you agree with him. I was under the impression, however, that in an examination of this kind, a surgeon's skill was required to fathom the depth of the soldier's infirmities; any old thing can discover the imperfections in his uniform, especially when he comes from the front; but as it seems to be otherwise, will you not kindly, and in my behalf, in making your report, inform the board that my uniform is not a part of my physical being, which fact may have escaped its notice, while you, major, have an ocular demonstration of its truth."

The surgeon replied very curtly: "I probably understand making my report, sir." I said: "Certainly, major, and if you care not to subject this poor old blouse and trousers to any further examination, I will again don the uniform of a private soldier in the American army." After which I was dismissed from the presence of the wise surgeon and the learned military board, and the same day returned to the Army of the Potomac.

The army had advanced in my absence, and I found my regiment south of the Rappahannock not far from the station of that name. There was much activity in the army. The weather continued fine, and in the latter part of November a general advance was made. Although Gen. Meade refused to give battle to Lee in October, north of the Rapidan and the Rappahannock, late in November he crossed to the south of the Rapidan with his whole army and went a-gunning for Lee in the vicinity of Mine Run; but the weather turned cold, and although we had some lively skirmishing, we returned to the north side of the Rapidan early in December without fighting a general battle, which retreat was, without doubt, the wisest and bravest act of Gen. Meade's military career. The First Corps crossed also to the north side of the Rappahannock, and there went into winter quarters, my brigade in the vicinity of Kelly's Ford.

We had just finished our beautiful cabin. I had secured an auger from some forgotten source, and was giving the finishing touches to our parlor walls, tastefully arranging our marble mantels, mahogany shelves and pictures by the old masters. It was about 10 o'clock a.m. of Dec. 12, 1863, six months to a day after receipt of my first permit from the war department to appear before Gen. Casey's board. Strange coincidence! I was called to regimental headquarters, where I received an official order, of which the following is a copy:

> Copy. War Department, A.-G. O.
> Dec. 5th, 1863.

Special Orders No. 540.—Extract:

XVL—The following named enlisted men are hereby relieved from duty with their respective commands, and will report in person without delay to Maj.-Gen. Casey, U.S. Volunteers, Commanding Provisional Brigades, for duty in connection with the organization of the U.S.C. drafted men and recruits being raised in the District of Columbia.

Corporal R. K. Beecham, Co. H, 2d Wis. Vols.

The quartermaster's department will furnish the necessary transportation.

By order of the secretary of war.

[Signed.] E. D. TOWNSEND, A.A.-G.

Headquarters First Army Corps, Dec. 11th, 1863.

[Signed.] C. KINGSBURY, JR. A.A.-G.

Headquarters First Division, Dec. 11th, 1863.

[Signed.] ROBERT MONTEITH, Capt. and A.A.A.-G.

Headquarters First Brigade, Dec. 12th, 1863.

[Signed.] J. D. WOOD, A.A.-G.

Headquarters 2d Wis. Vols., Dec. 12th, 1863.

A true copy.

[Signed.] G. WOODWARD, First Lieut. and Adjt.

The reader will notice that this order came to me through the "regular official channel," the secretary of war having discovered that in no other way could he reach a man in the army. It was dated at the war department Dec. 5, arrived at corps headquarters Dec. 11, and reached me on the 12th. Not very much red tape about that transaction, but for six months I had been in suspense on the red tape line of promotion, and it was, surely, about time to be getting to the end of the string.

Bidding farewell to my comrades and tentmates, most of whom I never met again, I was soon in the national capital, where I reported to Gen. Casey and was instructed to report there each morning until further orders.

Dec. 20 I received the following appointment:

War Department, Washington, D. C.,

Dec. 19, 1863.

Sir: You are hereby informed that the president of the United States has appointed you first lieutenant in the 23d Regiment of U.S.C. Troops in the service of the U.S. to rank as such from the 19th day of Dec., 1863.

[Signed.]

EDWIN M. STANTON,

Secretary of War.

A few days later I was ordered to cross the Potomac into old Virginia with a small squad of recruits to establish the nucleus of the 23d Regiment, at a point afterward known as "Camp Casey." On Dec. 23 I received the following:

War Department, Adjutant General's Office, Washington, D.C.,
Dec. 22, 1863.

Special Orders No. 566—Extract:

35. The following enlisted men are hereby honorably discharged the service of the U.S. to enable them to accept appointments in the U.S.C. Troops.

Corporal R. K. Beecham, Co. H, 2d Wis. Vols.

By order of the secretary of war.

[Signed.] E.D. TOWNSEND, A.A.-Gen. Vols.

Official—[Signed.] C. W. FOSTER, A.A.-Gen. Vols.

Approved: J. K. CASEY, Capt. and A.A.A.-G.

This order, which the reader will notice had passed through the "regular official channel," discharged me from my former lowly service as an enlisted man, and on receipt of which I was on Dec. 23, 1863, mustered into the service of the United States as a commissioned officer, henceforth to be honored among the mighty, with the magnificent privilege of snubbing a private soldier as much as I wanted to, and indulging in the senseless show of official "fuss and feathers."

I have given the full particulars of this little transaction, that the American people, especially ambitious young men, may see and understand how delightfully easy it is for a private soldier who possesses the physical manhood, the intellectual ability and the sand in his craw to get a commission in the American army.

Private George Washington, Twenty-third U.S. Colored Troops.

NINE

"Soldiers till the last man falls"

With the Twenty-third U.S. Colored Troops
January–June 1864

> God, that made the world and all things therein . . . hath made of
> one blood all nations of men for to dwell on all the face of the
> earth, and hath determined the times before appointed and the
> bounds of their habitations.—(Acts 17:24 and 26.)

Such was the language of Paul, the great Apostle to the Gentiles, as
he stood in the midst of Mars Hill and addressed the men of Athens
more than 1,800 years ago. Paul spoke with a knowledge from on
high and he was a firm believer in the universal brotherhood of the
human race.

We have a record of the brotherhood of man of still greater authority: And the sons of Noah that went forth of the ark were Shem, Ham
and Japheth: these are the three sons of Noah and of them was the whole
earth overspread. (Genesis 9:18 and 19.)

As before the flood "the earth was filled with violence," so after the
flood man was perverse, wicked and terribly cruel, and from the day
that Noah drank wine and was drunken in his tent, to the present hour,
"man's inhumanity to man" hath made countless millions mourn.

For long and dreary ages before the sublime doctrine evolved by the
Declaration of American Independence that "all men are created free

and equal," and that of their inalienable rights the most prominent are life, liberty and the pursuit of happiness, the strong and powerful had oppressed and enslaved the weak and helpless from the poles to the equator—from the rising to the setting of the sun.

In comparatively modern times we see the self-styled "enlightened nations of the world" turning their united power against unfortunate Africa and carrying her sons and daughters beyond the seas, condemning them to hopeless and, seemingly, everlasting bondage.

In the early history of our own America we find two records very diverse, the one from the other. The first reads: "It is curious to observe how largely this country was peopled in its earlier days by refugees for religious faith. The Huguenots, the Puritans, the Quakers, the Presbyterians, the Catholics, the persecuted of every sect and creed, all flocked to this home of the free."

The other record is from the chronicles of the first English settlement on American soil at Jamestown, Va., in 1607, and is as follows: "They were (i.e., the colonists who settled Jamestown) mostly gentlemen by birth, unused to labor . . . and came out in search of wealth and adventure, expecting when rich to return to England." Then, 13 years later, in 1619, we read: "The captain of a Dutch trading vessel sold to this colony 20 Negroes. They were employed in cultivating tobacco. As their labor was found to be profitable, larger numbers were afterwards imported."

This importation continued until the abolition of the slave trade in 1811, and 35 years before that event, or up to 1776, the year of the Declaration of Independence, 300,000 Africans had been stolen from their homes, imported into the British colonies in America and sold into slavery.

In 1620 the Puritans settled in Massachusetts; so we see that America had actually been made the land of the slave at Jamestown, Va., one year before the "home of the free" had been planted upon Plymouth's ice-clad rock in the old Bay State.

The African did not come to America of his own free will, as his Anglo-Saxon brother did; nevertheless, in the development of America the African and the Afro-American have borne an important part. For more than 200 years he was but the "hewer of wood and drawer of water" for the Anglo-Saxon brother, but it is stated by that eminent scholar and humorist, Judge Tourgee, that "in every American war the sons of Africa were always found defending the flag so far as lay in their power."

American history is very chary in speaking of the deeds in war of the Afro-American, but if we search its pages carefully we will find abundant evidence to sustain the truth of Judge Tourgee's statement. Beginning with the War of Independence, we find that the first attack on the British soldiers in Boston, March 15, 1770, was led by Crispus Attucks, a Negro runaway slave, and he was also the first man killed of the four who fell at that time. Some may except to the honesty of Crispus Attucks, because he ran away from his master, but the people of that day even so far forgot this blemish on his character, that they buried the man who loved freedom so well that he not only ran away from his master, but gave his life in the cause of freedom with his three comrades who died with him, the black and white together, and over their graves erected a monument that bears this inscription:

"Long as in freedom's cause the wise contend
Dear to your country shall your fame extend;
While to the world the lettered stone shall tell
Where Attucks, Caldwell, Grey and Maverick fell."

At the battle of Bunker Hill, Maj. Pitcairn, the British officer who caused the first effusion of blood at Lexington, as he mounted the American works shouting "The day is ours," was shot and killed and the British advance thereby checked, by Peter Salem, a Negro soldier of the patriot army. Many years after, at the unveiling of the statue in memory of Gen. Warren, who fell at Bunker Hill, Edward Everett, the orator of the day, said: "It is the monument of the day of the event of the battle of Bunker Hill; all of the brave men who shared its perils—alike of Prescott, Putnam, Warren and the colored soldier, Salem."

It is recorded of Maj. William Lawrence, who fought through the Revolution, from Concord until peace and independence were established, that at one time he commanded a full company of Negro soldiers, of whose courage, military discipline and fidelity he always spoke in highest terms of praise.

Other personal incidents might be cited, but these will suffice, with the substantial facts that during the Revolutionary period the colored population of the northern colonies did not exceed 50,000 people, yet of the 300,000 soldiers of the War of the Revolution who won for us national independence, 5,000 of them were Afro-Americans. They furnished their full quota of soldiers in the North, while in the South the Negro slaves assisted their masters in throwing off the British yoke.

The primal incident leading up to the War of 1812 was the capture of the American frigate *Chesapeake* in 1807 by the British frigate *Leopard,* when the *Chesapeake* was searched and three Afro-American seamen, Martin, Ware and Strachan, who had been impressed into the British service and deserted therefrom, were taken from her by the *Leopard*. In that war, the Afro-American soldier and sailor did his full share of fighting all along the line, and is entitled to his full and equal portion of the honor and glory of teaching England that she did not own and could not control the sea.

Before the battle of Lake Erie was fought in 1813, Capt. Perry found fault with the recruits sent him, from the fact that many of them were Negroes, and he made such complaint to Commodore Chauncey. In reply the Commodore said: "I have nearly 50 blacks on board my ship and many of them are among my best men," and later, Capt. Perry won the most memorable naval victory of the War of 1812 with his mixed crews of black and white sailors.

When the British were about to attack New Orleans with a superior force, Gen. Jackson called upon the free Negroes of Louisiana, and so nobly and promptly they responded that on Dec. 18, 1814, when Jackson reviewed his army of defense at New Orleans, consisting of about 6,000 troops, he found among them two battalions of Negroes, 500 in all, commanded by Maj. Lacoste and Maj. Savory.

Every American schoolboy knows the result of the battle of New Orleans, but how many of them are aware of the important historical fact that one-twelfth of Jackson's army that so heroically defended New Orleans were Afro-American volunteers?

We come now to the slave owners rebellion, the great American Civil War, where the Afro-American came to the front as a soldier in defense of national unity and national honor as well as in defense of his own inalienable rights, and there he truly earned the right to life, liberty and the pursuit of happiness, with each and every other right that belongs to any American citizen.

The American Civil War, one of the most terrible wars in all history, grew directly out of the question of slavery. The event of 1619 at Jamestown, Virginia, small as it seemed at the time—only the purchase and enslavement of 20 poor, friendless Negroes stolen from their African homes—had borne bitter fruit. The mills of the gods grind slowly, but they never cease to turn, and it matters not as to the quantity or quality of the grist, these everlasting mills of justice will grind it out at last.

For nearly two and a half centuries this boasted "land of the free and home of the brave" had been in fact a land of oppression for a whole race of people and the home of millions of slaves, but through all those guilty years the mills of the gods ground on, and the time came when, in the language of Abraham Lincoln, the liberator, the God appointed, the immortal, "every drop of blood drawn by the lash from the enslaved Negro's back demanded in atonement another drop of blood drawn by the engines and weapons of war from the heart of the Anglo-American."

But surely God demanded not that the victim of more than 200 years of bonds and stripes and unrequited toil should furnish his quota of that atoning blood? Here is the most remarkable fact connected with that great war—that the Afro-American came forward cheerfully and volunteered his strength, his brawn, his heart's blood to save the honor of the flag that to him and his race had been the symbol of every dishonor.

At first the government was not willing to give the Afro-American an opportunity to die for the Union and for liberty, but after a time it became evident to those in authority that we needed his assistance. Some regiments of colored troops were recruited in 1862, but it was not until January, 1863, that the United States began in earnest to organize such regiments. In May, 1863, a board was organized in Washington, D.C., for the examination of soldiers who were willing to accept positions as officers in these regiments, and it was owing to this fact that I am able to claim the honor of holding a commission in a colored regiment from December, 1863, until the close of the war.

During the last days of December, 1863, Lieuts. Warren H. Hurd, M. B. Case and myself, with 28 enlisted Negroes and a mule team loaded with supplies and camp equipage, crossed over Long Bridge from Washington into Virginia, and established the nucleus of the 23d U.S.C.T. at what was afterwards known as "Camp Casey."

Then began the work of organizing and drilling—of manufacturing soldiers out of raw recruits, many of whom had been slaves, most of whom had never handled a gun in their lives. As fast as men could be enlisted at the recruiting stations in Washington and Baltimore they were sent to us. Other officers reported for duty from time to time as the work progressed, and when the spring campaign opened in May, 1864, we had our regiment ready for the field, although some of the companies last organized had but slight knowledge of the handling of arms.

The recruiting station in Washington was run by Capt. Sheetz, and from him we received the original 28 men with which we organized Co. A. We learned later, when the first payday arrived and the paymaster visited the regiment, that a large majority of these first 28 recruits were marked on the payrolls as "deserters," and $30 charged up against each name. The men claimed they never had deserted, but when they enlisted the captain told them they might go home and remain for a few days until the camp was ready for them and that he would notify them when to return to the office for duty, and that afterward he so notified them by sending a guard to bring them back to the office. I took some pains to investigate the matter, and was fully satisfied, as all were who organized the regiment, that the men told the truth, and that about 20 of them had been robbed of $30 each, or an aggregate of $600. We reported what we learned to the paymaster and other officials, but so far as I was able to learn no attention was given to it, and the defrauded private soldiers, who were only Negroes, had to grin and bear it.

As the 23d was made up mostly of men from Washington and Baltimore, very naturally we found among them some pretty hard cases, the equals, perhaps, of what a regiment of white troops would show if recruited in the same cities; but as a rule the men were sober, honest, patriotic and willing to learn and fulfill the duties of soldiers.

During my service, while recruiting and organizing the 23d, and afterward while serving with it in the field, I had the opportunity to disprove some of the theories or ideas that are held by white people generally, and are frequently advanced, relative to the Afro-American race. One of these theories is that a Negro's foot is exceedingly large, with a heel out of all proportion to the rest of the foot and the foot out of proportion to the size of the man. From a daily paper published in Seattle, Wash.—the *Post-Intelligencer* of Aug. 1, 1899—I clipped the following, which illustrates this point and is certainly amusing:

> Booker T. Washington, the noted Negro educator, is visiting Paris, where he had a unique experience the other day. He went into a shoe store to buy a pair of shoes, but not a pair could be found large enough for him. The apologetic proprietor politely informed him that it was not the fashion to wear large shoes in Paris.

Of course, the above is only a revival of the stale joke on the size of a Negro's foot. I presume the same difficulty would confront me in a Paris shoe store, for I wear No. 9's, American make, and I have a brother who wears No. 11's. In the army I learned by actual experience that a company of soldiers, white or black, require about the same size shoes— i.e., a very few pairs of 6's, several pairs of 7's, a great many pairs of 8's and 9's, a few pairs of 10's and occasionally a pair as large as can be found.

One of the liveliest rows I had while in the service was with the quartermaster for filling a requisition that I made for shoes for my company, on the theory that no shoe was too large for a Negro, and he gave me all 10's and upwards. When I returned the shoes, informing him that my soldiers did not wear pontoons, he insisted that I should take them and issue them to my company anyway. Well, I didn't do it: consequently the row.

Another theory is that the Negro is a natural tippler—that they will all drink like so many fish when they get a chance. I had just one man among my whole company of colored soldiers that I ever saw drunk, or who gave me any trouble in that direction, and otherwise he was as good a soldier as ever wore the blue. Some of the boys drank occasionally, but many of them were strictly temperate. The 2d Wis. was not as sober and temperate as the 23d U.S. Colored Troops.

Another false theory is that the Negro is filthy. I found him the very opposite, and for that reason if for no other, I would prefer to command a company or regiment of black, rather than white soldiers.

During that winter, or rather in the month of March, I obtained a short leave of absence to visit my home in Wisconsin, and while there I married a little girl who had waited for my return since my enlistment in 1861, and for a wedding trip we journeyed back to "Camp Casey," and passed our honeymoon in teaching the men of Co. B, 23d U.S.C.T., to become good and efficient soldiers. What part did my wife take? you may ask. Well, there were but few of the men who could read and write, and the more a man knows the better soldier he makes, while it is especially convenient that noncommissioned officers should be able to read and write; so we organized an evening school, to which every man in the company was invited, and many of them attended, and my wife was one of the teachers. At first she had some prejudice against the Afro-American race, but long before the winter campaign was over she was willing to admit that the hearts of the boys of Co. B were in the right place at all times and under all circumstances.

Right here, I wish to say, because it is true, that there never was an organization of 1,000 men in all this broad, free America where a woman was held in greater esteem or her honor more sacred than in the 23d United States Colored Troops.

In the latter part of April, 1864, my regiment was ordered to the front, when we proceeded to Manassas Junction, where we became a part of the Second Brigade of the Fourth Division of the Ninth Corps. The Ninth Corps was commanded by Gen. Burnside, and comprised three divisions of white troops, commanded respectively by Gens. Potter, Wilcox and Ledlie, and a Fourth Division of Colored Troops, commanded by Gen. Ferrero. The Fourth was the smallest division of the corps and consisted of two brigades, the First commanded by Col. Sigfried, having four regiments—the 27th, 30th, 39th and 43d; the Second, commanded by Col. Thomas, having five regiments—the 19th, 23d, 28th, 29th and 31st.

The Fourth Division crossed the Rapidan at Germania Ford on the morning of May 6, 1864, and that night we held the extreme right of the Union line. The next day the division was detached from the Ninth Corps and assigned to the duty of guarding the roads, bridges and fords in the rear of Grant's army, and to see especially that no harm befell our immense supply train. A day or two later my regiment started out in charge of our supply and ambulance trains to Belle Plaine Landing, on the Potomac River, crossing the Rappahannock at Fredericksburg. When we passed through the city with our long trains, every ambulance and every wagon filled with wounded and thousands of wounded on foot, the people of Fredericksburg thought for a certainty that Grant's army was in full retreat. The rain was pouring down in torrents, the roads were next to impassable, and the battle of Spotsylvania was then in progress, for we could hear the cannonading and the awful crash of musketry. Really, the battle sounded as if not more than a mile away, and the people, no doubt, expected Lee's army was right at our heels, but the Army of the Potomac had crossed the Rappahannock for the last time. Lee's army was fighting with the same invincible spirit that had always characterized it, but Grant, the leader, had crossed the river to stay.

From Fredericksburg to Belle Plaine Landing was a horrible and never-to-be-forgotten trip. As we neared the Potomac the roads became worse, for the country is more hilly. The roads had been corduroyed in many places during the winter of 1862-3, where Hooker's army occupied this position, but the heavy rains of the previous winter had washed out these corduroys and gullied the roads in inconceivable shape; but over them we were obliged to go, with our long trains of wounded men. It was awful, not for us who were on foot, but for the helpless, who were compelled to ride over those horrible roads.

At Belle Plaine Landing, which was for a time our base of supplies, we loaded our trains with provisions and ammunition and returned as rapidly as possible to Grant's army. The day of our return we met and repulsed the first cavalry attack made on our train in our vicinity. The Confederate cavalry came on in some bridle path, through the woods, that was guarded only by a small detachment of Union cavalry, which the Confederates drove before them, and they were within 300 yards of our train when the 23d arrived on the ground, after double-quicking a half mile in order to reach it, and we hustled those Johnnies out of there in good shape, only losing a few men wounded.

From that date until its arrival in front of Petersburg the duty of guarding our trains against raiding detachments of Confederate cavalry was assigned to Ferrero's Fourth Division, and I have yet to learn of a single instance where the Confederates caught us napping.

While with the boys of the Black Division, as it was called, I always felt safe, just as safe as it is possible for a soldier to feel in the midst of dangers, and a soldier feels safe when he is with reliable men who possess the courage and the ability to meet any danger on the shortest possible notice and stand together like soldiers till the last man falls, if necessary. When in the field with the old Iron Brigade I never felt one whit safer than I did with the regiments of the Black Division.

From the Rapidan to the Pamunkey River the black boys marched and sang, but were not called upon to do any severe fighting. The last point held by the 23d previous to Grant's movement to the James River was on the Pamunkey not far from White House Landing. For several days I had been very much under the weather, and when we left the Pamunkey and were on the march southward, not far from White House, the Major and the Surgeon insisted that I should take a lay off for a few days, by going to White House and resting up, which I did.

In the American army an officer possesses many advantages over an enlisted man, and the higher his official rank the greater and more numerous are his advantages. Of course, no enlisted man would have been allowed to go to White House, or any other house, for a few day's rest, as I was. I am not registering a kick against the treatment of the officer, but only stating my reason for preferring the commissioned officer's privileges to the enlisted man's honors.

At White House I succeeded in getting some clean underclothing, and proceeded to make myself as comfortable as possible. I found there some old friends from Wisconsin, belonging to the 36th Inf., with whom I had a delightful visit. Now, as it so happened that Gen. Grant had already commenced his movement toward the James River in his last change of base during the campaign, and the day after my arrival orders were received to send all the sick up the Potomac, which order included me, although I was only comfortably sick, and believing that a trip to Washington would do no harm, I made no objection to the arrangement.

On the boat that carried us up the Potomac were a great many officers, most of whom were finely dressed, looking more like bandbox soldiers than men who had seen service. I wondered what so many officers were doing in holiday attire, and even to this day I wonder, for I never learned the mystery of it. Of course, I did not inquire into their business, but could not help noticing the fact that my "personal appearance was very much against me," in such a crowd of gentlemen, but being a commissioned officer, not even a colonel would think of telling me so.

Among these officers there was one genuine brigadier general. I speak of this fact to show in the connection the advantage of being a general instead of a common lieutenant. When the dinner hour arrived a waiter took his station at the dining room door with the bell in his hand, while an official of the boat politely waited upon the general and conducted him to a seat at the head of the table; then the waiter rang the bell for dinner, when all the minor officers walked in and found seats at the table, myself among the number. As I wore a common fatigue blouse without shoulder straps, and had just come from a 40-days' campaign, I certainly appeared a little out of place, and one of the waiters, concluding that such was the case, said to me in a low and polite tone of voice, "My dear sir, it is strictly against orders on this boat for enlisted men to sit at the table with officers, but the table will be reset for them when the officers have dined." Of course, I felt deeply humiliated at being mistaken for an enlisted man, but the humiliation was nothing to what it would have been to have lost my dinner; so, in the language of one of the large statesmen of America, I "told the truth" to the waiter just as politely, and he seemed to believe me without further question.

On our arrival in Washington, the sick, with whom I was numbered, were sent to Annapolis, Md., and there quartered in the Naval School Building, which was then being used for an officers' hospital. Here I had the opportunity of comparing my former hospital fare and treatment while an enlisted man with the fare and treatment of commissioned officers in an officers' hospital, and I am free to say that I greatly prefer the latter. My recollection is that we were charged $1 per day for board, and the table was well furnished. We had plenty to eat, and the service was sufficient to satisfy any man of reasonable judgment. Of course, this was the convalescent table, as I ate at no other while in this hospital, being a convalescent from start to finish, but this convalescent table was good enough for me, and I hereby advise all soldiers in the American or any other army, who are so unfortunate as to be sent to the hospital, to get into an officers' hospital, if possible.

My stay in the Naval School Hospital was during the cherry season of 1864, and never in my life did I enjoy a cherry season more. Within the Naval School yard grew a number of fine old cherry trees of enormous size, and just as full of large, luscious, ripe cherries as they could hang, and every day I climbed into the lower branches of my favorite and ate cherries to my stomach's content.

At the end of five or six days the surgeon in charge of the hospital called the patient convalescents together and selected a goodly number to return to the army for duty. I was among the number, and our orders were to report to our commands. There was a ship at the pier ready to sail the following morning, upon which I expected to go, but just after dark who should drop in upon me but my father, from Wisconsin, who informed me that a cousin, in Battery B, 4th U.S. Art., was wounded at or about the time of the battle of Cold Harbor, and had since died of his wounds in Washington, and that my brother, in the same battery, was wounded a few days later, and sent to the hospital at Washington: that he had searched through all the hospitals in that city without finding my brother, and seeing my name in the paper among those sent to Annapolis, he had made this trip for the purpose of finding me.

Well, I was under orders to report to the army, but being a commissioned officer I could select my own route, so my father stayed with me in the hospital that night, and I went with him to Washington in the morning. Together we searched all the hospitals in Washington and Alexandria, except the right one, but failed to find my brother, and I went down the Potomac the next day without seeing him, but my father, who left me at Alexandria, returned to Washington, and found my brother in a hospital that we had overlooked.

In returning to the Army of the Potomac via Washington and Alexandria, although I failed to find my brother, as I hoped and expected, I met with an experience which I otherwise must have missed, which I did not expect, but which had I missed I would have regretted all the days of my life.

When I reported to the provost marshal's office and asked for transportation to the army, I was told that a certain colonel, whose name I do not remember, had use for me on the way, and I was directed to report to him for duty. Upon reporting, the colonel informed me that he had been assigned to the temporary command of a thousand or more recruits, gathered there at Alexandria for transportation to Grant's army; that he was about to form his provisional regiment into companies, and wanted line officers to take command of them and that I should report to him at his headquarters the following morning at 8 o'clock, at which time he would form his regiment of recruits in line and march to the transport that would by that time be in readiness to convey us to Grant's base at City Point. The next morning I reported for duty, as ordered, and took command of the company to which I was assigned. Then, in due time, we succeeded in getting the regiment in line for the march to the landing. There were two or three line officers to each company, and as we marched down the streets of Alexandria, we presented the appearance of a new regiment going to the front, all freshly supplied with arms and equipments, new uniforms, etc. Of course, our regiment was not very well drilled, and we made no attempt at military evolutions, but there were certain semimilitary evolutions in which our raw recruits were not so raw. Most if not all of them were bounty jumpers and about as tough and reckless a gang of daredevils as was ever gotten together in one organization.

The colonel marched his regiment down the street toward the river, and when the head of his column neared the landing he learned that the transport was not quite ready to receive us, so he halted his regiment and for about two hours we stood at "in place rest," but for one I did not get much rest out of it, though I did get some fun.

Immediately every recruit wanted the privilege of going to a restaurant just long enough to get a "square meal" before going to the front; but all such requests were, of course, refused, as we expected to move at any moment. By watchful care we kept them pretty well in line, and I do not think we lost any men in the city. In a short time the huckster fraternity of Alexandria discovered that a "new regiment" was in their streets, and, of course, they were anxious to supply us with everything we needed. These recruits all had plenty of money, and they thought they needed anything and everything they could get, without regard to how they got it. To give some idea of the style of these recruits, I will relate one incident, as it happened only a few yards from me. A huckster with a handcart loaded with ice cream and various other articles to satisfy the needs of recruits, halted about midway of my company, and immediately opened up a lively business. In a few minutes a recruit who had purchased a dish of ice cream, after disposing of the contents, put the plate and spoon in his pocket for future use. The huckster wanted him to return the plate and spoon, but the recruit contended that he had bought and paid for them, and in fact, had paid more than they were worth and refused to return them unless his money was refunded. I was about to interfere in the interest of the huckster, and see that he had a fair deal, but the fellow could not wait for assistance. He thought he knew a thing or two himself, so he pressed the recruit closely and in trying to recover his plate and spoon, worth probably a dime, he made the fatal mistake of advancing one step too far, thus leaving his box of supplies unguarded. Quick as a lightning flash my recruits went through an evolution not found in the tactics, and when the huckster returned to his base, it was his base only, for his supplies had vanished and the poor fellow picked up his empty cart and departed. It was a hard company in which to enforce military discipline, and I was not sorry when the transport was ready for us to march aboard.

That night our transport was far out on the bosom of the broad Potomac, but when morning dawned the colonel found, or rather failed to find, about 25 of his recruits. Their guns and equipments were there, but the men had deserted, evidently by jumping overboard and swimming ashore, or drowning in the attempt.

We reached City Point the next day a short time before sunset, and camped our recruits on the shore of the James River, with a strong guard, furnished by the provost marshal, on the other side, with instructions to let no man pass out; but the next morning more than 200 of our recruits had disappeared. Their guns and equipments were scattered all over the campground. After breakfast the colonel got the balance of his regiment in line, and the march for the front commenced. It was a hot day, and occasionally our road led through pieces of woods where the shade was enticing, and from every woods and grove we emerged with our ranks depleted. I am sure we lost more men from that regiment that day than any other regiment even lost in one day during the whole war. Finally, along in the afternoon, when our regiment of more than a thousand men had dwindled to less than a full company, and I saw not far away the flags and badges of the Ninth Corps, I said to myself, in the language of Jack Falstaff: "If I be not ashamed of my soldiers, I am a souced gurnet. . . . I'll not march through Coventry (or up to headquarters) with them, that's flat," so I then and there deserted my provisional regiment and went in search of the 23d U.S. Colored Troops, which I soon found and rejoined.

Members of the U.S. Colored Troops at Petersburg after the Battle of the Crater. The Union suffered approximately 4,000 casualties during this disastrous battle.

TEN

"We'll show the world today that the colored troops are soldiers"

The Battle of the Crater
June–July 1864

On June 18, or a few days before my return to the army, the Fourth Division had been reunited with the Ninth Corps, and from that date until the battle of the Mine on July 30, we did such duties as were assigned to us; but as to what those duties were there is some difference between my recollection of them and what seems to be the general verdict of history so far as written. The Corps historian says: "While the Fourth Division was engaged in the trenches they were also drilled in the movements necessary for an attack and occupation of the enemy's works."

Gen Potter, commander of the First Division, in his report of the battle of the Mine, says: "Gen. Ferrero was informed that, in accordance with the plan of attack, he was to lead the assault, when the attack was made. He was ordered to drill his troops accordingly. . . . For three weeks they drilled with alacrity in the various movements—charging upon earthworks, wheeling by the right and left, deployment, and other details of the expected operations."

Then, again, Geo. L. Kilmer, who pretends to write historical sketches, in an article of that kind, entitled "The Siege of Petersburg," makes the following statement: "The colored troops were drilled especially to lead the assault, but the white troops were ignorant of what was expected of them, although camp rumor spread the news that a mine was to be exploded, and that the corps would charge the lines in front." In another place in his article, Mr. Kilmer says: "Some time after 6 o'clock Gen. Meade ordered a division of the Eighteenth Corps on the right of the Nineteenth, to charge the Confederate line and attempt to widen the breach. At the same time Burnside was ordered to send forward his colored division. This division was not on the ground, but was back in the sheltered ways behind the Union breastworks, and the outlets to the front were to all intents and purposes clogged, and men had to move out in pairs. These troops had never been under fire, though many of the officers (white) were old soldiers. It was 8 o'clock, or more than two hours after the explosion, before this charge took place. The men going in in confusion had no force for assault. Some of them ran into the pit for cover, others crouched behind the breastworks and log huts, and for the moment it looked as though the division that had been especially prepared for the attack was to meet with speedy ruin." Still further on Mr. Kilmer continues: "Mahone's Division, supported by portions of Johnson's, met the Colored Division when they made the farthest advance, and broke the force of their attack, sending them back in confusion upon the white troops in the captured entrenchments. This carried back part of Gen. Potter's Division of the Ninth Corps and Turner's of the Eighteenth Corps, and the Union advance was frustrated."

The foregoing extracts seem to show that the generally accepted belief is that the Fourth Division received especial drill and instructions relative to a certain battle in contemplation. My recollection is very different, and I was on duty with my company and regiment every day from the 22d day of June until after the battle of the Mine on the 30th day of July, 1864. I am prepared to say from actual knowledge derived from personal experience with the Fourth Division that the only duty assigned to the said division for more than a month before the battle of the Mine was work upon our trenches and fortifications. The Fourth Division during all that time was drilled especially in the use of pick and shovel, and in no other manner. Of this fact I do not complain. My complaint is, that while the Fourth Division worked ceaselessly, heroically, day and night, on the trenches to the neglect of every soldierly preparation for the battle, it has been falsely and persistently reported to have received special preparation for a particular battle.

The Corps historian of the Ninth Corps probably did not belong to the Fourth Division, and his statement is incorrect. Gen. Potter commanded the First Division, and would be a better witness of the purport of the orders received by himself than of those received by Gen. Ferrero, and he speaks of a matter of which he had no personal knowledge. As to Mr. Kilmer, he probably gives these statements as he heard them or gathered them from unreliable sources. At all events, his statements are untrue from beginning to end, so far as they relate to the Fourth Division.

From the 22d day of June until the afternoon of July 29, Gen. Ferrero never once had the Fourth Division together, let alone having a division drill of any kind, and during all that time I never once caught even a glance of Gen. Ferrero. During the same period we had but one brigade drill of the Second Brigade, which lasted about three or four hours, and consisted of the most common and simple of brigade movements. Our whole time was employed, day and night, in work.

About July 20 the regiment received a number of recruits, 10 or 12 of whom were assigned to my company. These men were dressed in new, clean uniforms, and their arms and accoutrements were polished and bright. Within a day or two Col. Campbell, who commanded the 23d regiment, and had a slight attack of swell-head, had them all on duty at his headquarters, where he kept them until the afternoon before the battle. Believing that a battle was imminent, and that these recruits would be in poor condition to render efficient service without some instruction and preparation, I went personally to the colonel and requested him to return them to their company, that I might give them such instruction; which request the colonel refused to grant, on the ground, as he stated it, that the men would receive more and better instruction by doing guard duty at his headquarters than I could possibly give them in the trenches with pick and shovel; so these men loaded their pieces for the first time on the morning of July 30, and went into the battle with us. With this incident indelibly stamped upon my memory, how is it possible for me to be mistaken with regard to our entire lack of drill and preparation for the battle of July 30?

Mr. Kilmer's statement that "These troops had never been under fire" is in keeping with his knowledge of the Fourth Division. Probably every regiment of the division at one time or another had been under fire before we reached Petersburg, and it is safe to say that from the 1st to the 30th of July not a day passed but some portion of the division was under fire. Work on the mine, according to Gen. Grant's *Memoirs,* began on the 25th of June, and from that date until July 31 it was exceedingly lively all along the front of the Ninth Corps, and to say that a division of troops worked all that time on the trenches and fortifications and was "never under fire" is the worst kind of nonsense.

The fact that Gen. Burnside selected the Colored Division to lead the assault is not proof that the "white troops were more ignorant of what was expected of them" than the colored troops were. Referring to this matter in his *Memoirs,* page 318 of volume 2, Gen. Grant says: "Burnside selected the Colored Division to make the assault, but Meade interfered with this. Burnside then took Ledlie's Division—a worse selection than the first could have been." Now, is it possible to suppose that the Fourth Division had been drilled for weeks to make a certain assault, and that Gen. Meade changed the order and substituted another division that had not been drilled on the eve of battle? If he did—and the Fourth Division could not have drilled for weeks for any purpose without Meade knowing it—then Gen. Meade was a bigger chump than I ever took him to be.

Gen. Grant further says on page 310, same volume: "I gave Meade minute orders on the 24th, directing how I wanted the assault conducted, which orders he amplified into general instructions for the guidance of the troops that were to be engaged." It must be conceded, I think, that Gen. Grant knew what he was talking about, and it certainly appears from his *Memoirs* that at least the four division generals of the Ninth Corps, viz, Potter, Wilcox, Ledlie and Ferrero, knew exactly what was expected of each of them and of the troops under their command.

During the early days of July, 1864, the Second Brigade of the Black Division, with which I had the honor of serving, was sent to the right of the army that besieged Petersburg, and employed for a number of days in building and strengthening the fortifications in that locality. The colored soldiers performed the duties assigned them there, as elsewhere, patiently and faithfully. Of course, we carried with us our arms and ammunition, with our other equipments, as any brigade of white troops would, although it was not intended that we should use them unless in case of the unexpected happening, and really carried arms more for appearance sake than anything else. When we arrived at our destination our arms were laid aside, except by the few who were required to do guard duty, and each regiment of the brigade furnished its daily or nightly detail which went forth armed with pick and shovel.

Nothing new or worthy of mention happened while we occupied this location, and later we returned to our old position in rear of the Ninth Corps lines.

Ah, that terrible battle, or rather disaster, of "The Mine!" How shall I describe it? What a butchery it was. What an awful deathtrap it proved for our brave boys, white as well as black.

Gen. Burnside was not a military genius nor a great general, but he planned this battle, or assault, well, and had it been executed with soldierly dash and courage the result would have been different. Col. Pleasants, of the 48th Pa., an old miner himself, in command of a regiment of miners, conceived the idea of blowing out of our way a fort in front of the Ninth Corps that was regarded as the key to the Confederate position. Burnside acted on Col. Pleasants's idea, and after securing the seemingly reluctant consent of Gen. Meade, the work of mining the fort began on June 25. A tunnel was run 520 feet long, terminating with laterals 40 feet in each direction, exactly under the fort, where 8,000 pounds of powder were stored and fuses laid for its explosion. Burnside's plan was to blow out the fort, and immediately after charge through the gap thus opened in the Confederate lines, and gain the commanding position of Cemetery Hill, in their rear. Burnside selected the Fourth Division to lead that assault, but this selection was made within a very few days of the battle, and although that fact must have been known to Gen. Ferrero, it was known to no one else in the division, and no preparation whatever was made by the division to carry out this arrangement. In fact, any such preparation was made unnecessary because Gen. Meade overruled Burnside and ordered that he should select some other division. Then, as Gen. Grant tells us, "Burnside took Ledlie's (the Third) Division—a worse selection than the first could have been." This was the first blunder, but others followed in rapid succession.

Under cover of the darkness of the night of July 29, the whole Ninth Corps was massed close up to the Confederate works, where we waited for morning and the strife that it was to bring. On the morning of July 30, 1864, the Army of the Potomac held within its very grasp a great and far-reaching victory, that would have given us the possession of Petersburg, the citadel of the Confederate capital. Before night we accepted in its stead a crushing and humiliating defeat, simply because the general officers of the Ninth Corps failed to obey and carry out in a soldierly manner the orders they had received.

The explosion of the mine was to take place at a quarter past 3 o'clock a.m., and before that hour arrived the troops were in column ready for action, but the fuse failed and there we waited for an hour and a half, until two soldiers of the 48th Pa. replaced or repaired the fuse.

At 16 minutes before 5 o'clock the mine exploded, blowing the whole fort into the air, leaving a great excavation or crater, 30 feet deep, 50 or 60 feet wide, and from 100 to 150 feet long. Immediately our artillery opened and the charging column swept forward, led by Ledlie's Division, and within 20 minutes after, we of the Fourth Division received orders to go forward, and followed the other divisions of the Ninth Corps into the breach. Geo. L. Kilmer's statements that "Some time after 6 o'clock Burnside was ordered to send forward his Colored Division. This division was not on the ground, but was back in the sheltered ways behind the Union breastworks," etc., are absolutely incorrect.

Just as soon as the troops in advance of us had time to get out of our way, so that we could move, we followed as in one continuous stream. We moved out on a double-quick, and 100 yards or less brought us to the outmost Union line; another 100 yards and we were abreast of the Confederate works. Then a strange thing happened: a movement was made that was to me unaccountable. My brigade—the second—had been formed left in front, which would indicate that as soon as we had gotten beyond the trenches we should move to the left and face the enemy by the front rank. Instead we were led to the right, passing over the rim of the crater into the Confederate works, fronting the enemy, by the rear rank, which movement would have a tendency to confuse anything but the best-drilled troops.

The First Brigade of the Colored Division, however, was led to the left over the rim of the crater in the opposite direction, thus separating our Fourth Division into two parts in the very beginning of the action; so that thereafter the Fourth Division did not and could not act in unison. As we passed over the rim of the crater I noticed that the crater was full of our soldiers, and though Grant tells us in his *Memoirs* that "Burnside's Corps was not to stop in the crater at all, but push on to the top of the hill," etc., and every soldier of common sense could see at a glance that the object of the charge must be to carry the hill behind the crater, nevertheless Ledlie's Division ran right into the crater and halted, and right there the assault failed. Grant should have withdrawn the corps immediately on learning that the division leading the assault had not only halted themselves but had really blocked the way of the passage of the divisions to follow; but we were not recalled. My brigade passed to the right of the crater and advanced as far as we could get, on account of the troops in advance of us who had halted, and then we halted also.

The Confederates soon recovered from their confusion and concentrated their batteries upon us, catching us like sheep in a slaughter pen, for there was the whole Ninth Corps crowded into a space where there was barely room for one division to operate, and there we stood from 5 o'clock in the morning, hour after hour, under a plunging fire from the Confederate guns, until the blistering July sun was high up in the sky, pouring his scorching heat upon us, sheltering ourselves as best we could from the missiles of death, and becoming every moment more mixed, confused and broken up, without even a chance to return the fire. Our generals had pushed us into this slaughter pen, and then deserted us. There was no one present with authority to lead or to direct. The highest officer in rank connected with the general and staff that I saw anywhere within that trap was Capt. Dempey, Col. Thomas's adjutant general.

The charge having utterly failed to push beyond the crater, it would have been wisdom and good generalship to order a withdrawal to our old line, surely within an hour after the assaulting division halted in the crater, but although Grant and Meade were both on the ground in person, in rear of the Ninth Corps, no such order was given. On the contrary, about 9 o'clock an attempt was made to carry the hill in our front by the Second Brigade of the Fourth Division alone, and thus accomplish the work that Grant had assigned to the whole Ninth Corps, and that, too, after we had wasted precious hours in inactivity, had frittered away our golden opportunity, and given Lee ample time to recover from his confusion and dispose his forces to meet and repel such a charge.

I do not know whence this order emanated, for if Gen. Ferrero or our brigade commander, Col. Thomas, were on the ground, I did not see either of them. The order came to us through Lieut. Col. Bross, who seemed to be in command of the 29th regiment of our brigade, and the highest in rank of any officer that I saw along our front of the line that day, and we accepted it without question.

Col. Bross formed his regiment in lead of the column as best he could in that jam of mixed soldiers—white and black together; and next in the column came the 23d. He passed along our front, carrying his regimental colors, notifying the brigade that he would lead the charge in person, and giving the order for us to follow. We did the best we could to obey that order, although every old soldier (and the officers of the colored regiments were nearly all old soldiers) could see that it was sheer and utter madness, and that the effort must fail.

The black boys formed promptly. There was no flinching on their part. They came to the shoulder touch like true soldiers, as ready to face the enemy and meet death on the field as the bravest and best soldiers that ever lived; but think for a moment of forming for an effective charge in that death valley, under a murderous fire, crowded, literally jammed in with the other troops, confused and broken up as we were. There was not one chance in 1,000 for success. An absolutely certain defeat, if not annihilation, awaited us, and we knew it.

As coolly as if on parade, Col. Bross shook out the folds of the stars and stripes in front of his column, and his voice rang out in clarion notes above the din and confusion that surrounded us. He said: "Boys, I want you to follow this flag. I am going to lead you to victory. We'll show the world today that the colored troops are soldiers."

I wondered at the time if the colonel realized that he was about to sacrifice his life for naught and lead his followers to destruction. O, it was grand, truly soul inspiring to behold that man, then in the full vigor of young manhood. There, with the old flag above him, he stood erect and fearless, nerved for the supreme effort, the soul of exalted courage, the very personation of the spirit of heroism! While I admired his lofty courage and resolved to follow his lead and do my utmost to make his daring effort a success, the thought—the conviction—was stamped upon my brain: "It is utter madness. That grand man will throw his life into the breach and death and defeat will be our reward."

Then along the column rang the order: "Forward!" and we moved out slowly; it was impossible to gain the speed and momentum necessary in a charge. There was an outer rim or earthwork which protected us somewhat and hid from our view the hill and ground beyond. Over this earthwork, with colors flying, Col. Bross led his regiment, and the 23d, which occupied the second line, had reached and was mounting this rim, when Col. Bross and his regiment received such a concentrated fire from the Confederate line that they were forced back upon us—but the colonel and his flag and many of his men never came back. Gen. Grant says in his *Memoirs*: "It was 9 o'clock before Lee got up reinforcements from his right to join in expelling our troops;" but when we attempted to make this charge we found them there in force. Mahone's Division had been posted in our front, while we were loitering in the Confederate works, receiving blows instead of giving them, and opened a withering fire upon Bross and his regiment the moment they appeared over the earthworks. Napoleon's Old Guard could not have advanced under that fire.

This was probably the charge to which Mr. Kilmer referred when he said: "Mahone's Division, supported by portions of Johnson's, met the colored troops when they made the farthest advance, and broke the force of their attack, sending them back in confusion on the white troops. This carried back a part of Gen. Potter's Division of the Ninth Corps and Gen. Turner's Division of the Eighteenth," etc.

But in this attempt at a charge we had but one brigade of the Fourth Division, and only one regiment of that brigade got outside the earthworks. The white troops were very readily carried back, when the repulse of one colored regiment would stampede a whole division of the Eighteenth Corps and part of a division of Ninth Corps, as Mr. Kilmer claims it did; but the truth is that Turner's Division of the Eighteenth Corps was not there.

From 700 to 1,000 of our men, of nearly all organizations in the Ninth Corps, rallied in the crater and held it until about 2 o'clock p.m., when the remnant left surrendered, and the Confederates reoccupied their old line completely.

That was a terrible day. The Ninth Corps's loss, according to official figures, was:

Killed, 419; wounded, 1,679; missing, 1,901. Total, 3,999.

The Confederate loss was probably less than half of that amount.

In this appalling loss in less than one day of battle, or rather butchery, for it was not a battle, the Fourth, or Colored Division, although the smallest division of the corps, sustained more than one-third. Our Division went into that deathtrap about 4,200 strong, and our loss was officially reported:

Killed, 176; wounded, 688; missing, 801. Total, 1,665. More than one-third of our entire force.

My regiment (the 23d) suffered the severest of any in the division or corps, losing 74 men killed. But these official figures, appalling as they are, do not show the worst features of the awful horrors of that bloody butchery; for while the report shows 801 missing from the Colored Division, the fact is that there were less than 500 Negro prisoners taken, and deducting 500 from 801 missing, leaves an additional 301 to be added to the list of killed, bringing the loss of the Fourth Division up to 477 killed, 688 wounded, and 500 prisoners.

The taking off of the last-named 301 would make a chapter of horrors too awful to be written. No wonder the people of the South deny the truth of the cold-blooded and inhuman murders committed by their soldiers that day.

In the late Spanish war they tell of the desperate fighting and fearful loss we sustained at Santiago and other places, but the Fourth Division alone lost more men killed than were lost by the United States in the whole Spanish war. The people of America do not realize, in fact, they do not know, that the Colored Division lost in that one battle of The Mine 189 more men killed than were killed in the whole American army during the war with Spain.

But not alone at Petersburg, nor in that one battle did the Afro-American give his blood and his life heroically for the Flag of our Union and the liberty of his race. Gen. Benjamin F. Butler, who commanded the Army of the James, and had in his command a division of colored troops that participated in a previous battle, many years after the war, in a speech in the House of Representatives, relative to the rights of the Negro race, paid the following grand tribute to the heroism of the colored soldiers of the Civil War:

> It became my painful duty, sir, to follow in the track of that charging column, and there, in a space not wider than the clerk's desk, and 300 yards long, lay the dead bodies of 543 of my colored comrades, fallen in defense of their country, who had offered up their lives to uphold its flag and its honor as a willing sacrifice; and as I rode along among them, guiding my horse this way and

that way, lest he should profane with his hoof what seemed to me the sacred dead, and as I looked on their bronzed faces upturned in the shining sun to heaven, as if in mute appeal against the wrongs of the country for which they had given their lives, and whose flag had only been to them a flag of stripes, on which no stars of glory had ever shone for them—feeling I had wronged them in the past, and believing what was the future of my country to them—among my dead comrades there I swore to myself a solemn oath, "May my right hand forget its cunning and my tongue cleave to the roof of my mouth if I ever fail to defend the rights of these men who have given their blood for me and my country this day and for their race forever;" and, God helping me, I will keep that oath.

From that hour all prejudice was gone and an old time state-rights Democrat became a lover of the Negro race, and as long as their rights are not equal to the rights of other men under this government I am with them against all comers; and when their rights are assured, as other men's rights are held sacred, then I trust we shall have what we sought to have—a united country, North and South, white and black, under our glorious flag, for which we and our fathers have fought with an equal and not to be distinguished valor.

The 30th of July, 1864, was my last battle. When I returned from the South and rejoined my regiment the war was over, the last battle had been fought, the Union had been saved, and the Negro race had won emancipation. My comrades who had lived through that awful day at Petersburg, many of them, had the honor of being among the first troops to enter Richmond, for the Confederate Capital was finally taken by Weitzel's Corps (the 25th), into which all the colored troops in the Army of the Potomac and the Army of the James had been consolidated.

In that terrible war that cost this nation millions of treasure and rivers of blood, who will say that the Afro-American did not do his full share? The official record stands in the adjutant general's office at Washington, D.C., that 178,975 Negro soldiers served in the army under old glory, and their losses in battle and from wounds and disease reached the sum total of 68,178 lives.

When the 29th colored regiment was repulsed and fell back from that foolish and useless attempt at a charge that no sane man or general could have ordered, close after them and almost upon their heels fol-lowed Mahone's Division in a countercharge. There was no earthly rea-son why we should abandon the works in our possession to Mahone's men if there was any advantage to be gained by holding them, and if it was the intention of the commanding general to abandon them he should have so ordered hours before, when we could have withdrawn at our leisure and without severe loss. Therefore I very naturally presumed that Grant wanted to hold what we had gained, and was planning to give us some assistance, and when I saw the stampede made by both white and black troops before Mahone's column, which was perfectly inexcusable on our part on any other grounds than the one I have al-ready mentioned, that our troops were so crowded, mixed and jammed together that it was impossible to resist a charge, I thought if we could hold one-fourth of our men until the other three-fourths, in their rush to the rear, cleared the ground sufficiently to give us room to form a line, we could repulse Mahone's advance; and so we could, but most of the men in that deathtrap who could run were wiser than I was, and they broke for the rear in almost a solid body.

A few of my colored boys, who knew no better, stayed with me, and we all got it in the neck, or where it answered the same purpose. As Mahone's men leaped upon the earthwork in our front, my first ser-geant, James A. Coats, shot their color bearer, and man and flag went down. The next moment the sergeant was shot dead and fell at my feet, while I was wounded and for a time disabled, and Mahone's men swept over us.

The ground where we had been standing was honeycombed with caves, ditches, and bombproofs, in which the Confederates had shel-tered themselves from our fire in days bygone, into one of which I fell when I was shot, and for a few moments I supposed I had received my deathwound. Possibly wounds that are not dangerous or really severe are as painful as mortal wounds; a man then being in the condition to sense every particle of suffering thus produced. In my case I cannot imagine how a mortal wound could more completely prostrate and over-come. For a few moments I lay at the bottom of the bombproof just as good as dead, without power to help myself, while if I had fallen into a boiling cauldron or fiery furnace, the all-consuming heat that seemed to overpower me could not have been more intense. I can account for this feeling only from the fact that my blood was as near the boiling point as it could well be, although I did not realize it until the pain produced by the wound concentrated and intensified in this heat. With this burning sensation came a thirst that no man who has not experienced it can comprehend or imagine. I believe it is necessary for a man to be wounded on a battlefield with his blood at a fever heat in order to know and understand the full value of a drink of water. In my case I did not have to endure the thirst for hours, as thousands of my comrades did while they waited for the relief which in many cases never came, for my canteen was full; but I got the sensation with all its unutterable agony in those few minutes, while I was recovering my nerve. Then I made a long and vigorous pull on the old canteen, and though the water it contained was as warm as a July sun could make it, it was the coolest and most refreshing draught I ever drank in my life. With the slaking of my thirst the consuming fire in my veins moderated. Then I examined my wounds and was absolutely surprised to find that I was not seriously injured.

A few minutes later a straggling Confederate, who loitered behind Mahone's line, which had passed me, took me in charge, stripped off my belt, and conducted me to the rear, a prisoner of war.

Lieutenants Alvan Lamson and Edward Sill shortly after their escape from the Confederate prisoner-of-war camp in Columbia, South Carolina, where Beecham was held. This photograph was taken shortly after Lamson and Sill arrived at the Union lines.

ELEVEN

"We're a sorry-looking set"

Prisoner of War Again
July 1864– March 1865

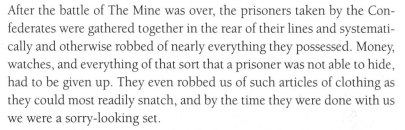

After the battle of The Mine was over, the prisoners taken by the Confederates were gathered together in the rear of their lines and systematically and otherwise robbed of nearly everything they possessed. Money, watches, and everything of that sort that a prisoner was not able to hide, had to be given up. They even robbed us of such articles of clothing as they could most readily snatch, and by the time they were done with us we were a sorry-looking set.

Many of the prisoners, especially the wounded, suffered for want of water, as no opportunity had been given us to procure a supply. Just after sunset an apparently kindhearted Confederate appeared among us and offered to fill our canteens. By this time I was in need of water myself, but having seen Confederate tricks played before that day, I had no confidence in his disinterested kindness, and told my comrades to hold on to their canteens, if they did not want to lose them. Some of my comrades resented this aspersion on the honesty of purpose of our Confederate friend, and called me a fool, and other pet names not necessary to repeat, and I said: "All right, gentlemen, you will probably have more sense yourselves when you've had more experience," and I doubt not they had, for they loaded the fellow up with canteens, which, for some reason or other, he failed to return.

Among our officers captured were several field and one general officer. This man, Gen. Bartlett, wore a wooden leg in place of one previously lost, and in the battle his wooden leg was broken, so that the general was unable to walk; the bearing of which will appear in the context.

We seemed to be within the jurisdiction of the Confederate Gen. A. P. Hill, for he was there in person both during the evening and the next morning, and it was noticeable that he was planning some scheme or arrangement in which he seemed greatly interested. About 8 o'clock a.m., Sunday, or the day after the battle—my recollection is that it was Sunday—this wonderful undertaking of Hill's materialized and proved to be for two objects; first, the diversion of the people of Petersburg; and, second, the humiliation of the Union officers who had fallen into his hands. The prisoners were therefore formed in column by fours consisting of alternate files of colored soldiers and commissioned officers, beginning with the highest in rank and continuing the formation as long as the supply of colored soldiers held out. As there were 500 colored prisoners and about 1,100 white officers and soldiers, the greater part of the column presented a fantastic and variegated appearance that, I am free to confess, was amusing. At the head, and as leader of this column, Gen. Bartlett was placed, on an old spavined horse, and the wonderful Sabbath-day's journey began.

We were marched through the principal streets of Petersburg, and so far as the humorous Hill's first object was concerned, affording a little innocent amusement to the good people of Petersburg, his arrangement was a success. In holiday attire the people sat in their windows and doors and on their wide verandas, or stood lined up along the streets, and with many jeers, flippant speeches and cutting remarks they watched our column pass by. O, yes, they were greatly amused, the people were.

As to Gen. Hill's second object, its effect was different from what people of the present day might imagine. I doubt if the white soldiers cared a straw about the matter, and the officers of the Fourth Division, who were accustomed to marching with Negro soldiers, could not be humiliated in that way, but it almost broke the hearts of very many of the officers of the white divisions, a majority of whom, I honestly believe, would have been glad to see the officers of the Fourth Division hanged or shot, if thereby they could have been relieved from the terrible humiliation of marching through Petersburg with Negro soldiers. This episode seemed to inspire a deep-seated hatred and prejudice in the hearts of the officers of the white divisions, against the officers of the colored divisions, and for a long time after many of them hardly treated us decently. Of course, they were not all built that way, but the highborn and aristocratic would often go out of their way to get a chance to call some officer of the Fourth Division a "nigger officer," with supreme contempt and lordly satisfaction. I doubt if A. P. Hill himself had any idea how completely his little joke worked as a humiliator among that class of Union officers, who knew for a certainty that God Almighty had taken extra pains to create them out of a superior clay.

After Hill had marched and countermarched us to his heart's content, until the dear people became weary of the show, we were placed upon a little island or towhead in the Appomattox River, separated from the mainland by a narrow channel, not to exceed a few feet in width. During the day many of the young bloods of Petersburg, who thus far had escaped military service, visited us, that is, they stood upon the mainland, the guards would not allow them to cross the channel, and were very ready to enter into conversation and argument with the prisoners on the status of the war, the constitutional rights of the South, and, especially the question of putting Negro soldiers into the field against them. One high-toned and haughty Southerner, of swarthy complexion, in particular, was loudmouthed and very emphatic in his denunciation of a system of "arming their slaves against them," and finally, when his talk had become wearisome, one of our boys remarked: "O, you need not put on such mighty airs. What, better than the Negro are you, anyway? If there is anything in color you are only a half-breed yourself." My, didn't that proud and haughty Southern bound? With an oath that he would shoot that Yankee _____, he grabbed the sentinel's gun and tried to wrench it from him, but the guard would not surrender it, and jerking it free from the grasp of the excited citizen of the Confederacy, the soldier said: "You git away from heah. You've no business heah quarlin' with these prisoners. If you'd been whar I was yesterday you wouldn't be 'round heah today fightin' with your mouth and tryin' to shoot some man who's got no gun. If you wanter do any shootin' you go out thar on the lines and they'll give you a gun and you'll find plenty of white men and niggahs, too, out thar with guns that'll give you all the shootin' you want." So he drove him, and all the other argumentative fellows away and during the remainder of the day and the following night we occupied our little island in quietness.

On the first day of August, 1864, we left Petersburg, and, taking passage in a fine train of box cars, journeyed southward. At Danville we halted for a few days' sojourn, where we were separated, the officers from the enlisted men, and the officers, a few days later, continued their journey by rail southward and were finally landed in Columbia, the capital of the great state of South Carolina, where we were assigned quarters in a beautiful three-story brick building, within the city limits, known as the Columbia jail, where we had the pleasure of residing for the next four months. Gen. Bartlett, Cols. Marshall and White, with two or three other field officers of lesser rank, were assigned quarters in the first story, while the balance of us (all line officers) were given the exclusive use of the second story.

In jail, as in the hospital and everywhere else in the line of service, I found renewed evidence of the advantages of a commissioned officer over a private soldier; also, the advantages of high rank, and presuming that this state of affairs exists all over the world, I advise all soldiers and other people everywhere, who contemplate going to jail, to first obtain an official position, and that of the very highest.

During the four months that we resided in Columbia jail, we did not live in very grand style, but no one starved or died of disease or exposure among us. The rations furnished were the same in quantity and quality furnished the enlisted men, but once a day hucksters were allowed to come to our door and sell us supplies of food in small quantities, which was of great assistance to us in eking out our daily allowance of provisions, besides, we were supplied with good, pure drinking water and were in a building that protected us from the heat and the rain.

All general exchange of prisoners of war had ceased nearly a year before, but although the United States and the Confederate States could not agree on a general exchange, where the interest and welfare of the enlisted man and the friendless line officer were at stake, they could readily agree on special exchanges, where the interest and welfare of general and field officers came in question. Therefore in about a month, Gen. Bartlett, Cols. Marshall and White and the other field officers with them were exchanged on a special agreement and returned to the United States, but we of the line remained in the Confederacy.

Where a man is under the pay of one government, and is being boarded and clothed by another, while at the same time his father-in-

law is providing for his wife, one might think that, as a business proposition, he had struck a snap. While that was the exact situation of many
of us, we did not seem to appreciate our good luck. I presume very few
men in this world know when they are well off.

Within a few days after we became settled in our comfortable quarters in Columbia, we organized a lyceum, or lice-see-em (I am not sure
of the correct orthography), which society every prisoner there, without
a single exception, joined, and every day we submitted a very important
question to a discussion of the committee of the whole—the most interested if not the most interesting of any society to which I ever had the
distinguished honor of belonging.

The gentlemen who had previously occupied our rooms did not
leave them in very attractive condition, but we soon put them in apple-
pie order, so to speak, by making them as clean and cozy as it was possible under the circumstances. There was, however, one discomfort
connected with our quarters that gave us much annoyance. The walls of
our jail rooms were built of brick, and at some previous time had been
smoothly plastered, but the former occupants of these beautiful apart-
ments had carelessly disfigured them by boring through the plastering
and drilling deep holes into the walls that it covered. Within the hol-
lows, crevices and dark recesses of these partition walls there resided a
whole generation—in fact many generations—of the genus Cimex
Lectularius, many of which were somewhat smaller, but were in shape
not unlike a sunfish, though they lived not in the sea. Well, to make a
long story short, these Cimex fellows would come out of their dens and
caves from within these old, mysterious haunts, through the doors that
had been opened in the walls, and in the early evening as soon as the
silent hours began and until the light of morning returned they made
night hideous with their wild pranks and war dances. Thus they continued to disturb and Lectularius until the Cimex became a burden, and
balmy sleep a stranger. How might we remedy this evil? Ah, the fraternal Confederate government, which guarded our every interest with kind
and watchful care, provided a remedy.

At that time the Confederate States were manufacturing a homespun soap that possessed wonderful cleansing and healing virtues. Probably no other soap in the wide world was equal to it, and I am fully
persuaded that if the Confederate government had put that soap on the
markets of the world then, the nations of the earth would have united as

one nation and declared and maintained the independence of the Confederate States of America; but not for wealth, glory or independence, even, would the Confederacy sacrifice honor. The comfort, health and happiness of her prisoners of war demanded her first consideration. Therefore she did not export any of this soap, but furnished us with a very liberal supply. We soon learned that when once this soap had hardened—which process required about six hours—there was no cement ever invented by man so absolutely impenetrable. Within a few days—just as soon as we could accumulate sufficient material—we had very puncture, crack and crevice in every wall of every cell in that dear old jail hermetically soaped, and thereafter the sweet-scented Cimex remained within their caverns, which we had thus transformed into tombs, and in the silent hours of night they did not Lectulari—us any more.

In connection with our jail there was a back yard, into which we were allowed to go once a day and there remain about an hour. Within this yard was a hydrant, and there we had the opportunity to wash our hands, faces and clothing, which was a great privilege that can only be fully appreciated by those who have been deprived of it. Just beyond this jail yard was located the subtreasury building of the Confederate States, where they manufactured Confederate paper money, worth at that time five cents on the dollar. It was a busy concern, and required many thousands of tons of paper to keep the Confederacy supplied with plenty of money.

Within this jail yard there was also a small outbuilding used to keep Union prisoners of war temporarily, who had escaped from other pens in the South and were being returned thereto. One day in the month of September, when we were admitted into the yard, I was agreeably surprised to meet an old comrade of Co. C, 2d Wis., who had been temporarily lodged therein. He informed me that he was captured at the Wilderness in May, had been confined in Andersonville, and had escaped therefrom about two weeks before. He told me of the prisoners belonging to the brigade, captured at Gettysburg, there was only one then living or alive at the time he escaped. I managed to find something in the shape of food for this comrade, which he ate with a relish—probably there is no other relish in the world equal to hunger, and this comrade looked mighty thin and in great need. He was still there under guard when I returned to my cell, but I never saw him again, and have never been able to learn whether he lived to return North, which is doubtful.

Sometime during the autumn the general officers' prison of the Confederacy, which had been located at Charleston, was removed to Columbia, and located across the Congaree River at a place designated by the prisoners there confined as "Camp Sorghum." Learning, or believing, that my old captain, Nat Rollins, who was captured at Gettysburg, was among those prisoners, I wrote him there, and after a time received a reply. On Dec. 12, a new camp having been established, we were turned out of our comfortable quarters in Columbia jail, while all the prisoners from Camp Sorghum were removed to our side of the river, and together occupied this new camp, but my old captain was not among them, as his time of service had expired, he had succeeded in getting out on a special exchange.

The material Confederate government, with an eye single to the health, comfort and longevity of her prisoners of war, had discovered that a constantly increasing danger of suffocation threatened the lives of all the Union officers confined in and around Columbia.

There were about 70 of us in the Columbia jail, which structure answered very well as a shelter during the summer and autumn, but for us to be shut in there, within those damp and chilly walls, though the dreary winter months was an awful risk that the Confederacy did not dare take.

The prisoners at Camp Sorghum were even in a more precarious situation. That camp had been located in the edge of a second growth, pine woods, as the illustration, drawn true to life by a soldier-artist, Capt. Robert J. Fisher, while imprisoned there, fully shows. There were thousands of square miles of such woods all over the South in those days, and especially was this true of South Carolina and Georgia. These sylvan shades, so conducive of health and comfort in warm weather, were all that could be desired in the balmy months of summer and autumn, but as the frosty nights and stormy days of winter approached, the inconsiderate prisoners cut down many trees on the hill sides, crafting the small logs thus obtained into rude dwellings which they covered with the branches and leaves, and mould from mother earth, filling the crevices between the logs with moss, which they cemented over with clay, thus making for themselves habitations which were as tombs for the living, and the precursors of tombs for the dead, which must certainly follow such lack or forethought and acts of rashness, if some plan was not immediately adopted to counteract these evils by the Confederate government. Besides, there were many trees left standing nearby which these careless prisoners might gather for fuel, and thus, overheating these shacks or tombs which they had so foolishly built for themselves, the mortality threatened was horrible to contemplate.

The Confederacy could never allow her prisoners of war to throw their lives away in that manner, much less to have the implication go abroad in the world that she had failed to guard her prisoners even against their own careless deeds; therefore, she gathered us even as a henhawk gathereth her chickens, all into one camp, where we might breathe the pure South Carolina winter air, free from all contaminating surroundings.

So, on Dec. 12, 1864, in the dead of winter, the doors of our dear old jail were thrown open and we marched forth to return no more. In the outskirts of Columbia, probably two miles from the jail, as the distance seemed to me, stood the insane asylum, to which we wended our way and through the gates were ushered into—not the insane asylum proper, for that institution was already full, while thousands of insane native South Carolinians were running at large; in truth, South Carolina was, and had been, from the days of nullification under the leadership of John C. Calhoun, one vast insane asylum—but we were ushered into the grounds thereof, which were inclosed by a solid and substantial brick wall about eight feet high. In one end of the parallelogram formed by this brick wall was situated the asylum buildings. Across the inclosed grounds from wall to wall, a wall or fence had been built of boards of the same height of the brick wall, separating the asylum buildings from the previously unoccupied ground, thus forming a square pen or yard containing probably three or four acres of land. Within this inclosure we found the prisoners from "Camp Sorghum," who had reached the ground before us, and some old tents, in the neighborhood of 60 in number, had been pitched in a promiscuous cluster in the center of the inclosure, and were all occupied. As there were somewhere from 1,000 to 1,200 of the "Camp Sorghum" prisoners, they were crowded into these tents like sardines in a box, so that there was a very poor chance for us jailbirds, who brought with us no sign of tent or covering, to obtain shelter.

Besides the tents, the Confederate authorities began the erection of barracks for the shelter of the prisoners, and the framework for a number of such barracks was constructed, only one or two of which were ever finished. For from one to two weeks after our arrival in this camp many of the jailbirds found it impossible to obtain shelter of any description, but after the completion of the first barrack, all managed to get under some kind of cover. There was one building inside of our camp that was used for a hospital, and we had a Confederate doctor of some kind in charge of it. I was never inside the hospital building. While in Columbia jail I was sick for a time, as well as wounded, but we had no medical attention of any kind there. While in "Asylum Camp" I was so fortunate as not to need hospital or medical aid.

In "Asylum Camp" we had the benefit of a sutler establishment within our walls, and any man who had money could obtain plenty of food. There was no lack of provisions in South Carolina in the winter of 1864–'5. With us there was a great lack of money. I was so fortunate as to have a comrade, Lieut. M. B. Case, who had taken the precaution to sew within the lining of his clothes a goodly number of greenbacks. He also secreted and saved his watch when captured, which later he sold for Confederate scrip. This comrade loaned me money, and during our stay in "Asylum Camp" we managed to buy about double the amount of provisions furnished us by the Confederacy, with all of which we managed to get two very moderate meals a day.

Our water supply came from the asylum, and was conducted through the partition wall by a wooden spout running into four wooden troughs, two of which we used for drinking and the others for washing purposes. The water was pure, and we always had an abundance of it.

One pleasant feature of this camp was "Chandler's String Band," consisting of four pieces—three stringed instruments and one flute. These boys gave us, free of all charge, some of the best, if not the very best, music that ever enlivened the ears of the weary. "Sherman's March to the Sea" was written by a comrade while we were in that prison. I made a copy of the song at the time on Confederate homespun paper, which was the best we could obtain there. The paper is dated "Asylum Prison, Columbia, South Carolina, Jan. 15, 1865," and I still retain the copy.

One member of the band set the song to music, and it was sung by him for the first time in that prison. The fame of this band was noised abroad in Columbia, especially "Sherman's March to the Sea," and several times a number of ladies came and stood upon a platform on the prison wall and listened to the music of the band and the singing of that song. Thus were these ladies as nearly within a Southern prison pen as I ever saw a lady, except at the jail in Columbia, where one huckster lady came almost every day to our jail door and under the eye and by the permission of the guard, sold us the bread of mortal life. This lady, though old, wrinkled and poorly clad, was one of the most beautiful women that I ever saw, for "handsome is that handsome does." These other ladies who stood upon the platform and listened to the music and the singing, were younger and more fashionably attired, but there was nothing especially attractive about their appearance.

Another pleasant feature of the asylum prison was the fact that the prisoners from Camp Sorghum, who were greatly in the majority, all treated the officers of the Fourth Division of the Ninth Corps as equals and as comrades. While in the jail we were made to feel somewhat lonesome, there being only about a dozen of us, but after we removed to the asylum prison we were with the majority, or rather the majority were with us, and our brother officers of the white divisions of the Ninth Corps, soon learning that conditions had changed, dropped their old arrogant and contemptuous ways toward us, and from that time on, while we remained in captivity, the term "nigger officer" was applied to us no more and disappeared from the prison vocabulary.

Delivering the mail occasioned more keen excitement than any other event within the asylum prison. There being more than a thousand of us, all of whom had friends in God's country who wrote us many letters, some of which we received, our mail at times was large, and required not a little time to deliver. This was accomplished by the adjutant of the prison reading the names of the recipients from the veranda of the prison hospital, around which hundreds of prisoners congregated anxious, as we all were, to get word from home. When a man's name was read he shouted "Here," and the letter was passed from hand to hand until it reached him. Our letters came unsealed, so that the Confederate authorities could examine them, and they were the brightest oasis of our desert of captivity.

We remained in asylum prison about two months, or until the evening of Feb. 14, 1865, during which time nearly if not quite all the Union officers imprisoned in the South were confined in this camp, but notwithstanding this fact, and the further fact that there were about 1,200 of us, there was not one general, only one colonel and but two or three field officers of lesser rank among us; all the others being line officers. These facts show the value of rank to the individual possessing it. For more than a year no general exchange of prisoners had been possible, but during all that time it had been possible to exchange generals who were prisoners.

On Feb. 4, 1865, Gen. John Winder visited us at the asylum prison. Gen. Winder was the man who established the stockade for enlisted men who were prisoners, at Andersonville, Ga., and who boasted of his purpose to make of that stockade the horrible charnel field for Yankee prisoners that it soon afterward became. At that time the old sinner—I am sure his dearest friends will not claim that he was a saint—was the general supervisor or commander of all the prisons and prisoners of war throughout the South. He inspected thoroughly every part of our camp, and I had the opportunity of getting a full and fair view of the man who was more directly identified with and responsible for the murder by starvation and exposure of thousands of Union prisoners of war than any other man, then living or dead, with the possible exception of Jeff. Davis. He must have been between 70 and 80 years of age. His hair was as white as snow and his face was like unto a mask of ice, reflecting the sympathetic throbbings of his heart; and from that face his cold gray eyes gleamed like musket balls imbedded in a tombstone. He seemed to retain his cold-blooded desire and determination to kill and destroy in his suave and gentle way every Union prisoner who came within his power, to the last hour—perhaps to the last moment of his life. The last order ever issued by the direction and at the command of Winder was issued on the afternoon of this day of his visit to our prison, and is as follows, viz:

Feb. 4, 1865.

Prisoners of War will take notice,

I am directed by Gen. Winder, commanding prisoners of war, that in case any more tunneling takes place in this prison he will remove all of the barracks and tents; so that it will be the fault of the prisoners themselves if they have no covering from the weather. They will furthermore take notice, that if any injury is done to any prisoner suspected of giving information, I shall use force for force and the guilty party will be punished.

[Signed] A. GRISWOLD,
Major, Commanding Prison.

Maj. Griswold commanded the asylum prison, and so far as I could learn he never of his own free will did an act to make the conditions surrounding us more intolerable and severe. He issued this order, as it shows on its face, by the direction and at the command of Winder. I copied into my diary at the time the order, just as it was written, word for word, and I still preserve it as a memento mori.

From asylum prison Winder went home, and that night God Almighty issued an order to him which he obeyed, and we prisoners rejoiced that God had called him hence before he had fully completed his great earthly work, that he had so carefully planned.

It was St. Valentine's Day in the year of our Lord 1865, and a day long to be remembered. For two months and two days, during the most invigorating portion of a South Carolina winter, we had enjoyed to its fullest extent the glorious sport of hunting South Carolina game, within our brick-walled retreat, in the suburbs of South Carolina's capital city. Ah! Such rare sport it was, such superb hunting! There were "millions in it"—i.e., of game in our camp. The comrade who joined not in the chase every day in the week, Sunday not excepted, possessed not the spirit of a true sportsman and was liable to possess no blood in his veins ere he was aware, for the game was bloodthirsty.

Within this quiet retreat we had dwelt for two long months, substantially carefree. We were all on the payroll of the United States of America, while the Confederate States of America had assumed all responsibility of providing our boarding house accommodations, all our necessary wearing apparel, which in that genial clime was not necessarily burdensome or abundant, and also for our medical treatment in case of sickness or accidents in the chase. Even the walls that enframed our cozy retreat were ornamented with picturesque watchtowers, equidistant from one another, and not far apart, throughout their whole extent. In each and every one of these watchtowers could be seen, at all hours of the day, and they were there also at all hours of the night, a faithful guardian of the camp, dressed in the gay and attractive uniform of a Confederate soldier, whose duty it was to watch over and protect us at all hazards—to cover us with their muskets from the inclemency of the weather, particularly from the night air, and from every other danger, both seen and unseen. Here we had enjoyed one continuous round of pleasure.

I have in my possession, and preserve with care, a beautiful and perfect illustration of that "happy hunting ground," sketched during leisure hours by the skilful hand of an artist comrade of those halcyon days of the long ago, to which I frequently turn, as a solace in the trying hours of adversity. Doubtless many an old comrade of that joyful winter, through the gathering clouds of neglect, poverty and ingratitude which hath o'erwhelmed him in the dear land whose battles he fought and whose flag he maintained, hath seen again and yet again, in his mind's eye, that cheerful and well-watered oasis as he hath journeyed in sorrow across the cheerless Sahara of his declining years.

But earthly joys may not last forever, and it was decreed that all our innocent amusement should suddenly be brought to an end; that we should shake from off our feet the sun-kissed soil of South Carolina and depart far hence to return no more forever.

During the days of our sojourn in this delightful retreat Sherman and his dashing raiders had reached Savannah and on the 1st day of February, 1865, they began their march northward through the Carolinas, which closed with Johnston's surrender on April 26, at Durham's Station, in North Carolina. During Sherman's march seaward and later, when he was marching landward, the newsboys of Columbia found ready sale for their papers outside of our camp, and it was seldom that the supply held out sufficiently that even one paper reached us, but sometimes, by a stray paper and sometimes by other means, we caught on to the condition of affairs and managed to keep pretty accurately posted as to Sherman's whereabouts and what he was doing.

For several days the Confederates had manifested a spirit of restlessness that plainly told we were approaching a crisis or that a crisis in the shape of Sherman's army was approaching Columbia. Then came St. Valentine's Day, and outside of our camp there was an unusual uneasiness. All the forepart of the day we were on the qui vive, and when the boom of distant cannon fell upon our ears we knew for certainty that Sherman was not far away. Then we were mustered in hot haste on the beautiful stockade campus and a train was hastily provided to bear us away to the northward. Gladly we would have remained to extend a welcome to Sherman and his brave boys, but that was strictly against orders. However, quite a number of our boys did remain, and joined Sherman on the 17th, when he entered Columbia. Gen. Winder's last order did not have the effect that it might have had, but for God's counter order, and from the 4th to the 14th of February, tunneling went on in asylum prison just the same and when Sherman's guns were heard many of our boys took the chances of stowing themselves away within the tunnels until Sherman's arrival. One of my comrades of the 23d U.S.C.T., who was in the hospital, escaped with others by secreting himself in the hospital garret. When Sherman took possession they came forth from their hiding and had things pretty nearly their own way in Columbia for a while. My comrade claimed that he had the satisfaction of applying the torch to the old jail where we had passed four months in captivity. As for myself and the great majority of us, when the gates of the asylum prison were thrown open, we, who had marched therein on Dec. 12, 1864, marched out again—the last time that we were to pass those gates—on that, to us, long-to-be-remembered St. Valentine's Day, A.D. 1865.

We traveled by rail from Columbia, S.C., to Charlotte, N.C., arriving at the latter place about noon on Feb. 15, 1865. As we rode all night, of course we took the sleeper, but as the sleeper was not first class, and as the railroad itself was somewhat out of condition, we were not thereby afforded a "heap" of rest. The train was also minus a dining car, and as it did not stop "20 minutes for breakfast" at any of the convenient towns along the route, we were somewhat weary and just a little hungry when we reached our destination, where we alighted in the outskirts of the city and were driven to our hotel, situated in a beautiful grove of scrub pines, made yet more lovely from the fact that "the beautiful snow" was quietly falling in quantities sufficient to give the evergreen foliage a variegated hue.

Once within the hotel, we proceeded to light the fires in the roomy kitchen with pine boughs gathered from the surrounding grove, for the purpose of preparing our dinner (which, by the way, did not materialize as one of our square meals). We were given the freedom of the grove, but not of the city, for the police had been instructed to allow no one to pass beyond that interesting limit called the "dead line." However, as we gathered fuel in the outermost parts, screened by the interlacing branches and blinding snow, many eluded the vigilant eyes of the police and passed into the outer woods, forgetting to return. Thus it happened that I found myself, in company with four comrades—Hill, Afflick, Stauber and Cramer—entitled to the freedom of the state of North Carolina, so long as we were able to subsist and keep out of sight.

Quickly we proceeded to widen the distance between ourselves and our kitchen fires, and right here, before I forget it, I wish to inform the reader that we ate no square meal that day. As the afternoon waned the snowfall turned into rain and after making rapid tracks northward as long as we could see, and until too exhausted to proceed further, we crept into a friendly thicket and slept the sleep of the most wretchedly weary,

> With forest leaves for a bed
> And dripping pine boughs overhead.

When the light of another day dawned we resumed our journey and within an hour fell in with a young Negro, who provided us with a cold lunch of hoecake, which we enjoyed greatly; but this was not one of our square meals.

The sky had now become clear, and it was pretty cold, so we took to the woods again, traveling until our clothes were dry and we were warm enough to rest comfortably, when we sought a quiet nook and slept and rested until dark. That night we tramped along the public road until nearly morning in a northwesterly direction, designing to reach eastern Tennessee in time, if we were not caught and good luck attended us. Our road finally led us to a village on the Catawba River, which we wanted to cross, but the dogs in the village were so thick and demonstrative that we turned back before reaching the bridge and once more took to the woods, going southward and leaving the village to our right.

When it became light we discovered a Negro of large and almost gigantic proportions clearing brush not far from his cabin. Attracting his attention, we motioned him to come to us, which he did, after arming himself with a stout club as a precautionary measure. When we had explained that were "Linkum sojers," just out of jail and nearly starved, he told us to keep in the woods until night, when he would put us across.

In the meantime he brought us a fair supply of hoecake and bacon, but not then did we indulge in a square meal. We ate sparingly and rested and slept until dark, when our guide came, and conducting us to a point on the river about a mile distant, he ferried us across in a dugout and directed us on our journey. Oh, those North Carolina Negroes were among the whitest of men to be found in Dixie by an escaped Union soldier in those days.

There were patches of snow on the ground here and there and the nights were bitter cold. As we had no blankets, we found it necessary to travel by night and rest by day, and every day when the sun shone the warmest we found some secure nook in the woods, where we devoted an hour or so to hunting the most numerous of all game to be found in Dixie's land. In these hunting excursions we were invariably successful, but, alas, the game we captured was too small and insignificant to supply our over-empty larder, and we ate no square meals in the woods of North Carolina. In fact, we found it so difficult to obtain food that we concluded to divide our party, as two or three could subsist where five could not; therefore, Afflick and Stauber left us, and we never saw or heard from them again. Hill, Cramer and myself made up the other party, but still the food supply was insufficient for our needs.

On one occasion when we were desperately hungry, we came upon a cabin in a lonely place in the woods, which we boldly approached. We were met at the door by four frightened women—an old lady and her three daughters—all alone, the male members of the family being in Lee's Army, as they later informed us. When we told them we were escaped Yankee prisoners of war how their eyes bulged, but on learning that we were peaceably inclined and very hungry, they skirmished around and dished up the best the house could afford for our dinners. They appeared to be "poor whites"—at all events they were white and so poor that the wonder was how they managed to live. I presume they had not eaten a square meal for months, and of course could not furnish such a luxury for us, but they pounded some corn in a mortar and prepared the everlasting hoecake, besides killing a poor, scrawny chicken, of which they had only a few, for our especial benefit, and our dinner was not bad to take. These women actually robbed themselves, and could not have entertained us more generously had we been their own brothers returned from the war. The girls also parched a quantity of corn for us to take in our pockets for future use and bade us Godspeed on our journey.

We had been about a week enjoying this winter outing in the woods of North Carolina when, one afternoon, we ran across an old farmer who took us for furloughed soldiers from Lee's army. He had in his possession a newspaper, from which we learned that an exchange of prisoners of war had been agreed upon and that our comrades whom we left at Charlotte had been sent on to Wilmington for that purpose. After parting with our informant, we concluded to find a safe place where we might surrender, as the speediest and certainly the most comfortable way of reaching the North. Following out this plan, we soon found ourselves in charge of a small party of old gentlemen with shotguns, who conducted us to the house of a well-to-do farmer whom they called Squire Strope, near the public road, requesting him to keep us overnight and on the following morning to take us to the railroad station, some five or six miles away, and deliver us to the provost marshal.

At first the old farmer seemed to object, saying that he had no gun in his house, and that there were three of us against one, as he was alone, except the old woman; but when informed that we were really peaceable Yanks and that he needed no gun, but a goodly supply of eatables instead, he accepted the charge. The Squire soon learned from us where we came from and how we had been faring for the past week. Then he called the good wife and after this manner introduced us; "Mother, here are three hungry Yanks; they don't appear to have horns, but I reckon they've got hungry stomachs. Get them a good square meal."

An hour later we sat down to supper—regular wheat-flour biscuits and plenty of them, with cow butter and homespun North Carolina molasses. What a feast we had! Would we ever get enough? Would the supply hold out? I do not remember what we had to drink, but drinks didn't count.

After supper we talked and argued with our host until a late hour, without coming to an agreement, except that the country needed peace, and then we retired to a shakedown, having advised our host that such an arrangement would be better for them and plenty good enough for us, for the very good reason that about our persons might possibly be lingering some uncanny specimen of the genus Grabax.

The next morning we partook of our other square meal for breakfast, which was about equal in size and finish to the supper, after which Squire Strope hitched up his team and gave us a free ride to the railroad station, which was the western terminus of that road, and from which point we were returned to Charlotte. As I bid adieu to the kindhearted old Squire and gave his hand a parting shake, the old man said; "When you-ns get back No'th, please send me a par of Yankee wool-kyards, as we don't get any in No'th Carolina no more."

I replied: "My dear old secesh friend, before 60 days have passed Lee will have surrendered, the war will be over, the Southern Confederacy will be extinct, and you will find Yankee wool-cards at every country store in North Carolina; if not, I'll not forget to send you a pair. Goodby." I never sent the cards.

From the little station among the North Carolina hills, back to Charlotte the train bore us, arriving there about noon on Feb. 22, 1865, but none of our fellow prisoners, with whom we had parted so hastily a week before, were there to meet us. They had been sent forward toward Wilmington to be exchanged. The only comrades we met in Charlotte were those who, like ourselves, had escaped and had been recaptured, of which there were of us about 30 all told, who had been brought in from one quarter or another. After waiting an hour or two—perhaps more—we were put on another train and started in pursuit of our comrades. Although our final destination was Wilmington, which city is about 200 miles east and 70 miles south of Charlotte, the route we were to travel was northeastward through Salisbury to Raleigh, thence southeastward to Goldsboro, and thence due south to Wilmington. Therefore, our first point was Salisbury, which place is situated probably 40 or 50 miles a little east of north from Charlotte.

Salisbury contained within, or near it, one of the notorious Southern prison pens of those days, where the captured soldiers of the Union armies were imprisoned, and in point of unutterable horror was exceeded only by Andersonville, in the state of Georgia. As an effective deathtrap for Union soldiers there confined during the fall and winter of 1864-5, I will have a word to say later.

In those days the Southern railroads were very much out of repair and the trains made poor time; the wonder was that they managed to run at all. We left Charlotte not later than 3 o'clock p.m., but it was well along in the night when we reached Salisbury.

We were in charge of a squad of Confederate soldiers commanded by a sergeant, and as he was getting us in line on the depot platform, after we had alighted from the train, who should pass but Lieut. Jones, carrying a lantern, which lighted up the platform and enabled us to recognize the lieutenant at a glance. Jones was Maj. Griswold's adjutant, and had charge of Camp Asylum at Columbia during our sojourn therein, and was always on friendly and even familiar terms with the prisoners. He was a long-haired, rollicking, harum-scarum Southern boy, about 19 or 20 years old, but was never known to do an unkind act to a prisoner, though he often talked pretty wild and extravagant.

When we left Columbia on St. Valentine's Day, Jones came along with us to Charlotte, and on the trip mingled freely with our boys, and many times assured us that there was a general exchange of prisoners agreed upon by the two governments, which would be carried into effect in a short time. We had, however, but little confidence in Jones's knowledge or truthfulness on the exchange question. On that very trip one of our boys attempted to escape by jumping from the train, when he was shot in the leg by a guard and, of course, recaptured. At that time Jones had said: "What's the use of you Yanks being such crazy fools? Heah, you're all going to be exchanged within 30 days without taking any risks, and still you can't wait, but must keep on trying to escape. Don't another one of you make a break like that; if you do you'll get shot, and I can't help it, and it will serve you right if you do."

Jones was never known to trump up an excuse to injure a prisoner, but always preferred an excuse not to harm him. He was always agreeable and condescending, but especially so after indulging a little freely in Paddy's eyewater, which he sometimes did, and on this occasion that was his exact condition. At all events, he proved himself remarkably humane and considerate; in fact, he surpassed all our expectations.

When the rays from Jones's lantern revealed his face to us I called out: "Hello, there, Adjutant Jones! Where are you heading for with that lantern?" Immediately on hearing his name called, Jones stopped, and discovering his old prisoners, came forward, and shaking hands all around, greeted us in language about as follows: "Hello, you crazy Yanks; back again are you? A nice time you all had, I allow, out in the woods, freezing and starving like a pack of fools, which you are, when you might have been in camp, where you were sure of the best fare I could get for you. Why didn't you have a little sense and hear the advice I gave you? I told you that within 30 days you'd all be out of this, and you see now for yourselves that you'll be out in half that time; but you knew too much yourselves to take good advice, and you got just what you deserved. I've a good mind to let them put you into that old prison pen tonight, and there's just where they would put you if I'd let them, but I reckon you've been punished enough for one offense." Then, turning to the officer in charge, he said: "Sergeant, these are all my old boys from Columbia, and I'll be responsible for them; so you just come with them to the provost marshal's office and I'll see the provost marshal myself."

Then we followed Lieut. Jones and his lantern to said office, which was near, and from which Jones returned in less than a minute and, dismissing the guard, said to us in his most happy and assuring manner: "Now, gentlemen, you may consider yourselves paroled. Come along with me."

Jones was great on pet names, but this was the first time he ever called us gentlemen, but we didn't care for that. With his lantern he lighted our way to his tent, which was not far away, and on arriving there he skirmished around and secured tents enough to shelter us, besides rations of cornbread and a pail full of blackberry juice. We soon had the tents up and, after disposing of our rations, retired for the night.

The next morning Jones found something for our breakfast, and about noon, when the train for Raleigh came along, he put us aboard thereof without a guard, on the honor of our parole, as he administered it the night before, and sent us on our way rejoicing. Jones himself remained in Salisbury, and there we bade him a last good-by.

The train that we boarded at Salisbury was composed of flat and box cars, loaded with a mixture of all kinds of freight. My two comrades, Hill and Cramer, and myself kept near one another and boarded the same flat, whereon was, among other things too numerous to mention, a hogshead or two of unrectified Southern plantation sugar. My comrade, Cramer, was a good forager, if he had half a chance. When we were in the woods of North Carolina, trying to make our escape some of our party considered him of little account and when Afflick and Stauber left us they barred Cramer out of their party. Cramer was only a boy 18 or 19 years old, and when he learned that the two comrades named did not want his company he thought we were all about to desert him, but I said, "You can stay with Hill and me, and we'll stick by you," and the boy paid us for it fourfold.

We had hardly stepped foot on the flat when Cramer discovered the sugar, and coming back to me, he said: "Give me your haversack, quick; I know where I can get some sugar." The boy had no haversack of his own, but I was more fortunate, and gave him mine without asking any questions. Within five minutes after, Cramer returned the haversack well filled with sugar. A moment later I noticed a Confederate guard over the hogsheads, but we had drawn our rations of sugar for that whole trip.

I have ridden many times, both before and since, on a freight and accommodation train, but invariably such trains were long on freight and short on accommodation. This was the only train of the kind, so far as my experience goes, where the accommodation was of the first order and superior to the freight. This, however, did not apply to all the passengers and the fact that it applied to our little party of three was all owing to the ability of the kid Cramer as a forager.

Our journey from Salisbury to Goldsboro was long and tedious. The distance is not so great—somewhere from 100 to 150 miles, but we did not reach Goldsboro until the evening of the 27th day of February, during which time no rations of any description were furnished us and we lived on what we could get, so that the haversack of sugar proved a godsend to us.

The first day out from Salisbury, Feb. 23, our train broke down before night, near a little station called High Point, and after waiting until dusk for it to move on again, we three, who had sugar to spare, started out to find a restaurant and lodging house. In my experience with Negro soldiers I had learned that sugar was an article of priceless value among the colored race, and we all knew that with or without sugar our best as well as our most numerous friends in North Carolina were Negroes, so we hunted up a Negro cabin.

When I asked the old auntie who met us at the cabin door if they could furnish three Lincum soldiers with supper, breakfast and lodging and take pay in sugar, she replied: "De Lo'd bless you, honey, is you-all Lincum soldiers? Come right in and I'll get you some supper." So we received the best the house afforded—corn dodgers and bacon for supper, a chance to sleep on a shakedown on the cabin floor, and bacon and corn dodgers for breakfast—which was far ahead of sleeping under the stars, supperless.

We left the cabin at an early hour the next morning, paying for our accommodations with three teacupfuls of sugar, which was considered ample payment by our hostess, and thereafter, although a haversack of sugar was a large and cumbersome purse to carry, we found that the purse contained a legal tender anywhere among the colored people. We lived on the fat of the land during the whole trip and had sugar left when we reached Goldsboro.

When we returned to the point on the railroad where we left our train the night before, lo and behold, the train was gone. Then we took a tie-pass and rode over the same road more rapidly than our train moved, for in about two hours we came up with it and climbed onto our flat again. O, the accommodation part of that train was perfect. Thus by slow stages we advanced toward our freedom, riding upon our train when we were not in search of food. We reached Greensboro that evening and again found hotel accommodations with our colored friends, for which we drew our usual check.

The next morning our old commander, Maj. Griswold, put in an appearance among us, having established headquarters at Greensboro, where our fellow prisoners whom we had left at Charlotte had assembled before us and had been regularly paroled by the major. Here we recaptured prisoners were also regularly paroled, and from this point we all traveled together toward the sea. Here another train was made up from which the freight was eliminated and which carried our whole party of paroled prisoners. We left Greensboro in the afternoon and passed through Raleigh about noon the next day. We made no stop in North Carolina's capital city, but rode right through, without feeding, toward Goldsboro. The road from Raleigh to Goldsboro seemed to be in a somewhat better state of repair, but there were many delays and breakdowns, thus affording the opportunity to gather supplies. We finally reached Goldsboro on the evening of Feb. 27, 1865.

After our recapture, and while we were waiting at the little station among the hills of North Carolina for a train to carry us back to Charleston, I fell in with a Confederate lieutenant who entered freely into conversation and gave me some information not written down in their archives by Southern historians.

This lieutenant was a middle-aged man, probably between 45 to 50 years old. He had been, as he informed me, on duty at Salisbury, in connection with the prison guards, ever since the stockade was established there. He also stated that the prisoners had all been paroled and the stockade was then vacant and, therefore, he was on his way home—which was nearby—on a short leave of absence.

The statement which this Confederate lieutenant made in this confidential conversation regarding the Salisbury stockade was as follows: "I reckon, sah, you officers received better treatment in Columbia than those poor fellows at Salisbury got, at least I hope you did. My God! sah. Salisbury was a horrible place; it was just awful, and no mistake.

"I would not believe that men could be treated so inhumanly if I had not seen it myself, day after day and month after month, until the horrors of that stockade will haunt me to the day of my death. When the wah broke out, sah, I believed, as all Southerners did, that we were in the right, and that God would be on our side, but God Almighty never stood by such awful, brutal inhumanity as I have seen practiced at Salisbury, and He never will. No, sah, the Confederacy will never be established. A government cannot be built up by wholesale murder, and all winter long wholesale murder has been carried on at Salisbury by the Confederate government. Those poor fellows have perished by thousands from cold and starvation, when we all know that No'th Carolina is half covered with woods and that there is abundance of food in the country to feed them. Now, the government has paroled the prisoners and sent thousands of them on foot to Goldsboro to starve and die along the road for the authorities all know that more than half of them were nearly dead before they started, and cannot tramp half way to Goldsboro to save their lives. They expect half of them to die, in fact they want them to die, and have planned that march for that purpose."

Later, I had ample opportunity to verify the Confederate lieutenant's statements.

Thank God and Adj't Jones, I was never inside the Salisbury stockade, but while enjoying the hospitality of Adj't Jones at Salisbury, I inquired of him as to the disposition of the prisoners confined there. Jones told me that they had all been paroled, and that while the sick had been sent forward by rail to be exchanged, the well, who were found on examination to be sufficiently strong and robust to make the march, had, on account of a shortage of transportation, started for Goldsboro on foot a day or two before.

From Salisbury to Greensboro the distance is about 50 miles, and be it remembered that on the same day that Adj't Jones gave me the above information, we started on our journey by rail to Goldsboro by way of Greensboro.

It seems that these Salisbury prisoners who were to make the march to Goldsboro on foot followed the railroad, of which fact I was not aware until we began to overtake them, and as truly as there is a God in Heaven we began to overtake them within an hour after leaving Salisbury. I verily believe we had not proceeded five miles on our journey before we came up with the first lot. As we proceeded their numbers increased, and all that afternoon and all the next day, until we reached Greensboro, we found them and passed them by scores and by hundreds, completely tired out, disabled, exhausted, fallen here and there by the wayside, in the fence corners, under the trees, in every sheltered nook, dying and dead!

I pray God I may never travel such a ghastly road again. These men were but as walking skeletons when they started out on that journey of a hundred miles or more to Goldsboro, without food or shelter on the way, and there could be but one result—they died by hundreds if not by thousands along that horrid road. As the Confederate lieutenant had said, "The Confederate authorities wanted them to die, and planned the march to accomplish that purpose."

We who were better clothed and had been better fed might have endured such a march ourselves, but to our starving and dying comrades we could offer no assistance. We passed the most pitiful sight that mortal eyes ever beheld, in silence. What could we do? How could a man even speak to a comrade under such awful conditions? What word of hope, comfort, or encouragement might one utter to starving and dying men on every hand for miles and miles along that dreary, ghastly track?

These boys left the stockade at Salisbury with bright hopes of home and the future, believing that they were able to march as of old. How cruel the disappointment, how inhuman the method. All along that awful road, upon the faces of the thousands that we passed there were two sentiments plainly depicted, the one or the other on every face—hope and despair. Hope beamed from the eyes and brightened the features of every face of every man as long as he was able to tramp that weary road toward home and freedom. Despair was as plainly stamped upon the face of every comrade who fell by the wayside, for the moment that his strength failed he knew for a certainty that the bitter end of his bitter captivity was near. No man asked assistance of a comrade, for all knew that no one could assist even a brother; so, when a man's strength failed, he crawled into the nearest nook and died without a murmur.

No horrible tale of olden time when all mankind were savage, that I ever read, could equal the awful reality of that road from Salisbury to Greensboro in February, 1865. From Greensboro to Goldsboro we were ahead of the marching column and saw no more of those ghastly sights which, during all the years that have followed, I have never been able to exclude from memory and from my vision.

Along this same road, about six weeks later, Jefferson Davis, with his cabinet, staff, and escort, fled southward from Danville, Va., after learning of the surrender of Lee's army, seeking safety and finding none. His bloody and inhuman policy, which had made this road the highway of horrors that no pen can picture, in the last days of February when I passed over it, failed utterly to establish the despotism of slavery, which was the dream of his cruel and crafty ambition.

On the night of April 9 Davis and his party reached the same old North Carolina town of Greensboro, where we were paroled on Feb. 25, in their official car, where they remained for nearly a week. On the evening of April 15, Davis and his cabinet held their last council of war with Gens. Joe Johnston and Beauregard. More properly speaking it was a council of surrender rather than a council of war, and Davis himself dictated the letter written on that occasion by Johnston to Sherman, which finally resulted in the surrender of Johnston's army. On April 16 the Davis party left Greensboro—not by rail in their official car, as they came, but in a train of wagons and ambulances, with a mounted escort. They passed through High Point, Salisbury, and Charlotte, so familiar to my memory in connection with this horrid road of death, and thence southward until captured by United States cavalry.

A well-known magazine in January, 1901, the first issue of the twentieth century—published a long account of this last effort of the Davis party to escape justice, written by Stephen R. Malory, Davis's secretary of the navy, while imprisoned in Fort Lafayette after his capture. Malory tells of the many hardships they endured and the terrible privations they suffered along that same road where starved Union soldiers while prisoners of war died like flies, and this magazine is ready and anxious to publish every scrap of writing, from all such sources, in the interest of history; but where is the magazine published in the United States of America in this twentieth century that could be hired to publish this sketch that I have given of that tale of unutterable horror that I witnessed along that same road?

They might lose a Southern subscriber, you know, and really the interest of history does not demand the publication of the truth concerning the suffering and wrongs endured by only common soldiers in the "last days of the Confederacy" to make the triumph of the flag and the Union cause possible.

We foraged around Goldsboro for about 20 hours and there we paid out our last ounce of sugar and our purse was empty, but it had served a noble purpose.

On the afternoon of Feb. 28, 1865, the Confederate government issued rations for the last time to our party of paroled Union officers, which by the way, was the first and only time that rations were issued to us after Adj't. Jones served us so kindly at Salisbury on the 21st, seven days before. Then, just before dark of the same day, we were directed to take the train for Wilmington, which proved to be our last journey in the Confederate States of America.

Wilmington, our destination, is situated on the Cape Fear River, about 20 miles from the sea, and about 75 miles due south from Goldsboro, but our train, which was really more aristocratic than any other upon which I had ridden during my happy sojourn in the land of cotton, made fast time, comparatively, for those days and conditions, and we reached a point not far from the "neutral ground" just at daylight, where we waited until 9 o'clock a.m. for the arrival of Col. Hatch, the Confederate commissioner of exchange.

This "neutral ground" was a strip of country lying between the lines of the two armies and occupied by neither, which was situated, in this instance, about 10 miles from Wilmington. When Col. Hatch arrived with his train, consisting of an engine and one coach, carrying a flag of truce, he led the way—our train following—within this "neutral ground" where our train halted, having reached the end of its journey, when we alighted and about 10 o'clock a.m., March 1, 1865, passed through our lines of cavalry, who received us at "present arms," and after seven weary months of captivity, I stood again beneath the Old Flag, though still on the soil of North Carolina.

Many were the demonstrations of joy by our comrades when we found ourselves once more beneath the protecting folds of Old Glory. Methinks there are many millions of American citizens in this year of our Lord, 1902, who could better appreciate the beauty, the grandeur, and protecting power of the American flag if they could be transported beyond the pale of its influence and enjoy the protection of some tyrannical rag for about six months. They might thereby learn that the thousands who gave their lives and their health to maintain the supremacy of that flag, had done them a personal service, for which they could at least feel thankful.

From this "neutral ground" we made our way to Wilmington on foot, and the next day at 11 o'clock we boarded the steamer that was to carry us back to God's country. That afternoon we ran down the Cape Fear River, and anchored in sight of Fort Fisher, over which the stars and stripes were flying. There our steamer remained until about noon of the following day, when she weighed anchor, passing over the bar and out to sea. The old Atlantic was not so very rough, but far as the eye could reach the rolling swells followed each other shoreward. Within 15 minutes after our steamer struck these dead swells that came leisurely and lazily rolling in to meet us, at least 1,190 of the 1,200 passengers (all returning prisoners of war), which the steamer carried were enjoying the various stages of seasickness. I had been to sea several times, and had never been seasick in my life, but on this occasion I got the sensation. As our good ship rose on the incoming wave, and then seemed to fall away from under our feet into the trough of the sea, it was accompanied by an unaccountable but not exhilarating uplifting of the whole inner man, which strange sensation passeth all understanding, and, to say the least, was not agreeable. When "uprising" became so monotonous as to be oppressive, I took my stand on the bow of the steamer in the teeth of the wind, thus preventing the uplifting of my spirits, and other things, in getting the start of me; but the great majority of my comrades were not so fortunate, and soon passed into the second and third stages of seasickness, so that, on the whole, I think it safe to say that our steamer carried the sickest lot of happy mortals that ever sailed the briny deep.

When the morning of March 5 dawned we found ourselves steaming leisurely over the more quiet waters of Chesapeake Bay. Most of the boys had regained their equilibrium, and though many of them still showed the effect of their late wrestling match with old Neptune, the deck of the steamer was soon covered, and anxious eyes were watching for the first glimpse of familiar landmarks. A few hours later we caught sight of the dome of the Capitol of Maryland in the distance, and soon the little city of Annapolis lay before us in beauty and in peace. About 1 o'clock p.m. we reached the dock, and to the music of "The Star Spangled Banner," played by a band assembled on the wharf, we hurried ashore as happy a lot of mortals as ever escaped captivity.

A half year in a Confederate prisoner-of-war camp had taken its toll on Beecham's health as can be seen in this 1865 photograph. Beecham captioned this image "Looking lank and feeling pale/Came home from jail."

TWELVE

"The paths and the vocations of peace"

March–June 1865

While we lingered in Annapolis, and within a few days after our arrival from the South, some comrade conceived the idea of organizing a fraternal society, or order, to be known as "The Society of Prisoners of War." In talking the subject over, we all felt favorable toward such an association, and therefore a meeting was called to take the necessary steps in forming such organization, which preliminary meeting was well attended by the returned prisoners of war. After freely discussing the objects and advantages of such an association, we seemed to agree unanimously that this was the proper action to take, and that no more opportune time would ever occur again, when so many of us were all in one city and could be so easily assembled. So a committee was appointed to draft a constitution and bylaws for our contemplated society, and report the same to an adjourned meeting, which was appointed to assemble a few days later, when the organization would be made permanent.

Our meeting for permanent organization was so well and extensively advertised that nearly all the prisoners of our old Columbia camp were in attendance, and it certainly looked as though our new society was destined to make an enthusiastic start on its life journey. The committee on constitution submitted a report, which was read, and a motion made to adopt the constitution as formulated by said committee. However, there was one article of the constitution which was not only a surprise to many, but most offensive to their ideas of justice. If my memory serves me, it was Article III, relating to the eligibility to membership, which was as follows:

> Officers of the United States Army, Navy and Marine Corps who have been, or may be, captured by the enemy and held as prisoners of war, at any time in and during the war for the suppression of the rebellion and the preservation of the Union, shall be eligible to membership in the Society of Prisoners of War.

Immediately a comrade arose and moved an amendment to this article, whereby soldiers, sailors and marines, as well as officers, should be eligible to membership in the new order. Then followed a somewhat lengthy discussion on the adoption of the amendment, and it was truly surprising to learn to what an extent the officers there present were impressed with their own importance, and believed that officers were the whole cheese in our army, navy and marine corps, and that enlisted men did not count when honors were to be considered.

There were some who espoused the cause of the private soldiers, and who stood bravely behind the man who stood behind the gun in the hour of battle. They argued that, as there was only about four percent of the army who were officers, there were not to exceed 10 percent of returned prisoners of war who were officers, and it was therefore inconsistent and manifestly unjust for a small minority thus to exclude the great majority of ex-prisoners from an association called "The Society of Prisoners of War."

Personally, I called the attention of the comrades there assembled to the great difference, in our favor, of the treatment received by the two classes of prisoners, which accounted for the awful death rate in the Southern prisons for enlisted men, and especially to the ghastly scenes we had ourselves, many of us, witnessed along the road from Salisbury to Greensboro, which proved that so far as privation, suffering and heroic endurance for and in behalf of the "preservation of the Union," as mentioned in this very article of the constitution, was concerned, we must all admit not only that our enlisted comrades outnumbered us, but they stood above us in every other respect and were surely entitled to be treated by us as comrades and as equals. In closing I said: "Gentlemen, for one I have no desire to, and never will, belong to a society of prisoners of war or any other society where one-tenth has excluded the other nine-tenths of their comrades, and if I should subscribe to that constitution as originally written, I would never again be able to meet an enlisted comrade who had been a prisoner of war and look him squarely in the face." But arguments were in vain; we were but casting pearls before not swine but hogs. I had long been aware of the fact that generals, in their own estimation, are the armies, and that colonels are just as surely convinced that without them there could be no regiments; but it was a surprise to find from 500 to 700 line officers who were just as certain that a company was composed of a captain and two lieutenants. So they voted down the amendment, and adopted the article which excluded enlisted men from "The Society of Prisoners of War."

After this vote was taken, about one-third of the assembly rose to their feet and seceded from the constitutional convention, and thereafter I learned nothing of their deliberations, but am happy in the knowledge that the order was short-lived, having died with the bighead, as it deserved to, and is long since forgotten.

In after years a society of prisoners of war was organized, which is still in existence and is not exclusive, but admits to membership all who suffered and endured as prisoners of war, excluding none, neither officer nor soldier, white nor black; to which society it is an honor and not a disgrace to belong.

Notwithstanding the failure of the officers in this instance to establish a permanent organization on aristocratic principles or ideas, this tendency of ex-officers of the army to arrogate to themselves all the honor, heroism and loyalty that existed, has met with some degree of success, and we have in the United States of America in the beginning of this 20th century several such societies, organized since the war of the rebellion, wherein the magnificent commissioned officer has barred the private soldier, who won for him all the laurels that he so proudly wears.

Once, many years ago, I attended as an onlooker, in Madison, Wis., a meeting of the "Society of the Army of the Tennessee," which proved to be a gathering of officers only, the private soldier of that army having been excluded since the war closed. Gens. Sheridan, Belknap and Hurlbut were there, but about 150 others, and I thought then what magnificent victories Sheridan might have won if he had excluded the enlisted men in the days of war, and led into battle a coterie of shoulder-strapped gentlemen.

It may be that the son of an officer is more worthy to wear the badge of loyalty in America than the private soldier who endured all things from all men for the sake of the flag and the Union, but I do not believe it.

To the honor of the private soldier be it said, that in no organization wherein he is in the majority has he ever attempted to exclude the officer, but always honors and respects him if he is at all worthy of respect. There is nothing snobbish about the ex-soldier. I wish I could say as much in praise of the ex-officer.

Once on a time I had an appetite. If it was not an appetite, what was it? I will not say I had a good appetite, although it was large and strong—my appetite was, and seemed quite able to take care of itself and, certainly, did not seem at the time to be so very bad, but since then I have often wondered if I really had what people call "a good appetite." That was many, many years ago when I had my appetite, and lost it, and I presume I'll never have another—not in this world. Still, I remember as distinctly as if it were only yesterday when my appetite would put to shame a whole family, if not a whole neighborhood of Koreans; I remember, with a commingling recollection of an aching void within my whole being, how I came by it; I remember, with a full sense of thankfulness in my heart, or, perhaps more appropriately, with a sense of thankfulness in my stomach, when I enjoyed it in all its perfection and glory; I remember also, without any vain regrets on my own part, and, I hope, not any on the part of my family and friends, the very day I lost it forever. I once read an old proverb which declared that "Eating takes away one's appetite," and I think some times that's true.

Now, the story of my lost appetite is as follows, viz: The day I arrived in Annapolis, Md., from Wilmington, N.C., after my wanderings in Dixie, was Sunday, March 5, 1865. Be it remembered that during the seven months wherein I had enjoyed the hospitality of the good people of the Southern Confederacy I had eaten two square meals and various other things too numerous to mention, and that during our three days' voyage from Wilmington to Annapolis our steamer was bountifully supplied with salt meats and hardtack, and that throughout said voyage I had not missed a meal. Therefore, I must honestly confess that I was not hungry and did not have my appetite when we landed in Annapolis; but my two comrades with whom I had roughed it in the woods of North Carolina and on the freight and accommodation train from Salisbury to Goldsboro, were both desperately seasick on that voyage from Wilmington, and having missed their regular meals through the upheaval of the sea and other things, were, as a matter of course, extremely hungry.

The little city of Annapolis is, or was in 1865, a Sunday town, all the restaurants and saloons (and all the restaurants were saloons in those days) being closed on the Sabbath day. Nevertheless, every saloon and restaurant in the city had a back door or two, which were not hard to find if one understood the combination. As I had been in Annapolis before, I knew where one of those concealed back doors was located, and volunteered to act as guide for my two hungry comrades. We soon reached and were admitted within our restaurant, where we found a number of town bums patronizing the bar. I said to the proprietor, speaking in behalf of my comrades, that we were just in from Wilmington by the last steamer, after a long sojourn in Dixie, and wanted a lunch. The proprietor asked if a cold lunch would do, adding in a kindly tone that he had nothing hot on hand except drinks. We said that we would not trouble him for hot drinks, but that he might bring on the cold lunch at once. The proprietor spread before us a stuffed and roasted swan, a large platter of baked fish, weighing from a pound to a pound and a half each, with bread, butter, cheese and crackers in goodly quantities, and right there and then, like a bolt of lightning from a clear sky, my appetite struck me square in the stomach.

It was fortunate that it did not strike while I was in Dixie, for surely, in that event, I had starved and perished there. Just as fortunately, it did not delay its coming too long and strike me late in life when too old to labor for a living, for how might an old soldier support an appetite on even so generous a pension as $8.62 1/2 a month? Fortunately, as it was bound to strike, it struck me then, when there was before me the wherewithal to, in part, appease it, and when there was eight months' pay due me from the government of the United States. Then we proceeded to carve that swan until there was nothing left thereof but the skeleton, beside eating three fish apiece, with bread, butter, cheese and crackers in proportion.

After partaking of this snack, I gave our names to the landlord and engaged board and rooms for ourselves and three other comrades, as the landlord kept a lodging house in connection with his restaurant, leaving orders to have supper ready for us at the usual hour.

From there we went to headquarters for paroled prisoners, where we registered our names, regiments, etc., and filed applications for leave of absence, and about 6 o'clock returned to our hotel with our other comrades. At supper, we three, who had lunched in the afternoon, held our own with, and ate as long and as wide and as deep as the three who had not lunched, and we all ate until the table was bare and nothing more in sight.

This was on March 5, when I found my appetite, and I remained in Annapolis just a week before receiving a leave of absence, during which time we, all of us, seemed to have appetites coined in the same mint, and ate three square meals every day, and at each and every square meal we rounded up everything in reach, while between meals we took our oysters raw, fried, stewed and steamed, besides other refreshments whenever and wherever we happened to find anything that tempted our fastidious appetites, and most every thing did.

The wonder was that we did not kill ourselves by overeating, but, strange though it may seem, no evil results attended or followed this inordinate gormandizing. We experienced a sense of fullness at times, and dreamed that we were full moons, which was rather pleasurable than otherwise, in comparison with the sense of emptiness that for months had been gnawing at our vitals.

Talk about a man controlling his appetite; that's all moonshine. The man who talks such stuff and nonsense never had an appetite. Our appetites were Boss, and no mistake. All we could do was to look pleasant and foot the bills.

On March 12 I started for my home in Wisconsin, which journey required about three days, during which time I ate my three square meals a day and as many more as I could get, and never once, from the moment that my appetite struck me so forcibly in the restaurant at Annapolis, did I feel satisfied as one may who has eaten enough, until I reached home. Then, the next morning I sat down to breakfast, and when I had finished my friends expressed surprise that a returned prisoner of war from Dixie and starvation, should not have a sharper appetite.

I was agreeably surprised myself, that at last I could eat a respectable meal, like other people, and feel that I had eaten enough.

Comparatively speaking, I have had no appetite since.

While enjoying my leave of absence with friends at home in Wisconsin, we received the glad tidings from the seat of war in the East that Richmond had fallen into our hands, which was followed, a few days later, by the announcement of the surrender of Lee and his army. While not with the Army of the Potomac in person when it achieved its final triumph I was there in spirit—which is really the most enjoyable way of soldiering. Very few of us who went out in '61 and were with McDowell and Sherman at the First Bull Run, were with Grant at Appomattox; but the fault, generally, was not ours.

Just after Lee's surrender I started back to Annapolis, and was in that city on the morning of April 15, 1865, when we received the saddest news that ever fell upon the ears of the American people—the announcement of the assassination of Abraham Lincoln. How vividly to my mind's eye that terrible news brought back the careworn, kindly face of the president the last time I saw him. It was in the early spring of 1864, while on duty at Camp Casey, Va., preparing the 23d U.S.C.T. for the field. I was in Washington one evening for the purpose of hearing a lecture by Bayard Taylor, who was, I think, our minister to Russia at that time, and Russia was the subject of his lecture, which was given at Willard's Hall. While the lecture in itself was interesting, a still more interesting feature of the evening, which did not appear on the bills, was the presence of President Lincoln. Taylor had been talking, in his smooth and fascinating style, for fully 10 minutes when the president and Mrs. Lincoln entered the hall, and for a few moments after not even the flowing, flowery speech of Bayard Taylor could hold that audience in silence. President Lincoln and his wife were entitled to a lively demonstration of recognition and they received it, although the noted lecturer and minister to Russia was interrupted for a few minutes. That was the last time I saw Abraham Lincoln, and not only when I heard of his assassination, but during all the years that have passed since that sad day, whenever I think of our martyred President, I see again the slightly stooping form and deep-lined, striking features of that man of iron nerve who saved the American republic as I saw them for the last time that night at Willard's Hall in Washington.

Then, too, the information that J. Wilkes Booth was the assassin brought to mind recollections just as vivid, but of a different nature, as they related to a different subject. I saw again that harebrained, heartless fiend who did the bloody deed as I had seen him, as an actor in various Shakespearean characters. During the same spring of 1864 I had frequently attend Ford's Theater, where J. Wilkes Booth was then starring and I remember him, particularly, in the characters at Petruchio, Hamlet and Richard III, in each of which he presented the same characteristics of foolishness or madness—very different from the acting of his brother Edwin Booth, Keene, Davenport, Forrest and other great actors of his time. It seemed as natural as to draw his breath for him to carry every part of his acting to the very extreme of madness—to make some display or break that no other actor had ever thought of.

In the scene where Katharine recites the "wife's duty to her husband," and Petruchio commands her with a kiss, J. Wilkes failed not to leave a great wad of tobacco on the fair Katherine's cheek which was simply disgusting, except to the very lowest class of theatergoers.

In the part of Hamlet J. Wilkes was a failure throughout the greater portion of the play, but he stabbed old Polonius through the arras with more than ordinary zest; and especially in the scene at the grave of Ophelia he was perfectly at home, and rolled out the following lines with the vehemence of a mad bull:

> Zounds, show me what thou'lt do;
> Woo't weep! woo't fight! woo't fast! woo't tear thyself!
> Woo't drink up Esile, eat a crocodile?
> I'll do't—dost thou come here to whine?
> To outface me with leaping in her grave?
> Be buried quick with her, and so will I:
> And If thou prate of mountains, let them throw
> Millions of acres on us; till our ground,
> Singeing his pate against the burning zone,
> Make Ossa like a wart! Nay, an thou'lt mouth,
> I'll rant as well as thou."

Ranting was really J. Wilkes's best hold, and he spoke the lines as though he found much delight in them.

In the character of Richard III, J. Wilkes Booth occupied the niche for which nature intended him, for he could "snarl and bite and play the dog" more true to life than any other actor that I ever saw attempt to personate Richard. His deformity of body was more picturesque, the hump on his back was larger, his crippled limbs shorter and his halting gate more noticeable, and he acted the part of a villain and fiend so naturally and enthusiastically that when I heard he was the assassin of the President I was not so greatly surprised.

About that time, and while still in Annapolis, I wrote some verses in commemoration of this event, entitled "The Assassin's Fate." The style and sentiment of my poem are very different from the poem, on the same subject, written by Col. Terrell, of the 6th Tex. Cav. Col. Terrell saw in J. Wilkes Booth the embodiment of the spirit of liberty rather the spirit of a fiend incarnate. Col. Terrell was ambassador to the Court of Stamboul, under the administration of Grover Cleveland.

At the time of the president's assassination there were many people in Maryland's capital in sympathy with the Lost Cause, but they were very careful and circumspect in their speech, as they had reason to be, for the city was full of Union officers, and we loaded our revolvers carefully for business the moment we heard of the assassination; but, I am happy to say, we had no occasion to use them.

Of all the demonstrations of sorrow for the untimely taking-off of President Lincoln, the most impressive, to me, was the simple and silent act of an old Negro. On the afternoon of April 15, as I was going from Annapolis to Camp Parole, about two miles out, where the paroled enlisted men were quartered, I met this old man who asked me in a choked and sorrowful voice: "Sir, is it true that they have killed Mistah Lincoln?" When I informed him that it was true, he spoke not another word, but simply stood there aghast, as if stunned by a mighty blow, gazing with a bewildered stare into space with a look of unutterable woe upon his dark features, that would defy the brush of the most skillful artist in the world to reproduce on canvas. When I passed out of sight that old Negro was still standing there, gazing into space, in the attitude of one whose whole soul was overburdened with sorrow.

In the latter part of April, 1865, we paroled prisoners of war were declared duly exchanged, and received orders to report for duty to our various regiments. Then our numerous family, endeared to each other after the manner of soldiers, by long association and untold hardships together endured, separated, most of us never again to meet on earth.

I found my regiment and the old comrades who had not fallen by the way, which I had left many months before, still in the vicinity of Petersburg, being then attached to the Twenty-fifth Corps. In revisiting or passing through Petersburg on my return a great change of conditions was noticeable, as compared with my former visit on the last day of July, 1864, nine months before. The Confederate general A. P. Hill, who so successfully planned the Sabbath day's diversion for the kind people of Petersburg, wherein I had figured as a part of the show, had passed in his checks at the last battle in defense of the city, and his soldiers, who had fought so stubbornly and fiercely for their ill-conceived rights, had passed from the stage of action, and the stars and stripes protected the Negro and the "nigger officer" as well as the white man, in Petersburg.

My stay with my regiment was short. On May 6 I was mustered as captain and assigned to the command of Co. H, my commission as such having been issued from the War Department on Aug. 9, 1864. But I was tired of war, and as everything indicated that the Twenty-fifth Corps would be sent to the Mexican frontier, on the Rio Grande River, as it soon after was, and as I had enjoyed all of Dixie climate and Dixie hospitality that seemed good for me, I tendered my resignation, which, on May 23, 1865, was accepted by the government, and I left the service forever. On May 24, I bid my old comrades farewell, and boarding a steamboat at City Point, made my last trip down the James and up the Potomac to Washington. Our steamboat reached Fort Monroe about 3 o'clock p.m., from which point Col. Pritchard and some of his riders, who had participated in the capture of Jeff. Davis, accompanied us to Washington, where we arrived at 6 o'clock on the morning of May 25, 1865.

From the 25th to the 30th of May I remained in Washington, squaring my accounts with the government. On the 28th I received from the second auditor's office my certificate of nonindebtedness to the government, and about noon of the 30th my final pay, which was the last, though not least, of the acts releasing me from service. During my sojourn in Washington the trial of the conspirators in the assassination of Abraham Lincoln was in progress, but I had no time to visit the court of justice.

On the afternoon of May 30 I packed my grip and at 7 o'clock p.m. left Washington for New York City, where I visited friends there and in Jersey City. June 2 I steamed up the picturesque Hudson, passing the great military academy of West Point, where thousands of swell heads and occasionally a man of common horse sense, are educated at the expense of the American people, to lord it over their sons in the days of war, when men of patriotism and courage are called to stand behind the guns and fight their country's battles. At 5 o'clock p.m. I reached New York's capital city, where I visited friends during June 3 and 4. About midnight of June 4 I left Albany for the West, or what was the West at that time—via Niagara Falls, stopping off to visit that wonderful American attraction from noon until dark, continuing my journey westward at midnight.

I reached my old home at Sun Prairie, Dane County, Wis., from which point I had enlisted for the war more than four years before, at 8 o'clock p.m., June 7, 1865. My days of war were over; before me were the paths and the vocations of peace.

INDEX

Afflick (prisoner of war), 204–6, 210
African-Americans. *See* Blacks; Slavery;
    United States Colored Troops
American Revolution, 163–64
Ames's brigade, 94, 109
Anderson's division, 74, 105
Annapolis, Md.: Beecham in, 219–24,
    225; Confederate sympathizers in,
    227
Archer, J. J., 72, 109
Archer's brigade, 72, 109
Arlington House, 15
Armistead, Lewis Addison, 106, 107
Armistead's brigade, 105
Attucks, Crispus, 163

Baltimore, Md.: Beecham arrives ill in,
    31–32; Confederate sympathizers
    in, 3–4, 31–32
Banks, Nathaniel, 25
Barksdale, William, 93
Bartlett, William F., 192, 194
Beauregard, Pierre G. T.: and Confed-
    erate surrender, 215; at first battle
    of Bull Run, 5, 6, 11, 12, 17
Beecham, Emma, 29, conducts school
    for USCT, xii, 168; death of, xviii;
    postwar life of, xvii

Beecham, Robert K.: in Annapolis, 219–
    24, 225; antislavery attitudes of,
    x; appears before examining board,
    152–56; at battle of the Crater,
    177–89; at battle of Gettysburg,
    71–78, 109; in Chancellorsville
    campaign, 54–56; as Confederate
    prisoner of war, xii, 121–41, 189,
    191–204; criticizes racist theories,
    166–67; death of, xviii; death of
    tentmate of, 118; early life of, x;
    enlists in Second Wisconsin, x, 3;
    escapes from Confederate prisoner
    of war camp, xii, 204–9; evacuated
    from Columbia, S.C., prison, 204;
    at first battle of Bull Run, 5–10;
    foraging expedition by, 41–52; for-
    mally exchanged, 216–17; ill-
    nesses of and military hospitals, xi,
    21–23, 26–35, 170–72; marches
    to Centreville, 17–18; postwar life
    of, xvii–xviii; problems with vac-
    cination, 15–16; promoted to cap-
    tain, xii, 227–28; recruits black
    soldiers, 165–66; refuses to join
    prisoners of war organization,
    219–22; resigns commission, xii,
    228; returns to Second Wiscon-

229